INDIAN INSTITUTE OF MANAGEMENT AHMEDABAD

BUSINESS BOOKS

Managers Who Make a Difference

Strategies
for Success

INDIAN INSTITUTE OF MANAGEMENT AHMEDABAD
BUSINESS BOOKS

Managers Who Make a Difference

T.V. RAO

RANDOM HOUSE INDIA

Published by Random House India in 2010

1

Copyright © T.V. Rao Learning Systems Pvt. Ltd.
Reproduced with permission 2010

Random House Publishers India Private Limited
MindMill Corporate Tower, 2nd Floor, Plot No. 24A
Sector 16A, Noida 201301, UP

Random House Group Limited
20 Vauxhall Bridge Road
London SW1V 2SA
United Kingdom

978 81 8400 137 2

Typeset in Cronos Pro by InoSoft Systems, Noida

Printed and bound in India by Replika Press Pvt. Ltd.

CONTENTS

Introduction

WHAT IS A MANAGER?

A manager is someone who gets things done. He starts with an objective given to him by others (organization, department, top management, superiors or bosses, etc.). He understands and interprets his goals. He sets out an action plan and mobilizes the resources (men, material, money or budgets and other support) required to achieve them. He then sets about achieving his goal, monitoring the progress along the way.

Once upon a time, that was the definition of a manager, Over the last couple of decades, however, the world has changed radically. Communication and connectivity has increased, cities have grown, and we have been buffeted by immense social forces. Here are just some of those changes that impact our workplace today:

- ▶ People's preferences have come into sharper focus
- ▶ Consumerism and commercialization has increased
- ▶ Economic activity has gone up leading to greater employment opportunities and accessibility
- ▶ Education levels are going up

- ▶ Talented people are scarcer
- ▶ People have become more conscious of their rights and have become less negotiable. Concerns about health and well-being have increased
- ▶ People have become more conscious of costs and benefits
- ▶ Choices have increased
- ▶ Relationships have become more complex. Divorces have increased and new phenomena like same-sex marriages, live-in relationships, and cross-cultural marriages have come into existence
- ▶ Modern organizations have become flat and yet some continue to be hierarchical
- ▶ Ethical issues have come into focus

The definition of a manager has to change with changing times. The implication is that a manager's job is to set new goals, new standards, recruit new people, mobilize new resources, review methods, set and reset new technologies, etc. The thrust is more on the dynamic process here. The manager is a dynamic entity and not merely an achiever of someone else's goals. The modern manager may be required to initiate new goals, define a vision, and chart out a course of action.

TYPES OF MANAGERS

From my work and interactions with managers I classify them into four categories:

1. **Doers:** These are managers who get things done. Though they are not extraordinary, they are necessary in the workplace. They do routine jobs. They take life as it comes.

They may not have ambitions, but they work hard enough to sustain their jobs and progress at a normal rate in the organization. Without them the company may not be able to run. However, if they leave, another manager will fill their position. The Doer Managers can be further classified into 'committed doers' and 'shirkers'. Shirkers try to find short cuts and try to do much less than what they are expected to do. We do not deal with them in this book. The 'Doer Managers' are sincere and hard-working managers.

2. **Achievers**: These managers do more than what they are required to. Many of them are outstanding. Achievers are smart managers and they work hard and get things done fast. They are noticed in the corporation and considered as assets. They have career ambitions but do not have a mission or purpose in life beyond that. They are willing to move to any company that pays them a higher salary or uses their competencies better. They are career managers. If luck favours them they may become CEOs at a relatively young age.

3. **Visionaries or entrepreneurs**: Visionaries are leaders. They are restless, creative, and they think big. They have long-term goals. They want to make an impact on the organization and are largely driven by creation of wealth for themselves and others around them. Thus, they make a lasting mark on society. These managers are found in various fields—government, social services, industry, trade, and commerce. They are often entreprenuers and empire builders. Personal wealth is often their distinguishing trait. Deepak Parekh, Kumar Mangalam Birla, Narayana Murthy, Kiran Mazumdar-Shaw, Venu Srinivasan, Anil Khandelwal, Shiv Nadar, Azim Premji, Sunil Mittal, Vijay Mallya, A.M. Naik, Mukesh Ambani,

Anil Ambani, and many IIM graduates like Sharath Babu all fit into this group.

4. **Missionaries**: These managers are mission driven. Their goals are not personal but more social and community related. They are highly driven by their goals, and there is an element of sacrifice involved in what they do. Mahatma Gandhi, Mother Teresa, Dr Verghese Kurien, A.P.J. Abdul Kalam, Ila Bhatt, Kiran Bedi, and Vikram Sarabhai are all examples of missionaries. Type 3 managers may also qualify to be in this category the moment they focus single-mindedly on social objectives rather than empire building. One such example is Narayana Murthy. As managers, our goal might usually stop at type 3—after all, the visionary is the archetypical manager and not all of us want to change society. However, all of us have missionary elements in our nature and it is important we acknowledge type 4 as the ultimate kind of manager.

The distinction between types 1 and 2 is sometimes blurred. The distinction between types 2 and 3 is clear. Type 2 managers are employees while type 3 are usually self-employed or employers. There are, however, various exceptions to this. For example, Deepak Parekh is mission driven but a professional manager and Verghese Kurien was appointed by the Government of India to head the National Dairy Development Board (NDDB) for several years and brought in the white revolution. Types 3 and 4 dedicate their lives to one cause. While type 1 and type 2 shift organizations when it suits their career goals; as they settle down and find their vocation or cause and substitute it as a mission they become type 3 and when they make sacrifices and influence large numbers of people they become type 4.

All four types described above are managers. Types 2, 3, and 4 are also leaders but the degree of their leadership varies. Type 2 managers demonstrate several leadership competencies in terms of setting standards and coming up with new ideas in their sphere of activity. Type 3's leadership competencies are in identifying new areas of activity and setting new goals. They are entrepreneurial leaders and their spheres may vary from small to large to empire building. Some of them may even rewrite the rules like Kiran Mazumdar-Shaw, Narayana Murthy, Deepak Parekh, Venu Srinivasan, Vijay Mahajan, and move closer to type 4. However, some of them may not yet be identifiable as type 4, as the most distinguishing feature of this type is being mission driven and making personal sacrifices for the sake of larger goals and not for personal wealth. Some of the characteristics of the four types of managers are presented in table 1 .

THE QUALITIES OF A GOOD MANAGER

Imagine the four levels of managers to be four rungs of a ladder. Your aim is to climb as high as you can. One of the objectives of this book is to help those in type 1 to move to 2, those in type 2 to 3, and the ones in type 3 to 4.

This book is based on two beliefs. First, that the better a manager you are, the bigger your vision is and the more value-led you are. While I will focus on the core skills you will need to be an effective manager, I will constantly point to the highest level to which all managers should aspire. Second, that the managers who make a difference exhibit certain qualities that can be emulated and developed. Their thought processes, outlook, values, and motives can all be acquired. Managers are not born, they can be made and each one of us has the capacity to extend ourselves. As a result I have emphasized human resource (HR) tools such as

TABLE 1: TYPES OF MANAGERS

Area	Type 1	Type 2	Type 3	Type 4
Life Goals	Do one's job, perhaps do it well; keep growing in career	To be outstanding and high achiever; to be noticed and make a difference; to do one's work well or to an outstanding degree that it gets noticed; build career; use one's potential	To be independent; to do something different; to serve a cause; to attain highest possible type in one's chosen field; to be a self-starter or self-employed; to provide employment and other opportunities for others; to create wealth for self, family, and others closer to them and perhaps society at large	To work for a cause; to be value driven; to think, dream, live the mission for which one is working; to benefit a large section of the society; to extend themselves and serve others; to work for unusual groups, weaker sections, poor people, the less fortunate, and so on; focus on super-orcinate goals

Mission	No mission	Career related; self focused mission	Larger mission; work for a cause; self-focused and at the same time integrates community or larger group goals into self	Totally mission driven; lives to achieve the mission; directed at others primarily and is willing to make sacrifices
Values	May or may not be specific	Articulates values and has clarity	Value driven; focused on culture; could be specialist values	Highly value driven; integrates mission and values; character, values, integrity, honesty, truthfulness, values required for a healthy society; Promotes actively these values among those who work with them

Time Management	Takes time as per the organization's or employer's requirements	Finds time for self-expression and creates time for outstanding things; works hard and works smart	Works hard; uses time for self-initiated mission and personal goals	Works hard; works with high commitment; uses all the time for things related to mission; eats, drinks, and lives the mission and cause for which he works
Dominant Motivation	Mixed; task motivated; could be dependent; may respond to controls; rules and regulations	High achievement and personal power; moderate; independence	High achievement; social power; independence; mild extension	High extension; high achievement; high social power; independence

PRD (Performance Review Discussion) and 360 degree feedback which help individuals improve through self-examination.

A summary of the qualities (implicit in our discussion of the four types) every manager must possess to a varying degree is:

1. Knowing and performing various roles and activities effectively (versatility)
2. High sense of efficacy or self-image
3. The ability to recognize that success or failure comes from their actions through hard work and perseverance (internality)
4. Value driven and highly ethical
5. Good team workers, collaborative by nature. They manage their teams well and help create good managers in turn
6. Engage with their colleagues and are trusted and respected by them (interpersonal engagement)
7. Strong and credible communicators with good networking skills
8. Good delegators who manage time and talent efficiently
9. Proactive, change oriented, and problem solvers (creativity)
10. Possess a powerful combination of motives and appropriate leadership styles and skills

Of these qualites, the following four are largely internal or character driven although they can be developed: self-efficacy, internality, values, and creativity. The following four are the practical skills every manager requires, although, as we will see, these differ from level to level: team building, interpersonal engagement, time and talent management, and communication.

In this book we will begin by looking in detail at the different qualities a manager must possess and then go through each of these qualites providing case studies, exercises, and tests where possible. We will end on a more general note looking at the different leadership styles a manager can work with and the motivations that push them. It is my hope that by the end of it you will become a better manager and aspire to change the world around you.

> You are the master of your thought, the molder of your character the maker and shaker of your condition, environment and destiny. Man is buffeted by circumstances as long as he believes himself to be the creature of outside conditions. But when he realises that he is a creative power and that he may command the hidden soil and seeds of his being out of which circumstances grow, he then becomes the rightful master of himself.
>
> James Allen, *As a Man Thinketh*

1

Versatility

ROLES AND ACTIVITIES OF EFFECTIVE MANAGERS

What do effective managers do? How do they spend their time? What activities ought they to perform if they are to make a difference and be called effective managers? The answers to these questions lead to one of the key differences between the various levels of managers. Almost all of us are given job descriptions when we join work, but to be effective managers we need to go beyond these tasks and aim to do much more. Some of these aspirations will be explored in greater detail in the following chapters. This chapter provides an overview and looks at how a manager can balance his core duties and the additional ones, between transformational and transactional activities, and how in fact the additional duties can help him graduate to higher levels of management.

THE MANAGER'S JOB: FACT AND FOLKLORE

What do managers really do? That's something people outside the corporate world know very little of. Ironically, managers themselves cannot always be sure what their primary functions are or ought to be. McGill's Henry Mintzberg identified some of

the common myths about managerial functions and compared
them with findings from his own studies. Here's what he found:

Henry Mintzberg, (1990), The Manager's Job Fact and Folklore, *Harvard Business Review*, March–April 1990, pp. 163–176	
Folklore	**Fact**
The manager is a reflective and systematic planner	Study after study has shown that managers work at an unrelenting pace, that their activities are characterized by brevity, variety, and discontinuity, and that they are strongly oriented towards action and dislike reflective activities
An effective manager has no regular duties to perform	Managerial work involves performing a number of regular duties, including rituals, ceremonies and negotiations, and processing soft information that links the organization with its environment
The senior manager needs aggregated information, which is best provided by a formal management information system	Managers strongly favour verbal media, telephone calls, and meetings over documents
Management is or is at least quickly becoming a science and a profession	Managers' 'programmes'— schedules, processes, decision-making tools, and so on—remain locked deep within their brains

Some of Mintzberg's other observations are worth noting here. He discovered that half of the activities engaged in by five chief executives lasted less than nine minutes each and only one out of ten activities exceeded an hour. In another study of fifty-six US foremen it was found that on an average they carried out 583 different activities in an eight-hour shift. This worked out to almost one activity every 48 seconds. And in a study where the diaries of 160 British middle and top managers were analysed, it was found that they worked without interruptions for half an hour or more only about once every two days. If you thought managers are particularly good at delegating responsibilities, think again. Mintzberg's studies indicate that managers seem to cherish verbal information, particularly gossip, hearsay, and speculation. Because of this preference for verbal transactions, a lot of strategic information is stored in managers' minds. It takes time—which they don't have—to convert it to a written form, hence the difficulty in delegating. *The inability to delegate means there are more things a manager needs to do himself, and he becomes more burdened than before and may be compelled to do certain jobs superficially.* More importantly by being bogged down by everyday tasks (transactional activities), the manager may be unable to look at the bigger picture and the larger goals (transformational activities) of his department or organization. Consider the following two case studies.

Case 1: The Finance Director

The chairman of a sugar manufacturing company once observed that most of his directors were not available most of the time when he needed their advice. He complained that they seemed to be busy with meetings all the time. This led the Finance Director to list all his activities and the time he spent on them. Some of these were:

▶ Presentation of accounts to the board every quarter and annually.
▶ The seemingly simple task of making accounts available on time every quarter in July, October, January, and April involved working with auditors to reduce delays and transaction cost
▶ discussing the audit reports with the staff and building their competencies; recruiting accounts staff, inducting them, and checking for gaps in SAP operation. (SAP is a form of enterprise resource planning—also referred as ERP—which manages all the information and functions of a business from shared data stores). It is a commercial software package that provides integration of all the information flowing through a company) operation.
▶ Making and meeting the financial strategy for business through fund management. This involved meeting potential lenders and bankers to explore and arrange alternative sources for prepayment; accessing funds through commercial banks and other agencies.
▶ The Finance Director listed about twenty different types of meetings he was required to attend (some every month, some quarterly, and so on, totalling over 150 in a year) such as project meetings, SAP steering committee, HR steering committee meetings, SBU (strategic business unit) incentive meetings, lenders' fund raising meetings, Director's informal meeting, accountants' meeting, new product sales review, project finance, meetings to schedule meetings, tender committee, tax status review, audit committee, board meetings, legal cases reviews, meetings to arrange direct payment to key suppliers, investor relations meetings, and so on.

▶ In addition to all this he had to perform many activities to ensure tax planning and tax management such as monitoring the internal and external audit (manning the internal audit, put in place an external audit agency, train internal audit staff), presenting the audit to the board, and setting up IT and SAP environment to facilitate business decisions.

Until he presented these points to the chairman and accounted for his time, neither he nor the chairman had an exact idea of how the Finance Director's time was being spent. Once listed, both realized that the Finance Director was involved in too many transactional activities.

Case 2: Branch Manager of LIC

When asked about how his time was spent, a Branch Manager of the the Life Insurance Corporation of India (LIC) who did not have an MBA degree gave the following list of activities that he undertook with the approximate time spent on them:

1. Discussing performance plans (PPs) with juniors in the group
2. Preparing and showing the performance plan to seniors
3. Reviewing their PPs quarterly
4. Monthly meetings to share ideas, experiences, and knowledge
5. Meeting top clients personally twice a year (about a hundred of them)
6. Contacting them over the phone on special occasions
7. Conducting training programmes for staff and development agents (once a week)

8. Accompanying agents and development officers (DOs) (ten times a month or more)
9. Monthly tour and visiting agents for eight days a month (5 hours a day)
10. Monthly meetings and recognition of outstanding performers
11. Weekly feedback and follow-up (3 hours a week)
12. Learning and developing of ideas (2 hours every week)
13. Data analysis and interpretation (one sitting every fortnight)
14. One unit meeting each per month for seven DOs (1 hour each)
15. Putting up stalls, etc., at local festivals
16. Organizing, managing, and supervising vehicle campaigns (once every 6 months)
17. Customer meetings through agents (once a month)
18. Monthly review meeting with all staff
19. Performance review meetings (twice a year)

Each of these activities has many sub-activities. For example, discussing PPs may include sub-activities like reading the PP, making notes and comments, fixing the meeting, making themselves available for meetings by fixing time for visitors accordingly, actual discussion, writing short notes, and so on. However, all these are grouped into one.

This Branch Manager classified all his activities under the following seven heads:

1. Performance planning for self and juniors (2 hours)
2. Customer relations development and sensitivity (10 hours)
3. Marketing team development (500 hours)
4. Business development (500 hours)

5. Branch management (20 hours)
6. Meeting and managing superiors (96 hours)
7. Motivating and managing insurance agents (3 hours a day and 260 days amounting to a total of 780 hours).

The time given in brackets is the actual time he spent in the previous year.

WHAT EFFECTIVE MANAGERS MANAGE

The two case studies we see are of typical 'doer managers' who ensure that they perform all their duties. But by doing so they are also making a number of mistakes. They are neglecting some critical activities that they are required to perform to provide leadership roles to their staff. For example, a Finance Director has to go beyond managing the finances of the company. He/She should be articulating the vision, communicating values, creating a team spirit and a work culture, meeting customers, and the like. The Branch Manager of the insurance company is engaging in few of the activities that can be considered leadership activities like developing juniors and meeting customers in the case of the insurance manager but that is not enough. Strategic thinking and collecting competitor information, benchmarking, vision development, change management, and the like, should benefit both Branch Manager of LIC and the Finance Director.

An old perception of managers may have been of someone who got things done. Indeed, this is still what is expected of the average doer such as the LIC branch manager and the finance director. But increasingly, managers are expected to make things *happen*. When it comes to achievers, visionaries, and missionaries, the focus is on transformation rather than simple delivery.

A competent manager is someone who discharges his/her day-to-day administrative responsibilities efficiently. These tasks often include planning, organizing things (labour, material, and other resources), monitoring the performance of teams or departments, taking decisions, directing and instructing, negotiating deals or projects, preparing strategies for business growth or marketing, mobilizing and scheduling resources, appraising performance, and conducting meetings to brainstorm about new ideas. Doers are usually adept at managing routine functions of this sort. These are essential activities, and central to an organization's performance. But if one seeks to make a greater and more lasting impact as a manager—as achievers, visionaries, and missionaries are constantly trying to do—one needs to develop a broader vision and a focus on certain other strategic and ultimately transformative activities, such as:

▶ Articulating and developing the vision and values of the company
▶ Ensuring adherence to the vision and values
▶ Collecting business information and formulating policies and strategies
▶ Planning and setting goals (long term and short term)
▶ Designing and introducing new systems
▶ Managing systems and technology
▶ Inspiring, developing, and empowering staff
▶ Culture building
▶ Teamwork and team building
▶ Understanding internal customers and servicing them
▶ Liaison with boss and top management
▶ Influencing the thinking of the boss and top management

▶ Ceremonial roles including networking, public relations, and dealing with government agencies

▶ External customer relations and client management

Henry Mintzeberg in fact identified ten roles that managers perform, and organized them into three categories:

A. Interpersonal Roles:

1. **Figurehead roles:** Ceremonial roles such as taking a customer or dignitaries out to lunch, or showing visitors round a plant;

2. **Leader roles:** These include hiring, training, motivating, encouraging, coaching, and setting a vision and goals;

3. **Liaison roles:** Here, a manager deals with people outside his vertical chain of command like peers or people outside the organization such as suppliers, consultants, etc.

B. Informational roles:

4. **Monitoring roles:** These find managers canning information, interrogating subordinates and others, and receiving unsolicited information;

5. **Disseminating roles:** This involves passing information on to others, particularly juniors;

6. **Spokesperson roles:** In which managers pass information to seniors, influential parties, and the government.

C. Decisional Roles:

7. **Entrepreneurial roles:** In which managers seeks to improve the functioning of the unit or department and adapt it to changing environment by looking for new ideas, implementing new ideas, initiating projects, planning new projects and activities;

8. **Disturbance handling roles:** In which the manager responds to pressures, problems, and emergencies;

9. **Resource allocation roles:** In which the manager decides who will get what, allocates work, authorizes important decisions;

> **10. Negotiator roles:** In which managers negotiate with customers, suppliers, contractors, team members, handle grievances, etc.
>
> Managers may not perform all these roles in an integrated way. Good performance depends on how well the person understands his job and has insights into it. Managers who are introspective about their jobs are likely to be effective in them (Mintzberg, 1990).

Some of the roles described above are clearly transformational and need to be undertaken for the future of any organization. The rest are largely transactional. Performing transformational activities is what creates a visionary leader. These activities are discovering new goals, setting new priorities, and are largely driven by vision. Achiever managers do transformational activities well or better than others and bring about improvements in processes.

ARTICULATING AND ADHERING TO A VISION AND VALUES

Every manager's job is to get work done by his/her subordinates. But employees tend to work better and with greater involvement if they work for a purpose. If they are convinced that their work helps others and if they have before them a larger goal than meeting a particular target or deadline, they will almost certainly work with greater motivation. As Robin Sharma points out, 'one's pay cheque needs to be linked to one's purpose, and purpose is the most powerful motivator in the world' (Sharma 2003: 51). A good manager ought to periodically remind people of their purpose—of the benefits people derive from their work and the large numbers of people they serve. This keeps employee morale high. Visionaries and missionaries in particular tend to inspire their colleagues through their unflinching sense of purpose and their desire to instil integrity, character, and courage in their colleagues. As Narayana Murthy remarks: 'Leadership is about creating vision, communicating that vision to one's followers, and exhorting them to move towards that vision.' (Chary 2002: 77) Under Murthy's leadership, Infosys has proved itself a paragon among Indian companies when it comes to preserving the dignity of every individual, maintaining the highest standards of corporate governance, strategic planning, and long-term goal setting.

An effective manager needs to:

▶ Communicate the top management's vision for the organization to all the employees in his/her department/ division;
▶ Develop and articulate values and a vision for his own department and monitor his staff to ensure that these are adhered to;
▶ Lead by example and practice what he preaches.

A key lesson for managers and business leaders is to reiterate their goals and vision for the future time and again, and engage employees in the *spirit* of the endeavour rather than simply in the endeavour itself. Leadership messages need to be communicated repeatedly until they are virtually internalized by a company's employees. Jack Welch, GE's legendary chairman, had the company's values printed and distributed to all the employees at every level of the company. Welch also included them in the annual letter to shareholders, mentioned them in his speeches to the GE board, and in his talks with the financial analysis teams. It is said that all the employees have the company's values guide with them in their wallet/purse. It means everything to them and they live by it. Do remember that as a manager and leader you are constantly under scrutiny by your subordinates and there must be a close fit between your words and actions.

The mission, vision, and values of the company as communicated and lived by the top management determines market perceptions and employee commitment. It communicates the DNA of the company to the outside world. Your DNA tells others who you are. Your mission tells them who you want to be. The vision consists of intermediate, measurable, and time-bound goals that you promise to yourself and your stakeholders. Annual plans and resource allocations flow from that and make sure that individual employee efforts are aligned to them. The vision and mission gives meaning to employees and enhances their engagement and enjoyment at work.

FORMULATING POLICIES, PLANNING, AND SETTING GOALS

Narayana Murthy famously commented that Infosys takes a long-term view of business and life. 'We remember that success is ephemeral. We remember that we are as good as the results of our last quarter. We fully believe that we are running a marathon, not a sprint; and our strategies and policies reflect that.' As a manager you need to set both short- and long-term goals for your department or unit. This means that you have to be discerning and resourceful enough to collect critical information about the business development, strategy formulation, and performance improvements. You also need to take a close look at matters such as systems, services, quality costs, recoveries, and innovation. Of course, the sort of goals you will find yourself setting will depend on not just the type of manager you are, but also your position in the organization. If you are a doer or a achiever, your strategies are more likely to relate to the short term. Achievers will probably look for smarter ways to achieve their short-term goals and may even try to raise the level of the goals they set themselves and their department.

Visionaries and missionaries will probably have their eyes trained on the medium and long term. Hence CEOs tend to be involved primarily with creating and implementing the firm's long-term strategy, and spend much of their time dealing with issues outside the firm such as competitors, customers, market trends, and technological developments. They delegate day-to-day operations of the business to other managers and senior colleagues.

Make sure that you include every part of the company when you are rethinking the corporate strategy or making other far-reaching changes. In these turbulent times, you cannot afford to leave any division, unit, or individual on the sidelines. In 1992, IBM's then CEO John Akers had developed a plan to break up his company into several small units. But on Gerstner's (CEO, IBM) first major decision upon taking the reins ran in the opposite direction. He decided not to break up the company, arguing that implementing the plan would splinter IBM into a collection of piece-part providers. 'There wasn't going to be an IBM; there was going to be six or eight IBMs—effectively no IBM. So we made a very early decision—the most important decision I'll ever make in my business career—to reverse that direction and keep IBM whole.'

Whether you're a doer or a visionary though, you need to think and act like a chess player who sees two or three moves ahead. So whatever the level at which you operate, you will find yourself a wise leader, looking into the future for the role you will be playing and arming yourself with the skills you'll need in those new roles.

If you do not continuously collect business-related information and keep making new strategies and business plans to exploit opportunities your corporation will be left behind. This role, therefore, is critical for the survival of an organization in a competitive world.

MANAGING TECHNOLOGY AND SYSTEMS

Today, managers must be technologically savvy as they are expected to understand the IT system requirements of their department and ensure that these are in place. They must also try to build the necessary development capabilities in their staff. IBM's Lou Gerstner says, 'The Internet is ultimately about innovation and integration. But you don't get the innovation unless you integrate web technology into the processes by which you run your business.' Having instituted the required systems, however, a certain amount of awareness, training, and commitment is needed to ensure that employees use them to operate with maximum efficiency. Azim Premji remarks that technological knowledge becomes obsolete very fast indeed, so it's imperative to keep reading, attending seminars, and teaching and training others to remain updated. Managers need to be aware of the ways in which new developments in technology make older management methods redundant. In larger firms, what managers should aim to create is an effective corporate memory—a digital resource centre that allows teams or individuals to retrieve earlier records of projects similar to the one(s) they may be working on themselves. A firm may have a large corporate memory but unless these digitized documents can be easily be retrieved or searched, the database isn't really an asset.

A T. V. Rao Learning Systems (TVRLS) study of 174 senior-level Indian managers seemed to indicate that they are generally rather slow in upgrading themselves and their departments as compared to their Western counterparts. Among India's top-notch professional managers there were alarmingly few who had actually recognized the benefits of a tech-savvy organization.

To return to our typology of managers, we find that doers are usually happy enough to maintain the status quo and are not overly keen on new technological innovations within a department. Achievers are highly technology driven. IT systems are an integral part of visionaries' and missionaries' goals for the future—they are usually quick to leverage these to their advantage.

Indian public sector banks (PSBs) are one good example of how managers can leverage technology to command superiority. In the early 1980s most PSBs could not introduce computer-enabled services for fear of unions who felt that IT would create job losses. Even the Reserve Bank of India (RBI) failed. The scenario has totally changed today. As the recently appointed HR Committee on PSBs observed:

> Though initially slow and halting, PSBs have caught up with technology, e-channels, and other customer-centric innovations in the last decade or so. Almost all PSBs have deployed advanced technology and networked their branches, rolled out core banking, set up a vast network of ATMs, launched many innovative products and enlarged the basket of offerings to the customer. Marketing and sales are becoming the buzz words in many PSBs and they are repositioning their key branches as sale and service outlets. Decision-making machinery has been fine-tuned and many have improved their response time.

As a result PSBs have provided strong competition to the PSBs that are emerging in the country and have improved their financials in recent times . A large part of this credit goes to people like C. Rangarajan, former Governor of RBI and innovative CEOs of banks like the State Bank of India, Bank of Baroda and so on.

To summarize, therefore, an effective manager:

- ▶ Introduces new technologies relating to the department's function
- ▶ Builds the technological competencies of employees in a department through training, and so on
- ▶ Keeps abreast of technological developments in related industries and functions both in the country and globally
- ▶ Introduces new systems of management to manage various activities and operations effectively
- ▶ Monitors the effective implementation and utilization of systems and processes relating to his function

INSPIRING, DEVELOPING, AND EMPOWERING STAFF

'If you create an environment where people truly participate, you don't need control,' says Herb Kelleher, CEO of Southwest Airlines. 'They know what needs to be done, and they do it. The more people devote themselves to your cause on a voluntary basis, the fewer hierarchies and control mechanisms you need.'

People management is a large part of every manager's responsibilities. Normally managers have a definite jurisdiction or span of control—this could be about eight to ten people (or perhaps more) in a department. The addition of large numbers of juniors often puts a manager under pressure to devote more time in supervising and mentoring. But management and mentoring isn't a one-way process—you need to value your subordinates' ideas purely on their merit rather than their status or credentials. The ideal result of effective mentoring is to help people articulate ideas and strategies that are clever, original, and workable. By doing this you lessen your load as a manager. Wipro takes the idea of teaching, training, and developing people very seriously indeed.

Azim Premji notes that over 40 percent of Wipro's revenue is spent on compensation, and 6 percent of its compensation is invested in teaching. The company runs a training and development unit which is about three times the size of the Indian Institute of Management, Ahmedabad (IIMA). 'I believe that helping people in building careers by paying careful attention to their development is very important,' says Premji. 'One of our major deliverables at Wipro has been to persuade and attract excellent managers and leaders to work for us.' (Chary 2002: 56–57)

As a developer of teams and talent, every manager must:

▶ Plan and organize various activities for the development of staff
▶ Act as a role model, motivate and inspire juniors, guide and counsel them
▶ Provide a sense of ownership and importance to employees
▶ Set clear-cut performance goals for the department
▶ Provide the information and resources necessary for tasks to be performed well
▶ Monitor staff performance
▶ Provide periodic feedback and encourage innovativeness
▶ Handle staff grievances, resolve conflicts, and help staff members resolve conflicts
▶ Maintain consistency and objectivity in relation to staff decisions (rewards, promotions, placements, and so on)

G.V. Prasad, CEO of Dr Reddy's Laboratories, is a good example of a manager mentoring his juniors in a systematic way. After discovering his strengths as strategic and entrepreneurial thinking and mentoring through a 360 degree feedback, he extended his mentoring efforts to cover a large number of young managers by appointing them as his executive assistants and providing them an opportunity to observe him and learn. He reports that this enabled him to develop a pool of competent managers in his company. Every few months he appoints new managers to work with him and sends the ones he has already mentored to other departments. This also creates a positive culture.

Building juniors into potential leaders requires a manager to be a careful and compassionate listener, keep promises, recognize their efforts in a routine way, and reward them for their work through genuine and heartfelt appreciation. Building on these qualities helps managers to become excellent coaches and mentors.

While there is a separate chapter devoted to this issue, as this also requires special skills, it is sufficient to say here that there are a number of activities to be performed by a manager in a planned way to achieve the objectives of the organization. Most managers, for example, don't undertake simple activities like providing periodic performance feedback to their juniors and a few of them don't even think of listening to employee grievance as part of their job and delegate it to the HR department. As a result there is a gap in credibility and morale issues. The questionnaire given at the end of this chapter lists at least fifteen different activities that could be undertaken to inspire, manage, and motivate employees. Doers carry them out as per requirements. Achievers do them skilfully but find it difficult, sometimes, to find time. It is visionary and missionary managers who give adequate attention to the activities and perform them well.

CULTURE BUILDING

In 1989, GE's CEO Jack Welch launched a countrywide 'Work Out' programme. Its purpose was to foster a new boundary-less culture characterized by speed, simplicity, and self-confidence. GE's work culture was to be made more informal and open, everyone was expected to share ideas and learn from each other. These meetings used to be for three days. Before one of the Day 3 meetings began, Welch noticed a man standing outside the meeting hall and asked him what he was doing there. The man said he was there in case the bulb of the overhead projector needed to be changed. To this Welch replied that there were five engineers including the chairman and one of them could certainly replace a light bulb.

An organization's culture is a set of key principles and values that holds the organization together, by providing standards for its members' behaviour. Pareek likens organizational culture to a strong rim for a fast moving wheel, which integrates several factors and binds them together so that difficult and unpredictable terrain can be negotiated. If articulated clearly and well, an organization's culture becomes much easier to promote and helps reduce the inconsistency of people's actions.

Good managers focus on building a strong culture and set of values at their workplace. But they shouldn't expect to be rewarded in the short term for this contribution. It's only in the long run that the culture a manager has fostered distinguishes him/her from others. They prepare the ground for the performance of other employees—as such their beliefs and practices have a lasting impact. If you are in a managerial position, and want to inculcate a certain work culture, you have to walk the talk and live that culture yourself. Venu Srinivasan, CEO of TVS, maintains that culture filters down to the lower levels of an organization only when department heads and the top management are seen to behave in a consistent and credible way. Much like the methods needed to empower staff, managers need to:

▶ Articulate the culture (norms, values, and organizational processes) that should characterize the department

▶ Periodically remind members about the organization's culture

▶ Set a personal example, monitor that employees fit with organizational values, and institute processes and mechanisms to build the desired culture

Visionaries and missionaries are highly culture driven. In the case of missionaries in particular, a certain work culture guides their actions, the way they live and what they stand for. Parry's M.V. Subbiah, Ravi J. Matthai, Narayana Murthy, and A.P.J. Abdul Kalam have built a reputation for themselves for their simple living, high thinking, approachability, and the consistency between what they preach and practice.

Certain tools allow managers to, subtly and effectively, communicate an organization's culture to its members. In your interaction with juniors, draw upon stories that have to do with the organization's founders and anecdotes of how the workforce tided over troubled times. These narratives reflect a company's culture and values, and legitimize current patterns of behaviour. Try to establish certain *ritual practices:* for instance, it is an unwritten 'law' at McKinsey that one employee should return a phone call or respond to a message from another within twenty-four hours. These are not formal rules but evolved through consistent practice. It is also a good idea to encourage your team to internalize some of the *lingo* particular to your organization. This helps create a shared culture towards which loyalty grows steadily over time. 'MECE' is a hugely popular catchword at McKinsey, and a principle the firm's consultants swear by. This is an acronym for 'Mutually Exclusive, Collectively Exhaustive', and is how consultants refer to their collection and organization of business data before they begin to apply their problem-solving techniques.

> The culture of Southwest is probably its major competitive advantage. The intangibles are more important than the tangibles because you can always imitate the tangibles; you can buy the airplane, you can rent the ticket counter space. But the hardest thing for someone to emulate is the spirit of your people. Our esprit de corps is the core of our success. That's the most difficult for a competitor to imitate. They can buy all the physical things. The thing you can't buy is their dedication, devotion, loyalty—feeling you are participating in a cause or crusade. (Herb Kelleher, CEO, Southwest Airlines in Jeffrey 2003: 178)

TEAMWORK AND TEAM BUILDING

Jack Welch always believed that middle managers had to be the best of team members and coaches. He felt that if GE had the best manufacturing person with the best numbers, who produced high quality goods on time, but wouldn't talk to people in engineering and manufacturing, then someone would replace this person—someone perhaps not quite as perfect, but who was a team player and would lift the team's performance. Whereas the earlier person worked at 100 or even 120 percent, he got only 65 percent out of the team. But under his replacement, the team operated at 90 to 100 percent. Ultimately, the latter was far more important.

Business leaders recognize the huge importance of teams and teamwork. Herb Kelleher's mantra for recruitment at Southwest is: 'If you're an altruistic, outgoing person who likes to serve others and enjoys working with a team, we want you.' (Chary 2002: 98) But the most successful managers also realize that strong leaders build strong teams. Effective Managers are those who can exercise initiative and leadership independently, and can operate as colleagues or associates rather than submissive followers. Moreover, they are adept at the art of team building—selecting the right people with the right skills, positioning them so that they can make the greatest contribution, and fostering their sense of mutual responsibility for achieving the organization's mission and vision. The careful allocation of responsibilities within a team—factoring in members' strengths and weaknesses—is a critical managerial function and decides the efficiency of outcomes. As Narayana Murthy points out, 'A strong team brings together a set of complementary skills, expertise and experience. It is essential that the team operates on a common value system and maintains the dignity and respect of every individual in every transaction.' (Chary 2002: 98) Strong and cohesive teams are the most important development tools an organization could have. Hence managers need to engage actively in the following team-building activities:

- ▶ Fostering team spirit through group meetings, feedback, and directions
- ▶ Creating a feeling of oneness (a 'we' feeling) and a collaborative culture
- ▶ Managing different viewpoints among their own team members
- ▶ Providing information and assistance required by colleagues to facilitate teamwork and collaboration
- ▶ Acknowledging the contributions of every team member

Venu Srinivasan maintains that team building, right from (QC) circles to suggestion schemes, to cross-functional task forces, all help in defining the individual roles of people.

Increasingly, organizations are recognizing the need to build teams. They use outward-bound programmes in which the entire team of managers is taken out on an expedition to an unknown place where they undertake unusual activities and are all required to work as a team. These unusual activities may include construction of their tents, cooking, mountain climbing, and so on. These activities help them shed their inhibitions and get them closer to work as a team.

Most organizations offer team rewards in addition to the individual rewards to promote teamwork and ensure energized, enthused, and motivated teams. One example of a team reward instituted by an organization is the Quest for Excellence award instituted by Moser Baer to recognize outstanding achievement in business results. Tata Motors also offers quality-linked payments for achieving high productivity in the manufacture of vehicles, given in groups based on the ratings of cross-functional teams. For example, a team award was given when the truck ACE was produced in record time. The Trailblazer team award has been instituted by Dabur India for recognizing best performing teams. In February 2009, they recognized the good work done by their Jammu unit team during the political and social turmoil which lasted for about two months. The team ensured that the production schedules were adhered to consistently despite the constraints, while ensuring the safety and security of the employees.

LIAISON WITH THE BOSS AND TOP MANAGEMENT

Understanding, influencing, and managing your boss, and meeting his/her expectations is likely to take up much of your time as a manager. You will need to communicate and liaise with the boss and other top management to keep them informed of various developments and decisions. You have to be both sensitive and diplomatic to get your boss's or the top management's support, and win the resources you might need. Be candid, but also be open to any good advice or guidance that your superiors might have to offer you.

You might think that managing a person or a body who is your superior is inherently problematic, and indeed it usually is. But that's when some careful strategizing may help you convert your problems into opportunities. When the Ministry of Petroleum introduced the concept of memorandums of understanding (MoUs) in the late 1990s, and pushed oil companies to set and achieve annual targets, the Indian Oil Corporation included an 'organizational climate and employee satisfaction survey' in its MoU. The petroleum ministry felt that it might indeed be a good idea to survey employee satisfaction and organizational culture. The survey indicated clearly that the absence of a reward system and incentives for good performers was a major reason for dissatisfaction. The ministry read the report and asked the oil company what their plan of action was. The company responded by saying that as they had no freedom to recognize and reward outstanding performers, they could not provide an action plan. The ministry ended up granting them the autonomy to reward employees through special incentives. Thus the CEO of this company used a government requirement to 'manage' the government and get what he wanted for his employees.

The ability to influence your superiors is a significant aspect of leadership. Visionaries and missionaries are often their own bosses—rather than managing individuals who are hierarchically their superior, they need to manage and negotiate with governments, policymakers, and regulatory bodies. For doers and achievers though, the matter of managing individuals is a very real one, and something they have to deal with frequently.

CEREMONIAL ROLES, NETWORKING, PUBLIC RELATIONS, AND DEALING WITH GOVERNMENT AGENCIES

In another critical role, managers participate in receiving information, learning about the environment, meeting government officials and other regulatory bodies, suppliers, and other parties. Senior managers are also required to perform ceremonial roles such as inaugurating branches and institutions, giving speeches, attending social gatherings, festivals, etc. These bolster his position as an important member of the community. The image of a business leader or senior manager as an involved and compassionate citizen tends to build the organization as a brand, raises the morale of employees within the organization and disseminates information about the organization's mission and vision.

Nominal roles are generally taken very seriously by Indian business leaders. When K.V. Kamath accepts the chairmanship of the Confederation of Indian Industry (CII), Narayana Murthy the chairmanship of the Bangalore International Airport, when Deepak Parekh accepts to be on committees to award business excellence awards, or when they agree to help turn around Satyam Computers, not only are they conscious of the larger social good, they are also discharging some of their social responsibilities. Visionaries try to use every ceremonial position strategically.

For example, in the thick of heated discussions and security concerns after the Gujarat riots, Azim Premji addressed the convocation at IIMA. During his visit, he made it a point to meet his customers. When he was offered security he was reported to have said that he needed no security to meet his customers. While addressing the workers of the Bhilai Steel Plant on his first visit there, Dr V. Krishnamurthy found himself surrounded by the press. He kept silent for a while and let the photographers and cameramen do their job. Then after a few minutes he asked them to leave the room saying, 'I don't want to have anyone between me and my managers'.[1] This statement established his mission in one line for the rest of his tenure. Coming from the heart, this was a strategic statement that won over the other managers.

Missionaries can lobby for a licence, a change in policy, or disseminate their vision. They will use them to influence the public at large, clarify their mission, and reach out to more followers from various sections of society. It's important for aspirants to senior managerial positions to try to become involved with a few ceremonial activities as these are terrific networking opportunities.

EXTERNAL CUSTOMER RELATIONS AND CLIENT MANAGEMENT

'There is only one boss,' says Sam Walton, 'the customer. And he can fire everybody in the company from the chairman down, simply by spending his money somewhere else'. (Sam Walton in Krames 2003: 197)

Visit any branch of a nationalized bank in India, and you'll find a picture of Gandhi with the quote: 'The customer is king.' Professional researchers, managers, marketing specialists have all come to the same conclusion. Organizations, companies, non governmental organizations (NGOs) and governmental organizations (GOs) all exist to serve their customers. If you're a manager, you certainly need to understand your customers, their needs, and perspectives. You also need to meet external customers and suppliers frequently, get to know them better, evolve strategies to improve customer satisfaction, communicate with other staff about customer requirements and concerns, understand

---

[1] Author was present a that time.

the difficulties commonly faced by customers, and act on their feedback.

Michael Dell says that the secret of his company's success is its customer base. 'From the start, our entire business—from design to manufacturing to sales—was oriented around listening. Around listening to the customer, responding to the customer, and delivering what the customer wanted.' (Krames 2003: 42) Here's what you can do to cultivate closer relationships with the end-users while also generating key information and product feedback:

▶ Spend more time with the customer
▶ Use your time with customers wisely—get specific feedback about their needs and preferences
▶ Invite key customers to speak to key units
▶ Use the Internet and other non-intermediated means to create an ongoing customer relationship
▶ Make a commitment to learn more from your customers

If your company doesn't already do so, try to conduct at least one customer satisfaction survey each year in an area that would benefit from increased customer knowledge.

The very word 'customer' implies a degree of transaction. But it would be a grave error to think of your customers' needs as incidental. You need to broaden your perspective and think of customers not just as partners but close associates. Deepak Parekh, chairman of HDFC, uses the word 'affection' in a somewhat specialized sense to refer to the mindset with which a manager ought to approach his customers. It is hardly surprising then that old-timers who have met Parekh personally and benefited from the visionary's home loan reforms, still refer to him as 'apna Deepak'. Visionary leaders are intensely customer focused, but missionaries take their customer orientation to an altogether different level. At Kurien's cooperatives and at Sewa, beneficiaries of the organization's services are referred to as 'line members' or 'participants'.

CONCLUSION

Clearly, managers have to be agile and versatile—their job demands them to multi-task effectively. Given that their hectic schedules leave them with very little time—only about 2,000 hours a year— all their actions need to be focussed. Careful planning and time management are of the essence and we will devote a chapter on helping you build these skills. If you want to be an achiever-manager (and become a visionary) focus on the transformational activities discussed in this chapter. However, irrespective of what kind of manager you aspire to be, you should try and perform all these activities. Versatility is the key to becoming an effective manager.

You might want to list the activities you need to perform, organize them under different roles, keep track of the time spent on various activities, take stock of what you have been doing and what you think you should actually be doing, and enlist the help of a secretary or assistant to ease your workload. Don't lose sight of the fact that you are a team leader—so while you introspect about your tasks by yourself, don't forget those regular debriefing sessions with subordinates. Use their analytical inputs to step back and see the larger picture. Respond to issues thoughtfully rather than hastily or superficially.

Adopt a step-by-step approach.
► Have a clear vision of your outcome
► Create positive pressure to keep yourself inspired
► Never set a goal without attaching a timeline to it

If this involves the adoption of a new work routine, you might need to maintain it actively for three weeks before it crystallizes into a habit. Once you have a schedule, a routine, and a timeline in place you will find it a lot easier to streamline your activities so that you can focus on the ones you really need to. As Yogi Raman says, 'The golden key to time leadership is really doing what you planned to do, when you planned to do it... . The starting point is self-discipline.' (Sharma 2003: 183)

MANAGERIAL AND LEADERSHIP ACTIVITIES QUESTIONNAIRE

Assess yourself on how versatile you are as a manager by assessing how well you are performing the following managerial and leadership activities. You may use a 6 point scale for each of the purposes: (5 = I am performing this activity extremely well; 4 = I am performing this reasonably well; 3 = I am performing this somewhat satisfactorily, 2 = I am not performing this to my satisfaction; 1 = I am not at all performing this activity satisfactorily; 0 = I am not performing this activity at all.

I. Vision and values

☐ Articulating or developing a vision for one's department/section/unit

☐ Communicating the top management's vision of the organization or business to all employees in the department/division/unit

☐ Clearly stating the values of the department/section/unit. For example, customer service, service quality, punctuality, cost effectiveness, etc.

II. Policy formulation, planning and goal setting

- ☐ Securing critical information required for business development, strategy formulation, and performance improvements of the department/section/unit
- ☐ Setting long-term goals and objectives for his/her department/unit/section
- ☐ Setting short-term tasks and targets and clear-cut performance goals for his/her department/section/unit in various areas of operation
- ☐ Fair allocation of work to staff in his/her department/section/unit
- ☐ Formulating strategies and thinking strategically for getting results through systems, services, quality, costs, recoveries, innovation, etc.

III. Technology and systems management

- ☐ Introducing new technologies relating to his/her function.
- ☐ Building technological competencies of employees in the department/unit through training, etc.
- ☐ Keeping in touch with technological developments in related industry and/or function in the country and globally
- ☐ Introducing new systems for the effective management of various activities and operations
- ☐ Monitoring the effective implementation and utilization of systems and processes relating to his/her function
- ☐ Thinking globally, communicating global thinking and awareness of global standards and benchmarks to others in his/her areas of work
- ☐ Achieving goals, meeting targets, and delivering results

☐ Thinking entrepreneurially, coming up with alternative, cost-effective, time-saving, competitive methods to achieve plans

☐ Show high degree of ownership and commitment in whatever he/she undertakes

☐ Setting personal example and being a role model for others to imitate

IV. Inspiring, developing, and empowering staff (juniors and others reporting to her/him)

☐ Investing time and effort in the growth and development of staff

☐ Motivating and inspiring them to be excellent performers

☐ Providing information and the resources necessary for the staff to perform their tasks well

☐ Monitoring staff performance

☐ Providing periodic feedback, guidance, and coaching to enhance their impact and performance

☐ Recognizing and encouraging good performance of employees and providing a sense of ownership

☐ Listening to problems, grievances, difficulties, and conflicts of employees/staff, and diagnosing issues

☐ Handling staff grievances and resolving problems and conflicts

☐ Maintaining consistency and objectivity in relation to staff decisions (rewards, promotions, placements, etc.)

☐ Encouraging innovativeness among the staff

V. Culture building

☐ Articulating the culture (norms, values, and organizational processes) that should characterize the department/unit

☐ Setting personal example in terms of following the norms, values, and culture

☐ Instituting processes and mechanisms in the department/unit to build the desired culture

VI. Teamwork and team building

☐ Fostering a spirit of teamwork and collaboration among the staff in her/his department/section/unit

☐ Creating a feeling of oneness ('we' feeling) and team spirit among the employees of her/his department/unit/section

☐ Developing methods and systems (incentives, reviews, etc.) to foster teamwork and team spirit

☐ Acknowledging the contributions of every member of the team periodically

VII. Management of colleagues/internal customers

☐ (Colleagues = peers, internal suppliers and other functionaries having interdependencies)

☐ Developing good working relations with colleagues—by interacting with them, respecting them and being polite and frank

☐ Understanding the needs, expectations, and requirements of the colleagues/internal customers

☐ Meeting the requirements and expectations of colleagues in the organization wherever possible

☐ Acknowledging the contributions of colleagues and internal customers and getting their co-operation

☐ Learning from colleagues/internal customers and benefiting from their experiences

VIII. Liaison with boss and top management

☐ Communicating and liaising with the boss/top management to keep them informed about various developments, decisions, issues, etc.

☐ Understanding the expectations of the boss and the top management

☐ Influencing the thinking of the boss and getting the necessary support and resources

☐ Taking guidance and learning from the experiences of the boss and other seniors

☐ Getting the support needed from the boss and the top management

IX. External customer relations and client management

☐ Meeting external customers/suppliers frequently and getting to know them better

☐ Evolving strategies to improve customer satisfaction

☐ Communicating to other staff about customer requirements and concerns

☐ Understanding the difficulties and solving problems of customers

☐ Seeking suggestions from customers in order to improve services provided by the unit and taking the suggestions seriously

Add your scores. If your scores exceed 200 points you are a highly versatile manager. Those who score below 100 need to step up their effort to perform some of the critical roles. Perhaps they are acting at the level of doers rather than as achievers. Discuss with your seniors and rate each item on its importance to your job.

Research by Dr Raju Rao at TVRLS has indicated that star performers are rated by their seniors, juniors, and colleagues as performing each of the activities mentioned in this questionnaire far above the average performers.

Those who perform well on these items are showing a tendency to be leaders and perhaps are likely to move into the visionary category from that of the achievers: 1, 2, 3, 4, 5, 8, 9, 10, 11, 12, 14, 16, 18, 19, 21, 22, 24, 28, 29, 30, 31, 34, 40, 43, and 47.

Visionaries and missionaries may not perform some of these activities well but focus on doing some of them to an extraordinary degree. They are likely to become versatile visionaries and missionaries if they also master performing a number of the activities mentioned in this tool.

REFERENCES

A. Krames Jeffrey (2003), *What the best CEOs Know*, New York: Mc Graw Hill, pp. 42 and 178.

Robin S. Sharma (2003), *Leadership Wisdom*, Mumbai: Jaico Publications, p. 51.

Robin S. Sharma, *Leadership Wisdom*; p. 183.

S.N. Chary (2002), *Business Gurus Speak*, New Delhi: Macmillan India.

Ibid., pp. 56–57.

Ibid.

Sam Walton, in Krames A. Jeffrey (2003), *What the Best CEOs Know*; New York: McGraw-Hill.

2

Efficacy

In the first chapter we have presented an overview of the key qualities a manager needs to possess. In the next four chapters we will look at some of the internal drivers that shape a manager's effectiveness. The more aware we are of these, the more we can develop them. This chapter deals with the 'sense of efficacy' or the self-image managers project about themselves. Efficacy can be measured by various methods. A simple question like 'Who am I?' or an essay written by the individual about himself is one good indicator. People with a positive self-image—and thus those who are more effective—view themselves differently from those who are less so.

WHAT IS A SENSE OF EFFICACY?

Consider the following three examples of managers who were asked to write an essay titled 'Who Am I?'

> I am Sampath Bapatla, 42 years old. I am manager in Finance and Accounts in ... I was born in an ordinary family of teachers. Both my parents were teachers. My father was highly respected for his teaching in the village. He was very popular in the area. I had all the good things in life. He was able to educate me well. He always

dreamt that the family should go abroad and earn as much as possible. He had been through a very tough life and he wanted the family not to suffer like him. He did his best to get us educated. Now I am a senior-level manager in a software company. I would like to make sure that my parents who suffered for us so much have a decent life. My aim in life is to have a good family and look after my family well.

I keep asking myself this question. This question is being asked for hundreds and thousands of years and by all kinds of people including sages and great gurus. I am afraid there is no easy answer for this. Sometimes I feel that there is no point in asking such questions. However, since you asked me the question let me attempt an answer. I am one of the millions that come to this earth unannounced and vanish. I am a drop in the big ocean called humanity. I like to do things in the way I am expected to. I like to be a good husband to my wife, a good son to my parents, a good parent to my children and most of all a good human being as expected by society. I believe in taking life as it comes. There is no point struggling hard and aiming for big things. I don't have ambitions to be a great person like some people. I am satisfied with what I have. I want to do my duty and exit from this world when my time comes. Many people who want to be great are really not that great. Behind most people who are claimed as great, there was someone who sacrificed and suffered for them. I don't want such greatness. I am fine as an ordinary human being.

I am a person with great values and I am grateful to my parents, friends, and teachers for giving me these. I am an engineer by background and subsequently did my MBA. While studying engineering I had to choose between doing well in my degree or to prepare for the IIM entrance tests called CAT. I preferred to do well in my BE and stood first in engineering though I could not make it to any of the IIMs. I got into Jamnalal Bajaj which is a decent management school located in Mumbai. In my management school, I took up marketing and stood first in the class. I was sent to America on an exchange programme where I made a mark. I got a job in one of my dream companies and developed new brands and made record sales in my early years there. I was posted in small towns for the first three years. That was a great experience for me for I learnt what real marketing means. Once I was posted to a big town and was given high targets to meet. I had no time even to search for my accommodation and decided to stay in the company guest house. One day the HR head of my company visited the company guest house where I was staying. He was surprised to see me there because apparently the guest house was meant for higher-level officials and not for juniors like me. Instead of appreciating the work I was doing and encouraging me he asked me to vacate the guest house as it would set a wrong precedent. It is at that time I decided that I would change the thinking of such HR people who seem to make the lives of others miserable. I decided to become a trainer of HR managers. Now I am one of the most respected coaches in the country and I help young men and women enhance their effectiveness and lead a peaceful and enriching life. My purpose in life is to make some difference to others all the time. I enjoy music. I enjoy being with people. I enjoy sharing my experiences with others. I have a lovely family who always support whatever I do and I support them in their life. I get a lot of positive feedback and it makes me feel happy when someone says that I was the turning point in their life. The younger generation is living in a complex world. They need constant guidance. I can understand their hearts and souls. I hope I can make a difference and make the lives of others more meaningful. That is what makes my life meaningful.

A sense of efficacy is the feeling of inner worth and effectiveness that the individual always carries with him. Such people take more initiative, approach situations with confidence and optimism, and therefore are likely to succeed better than others. (See the appendices on how to measure your efficacy.)

THE FOUR CHARACTERISTICS OF EFFICACY

A person with a high sense of efficacy usually exhibits certain characteristics. Pfizer (1971), who developed a manual for scoring an individual's sense of efficacy, listed them as follows:

- ▶ Action goal orientation or goal making
- ▶ Internal locus of resources or the harnessing of inner resources
- ▶ Problem-solving
- ▶ Taking initiative

Now let us examine these in detail.

Action goal orientation

People who are driven by goals are often very active. This is because having a goal makes us focused. It allows us to use our competencies and talents in more directed ways, reduces wastage of time and gives meaning to life. Goals may be of any kind. They could be organization related, team related, friends and family related, societal, competency building, service goals, etc. Goals are either long or short term. Long-term goals may include becoming a CEO of a company, changing the values and culture of an organization, reforming society, getting rich, serving the nation, and the like, while short-term goals refer more to the immediate circumstances of a person—passing an examination or doing better than the previous year, overtaking someone else, getting a decent job.

Here's Shantanu Prakash (IIMA 1988), the creator of Educomp, a multi-crore organization influencing and providing quality education to millions of children across the country.

> I remember, the first office didn't even have a fan. But I didn't seem to mind at all at that point of time. I was so completely obsessed with what I was doing and what I was building. So when I look back, I think that was the coolest year of my life. That I was planning to do the most significant things that I could ever hope to do.

Vijay Mahajan (PGP IIMA 1980) is another example of a long-term action goal-driven individual. Ten years before C.K. Prahalad came up with his notion of 'bottom of the pyramid', Vijay Mahajan established an organization doing just that. He created Basix, a microfinance institution that serves the poor and empowers them to enhance their earnings. Mahajan had his encounters with poverty while he was in school at St Xavier's, Jaipur, and while he was an undergraduate at IIT he sought to solve the problems of the poor through technology. After his graduation from IIM, he moved away from the corporate world creating an NGO called PRADAN. He went on to become a consultant specializing in rural livelihoods before setting up Basix. Each of these actions shows an individual working towards a long-term goal.

Short- and Long-term Goals: These goals may coexist in a person. For example, a student may have a long-term goal of becoming rich through a good posting and a career in an MNC and a short-term goal of doing well in his or her exam. Many people may have multiple goals: getting a big salary, a foreign posting, a job in a prestigious company, etc. If the short-term and long-term goals are linked, they become an even stronger force for motivation for the person. For example, doing well in one's exams (short term) will most likely lead to getting a job in a good company (long term). Conversely if one's multiple goals are contradictory, one's sense of efficacy is hampered. For example, becoming rich and serving the poor by starting an NGO could be contradictory goals and require a lot of high-level competencies to achieve both simultaneously. At some point one of the goals will inevitably become stronger than the other. The individual will oscillate between the two and may experience guilt while placing one over the other. In such cases a person's energy and drive will diminish and his sense of efficacy will become less. Thus, it is always better to pursue mutually compatible goals and to be clear-sighted about them and plan them for particular durations. For example, a person may decide that he should focus for the next ten years on getting rich. He may say to himself that 'once I get rich without sacrificing my values I will start an NGO. It may take place when I am 50 or when I am 45 but not when I am 30.'

Superordinate goals: These are not ordinary goals. They are meant to serve a larger principle. In creating and working towards these goals, a person derives satisfaction from the feeling that she is existing for a cause. Perhaps she was born for that. As one starts doing good work, others begin to appreciate them. With every good deed the person gets more power, appreciation, and recognition and this has a tremendous force. Take the example of Sarath Babu, the IIMA graduate who decided to set up his own 'idli factory' immediately after his studies at IIMA instead of taking up a high-paid, secure job. He has become a success story and a role model for many management graduates to emulate. Recently he narrated an incident about a troubled young girl who was about to end her life. She came across Sarath Babu's story and was so inspired by his achievements that she decided to live and make something of herself. It is incidents of this kind that help build one's determination to work for superordinate goals even though they may be weak at first.

Superordinate goals give individuals a high sense of efficacy. Mahatma Gandhi worked for India's independence while adhering strictly to the principle of non-violence. This was the driving force that enabled him to make several sacrifices and it was this ability to make sacrifices, not seeking power for himself and leading a simple, non-materialist life that made him the greatest leader on earth. Dr Verghese Kurien is another example of a superordinated goal achiever. He worked single-mindedly to make India self-sufficient in milk production and was the architect of Operation Flood, the world's largest dairy development programme. Narayana

Murthy of Infosys started with a long-term goal of liberating IT and generating wealth to be distributed among a large number of those who work for Infosys. After creating Wipro, Azim Premji started devoting his time to nation building and has been promoting education in rural India. They are all examples of superordinated goal seekers.

Action goals and essence goals: Action goals are also powerful goals, although they fall below the superordinate category. They refer to those goals where the person sees himself as *doing* things once he achieves the goal. Action goals in short represent a state of doing rather than being. For example, someone may want to become the CEO of the company so that he can bring a change in some of its policies or practices, or change its direction. Conversely, someone may want to merely be in the position of CEO of a company because he or she enjoys being the head; once he achieves this, his goal will be to protect the 'being called CEO' than actually do something in the position. Doing makes one restless. Being makes one enjoy that achievement and protect the state. Doing goals make one efficacious. Always change your being goal into a doing goal.

What makes a person a good manager is a high sense of personal efficacy and this arises from the way their goals are oriented— superordinate, action, or essence. People who approach life without any goals waste their time and talent. Effective managers are goal driven. Where there are no goals they discover some and make them a part of their life.

Locus of resources

Human beings are complex and competent. Every day we discover new things. Our learning comes from actions, interactions, observations, reading, reflection, assimilation, conceptualizing or abstractions, etc. An individual who keeps himself isolated from his environment has limited learning; those who use multiple sources, senses, and the processes mentioned above learn more. And as we learn we develop our faculties. That is how competencies are formed. And as we grow, our consciousness or awareness of our strengths and weaknesses becomes enhanced. *Awareness of our strengths and weaknesses—in short, our inner resources—helps us in making conscious choices and enhances effectiveness.*

Two behavioural scientists, John Ingam and Harry Luft, created an interesting method popularly called a Johari window. Ingram and Luft argued that our personality can be viewed as, of conceptualizing ourselves four parts. These four parts are a combination of those aspects which are known or unknown to us about ourselves and those aspects that are known or unknown about ourselves to others.

An **open** or **public self** consists of those aspects that are known to yourself and also known to others. Many of our strengths and faults for example are known to us as well as to those who interact with us. Someone may be an expert in IT and most of her colleagues would be aware this. A talkative person, an introvert, a sociable person, etc. would be regarded as such by both themselves and others. These are, in short, qualities that constitute our public self.

A **closed** or a **private self** is made up of those qualities of which only the individual is aware. Most of us have strengths, weaknesses, and habits which are not known to others as we may not like to talk about them. For example, most people don't openly discuss their religious views and prejudices. Modesty also prevents most people from sharing their strengths with others. As a result talents exhibited in early years go unnoticed later unless a situation is created to use them. An HRD manager in one company may have worked in an earlier company as a materials manager and done a great job of vendor development. However, as he has been recruited to head HRD, he may never get an opportunity to apply his talent in vendor development.

A **blind spot** is an aspect of themselves which the individual is not aware of but which others are. We all have strengths and weaknesses which others perceive in us but which are not known to us. In relationship-valuing societies and cultures like the Asian cultures, people will normally tell you things that please you and refrain from giving negative feedback. In such societies people may have a sizeable chunk of blind spots. An individual may pride himself on being flexible and creative while the same behaviour may be interpreted or experienced by his subordinates as inconsistent and unreliable (as he keeps changing his views due to his creativity, others affected by it may perceive the inconsistency in the ideas, etc.).

A **dark** or **hidden** part is the aspect of themselves which neither the individual nor others are aware of. This is because we may never get an opportunity to experience what we are capable of. Indeed during our entire lifetime we may discover just a small part of our potential.

How can you use the Johari window to assess yourself? Consider the following points:

▶ Too many blind spots impede effectiveness. These can be reduced by seeking feedback from others, accepting it, reflecting on it, and using it to improve oneself.

▶ Discovering more of your dark arena helps bring out latent talent. Your dark arena can be reduced by undertaking new tasks, activities, exploring new methods of working, experimenting, job rotation, etc.

Leaders, effective managers, and effective people constantly explore their dark arena and attempt to reduce blind spots. *The greater our self-awareness and our striving towards it, the stronger our sense of efficacy and thus our performance as managers.*

In January 2003 Mr Vanikkar (name changed), Chief of ABC Consumer Products Manufacturing Unit, decided to get himself profiled using a 360 degree feedback. A 360 degree feedback is an anonymous assessment of the candidate by his boss, subordinates, peers, and others who work with him. It also includes self-assessment. The HR firm sent him a set of fifteen questionnaires to be distributed to his associates (boss, subordinates, and colleagues). Of them ten sent their assessments. The analysis of the data suggested that there were both similarities and differences between Vanikkar's self-perceptions and his colleagues' views of him. Vanikkar assessed himself as good at delegation, in inspiring and empowering staff, keeping in touch with the technological developments, teamwork and team building, and being well organized. His weak areas he felt were meeting external customers/suppliers, not being sufficiently flexible, proactive, receptive and sociable. His juniors assessed him as technologically sound and highly systems driven but not flexible, receptive, and proactive. They also assessed him as weak in delegation and in inspiring and empowering juniors. They felt that he was well organized but soft spoken and not assertive. It was clear by this 360 degree assessment what Vanikkar's blind spots and open areas were.

Initiative and proactiveness

The third factor that contributes to our sense of efficacy is initiative and proactiveness. Initiative is the ability to do things on one's own. Proactive people are self-driven and act on their inner convictions. These are important qualities for leaders and managers.

If a manager spends his waking life doing what others want him to do, a large part of his talent may get wasted. It is not how much initiative you take that is important but your self-perception as being one who takes initiative. People who view themselves as proactive are likely to take more initiative than those who see themselves as conformists. Conformity and discipline are important for any society. However, if you live only to meet the expectations of others then you may end up wasting a large part of your talent. We must constantly strive to discover what we are capable of doing.

This is what the American psychologist Abraham Maslow called self-actualization. Maslow wrote his paper in the 1940s. The context is different now sixty years on. One need not wait for old age to become self-actualized. Today's generation have many avenues to take care of their basic needs (in Maslow's pyramid an individual has to go through a few stages before they can achieve this final one) and so they can move to self-actualization earlier. In fact one's search for self-actualization could start in school and college days even though it may be resolved later.

Proactive people are doers. They take initiative and make things happen.

Dr V. Krishnamurthy, former chairman of SAIL, member of the Planning Commission, and current chairman of the Commission for Manufacturing for the Government of India, is a great example of an initiative-taking manager. When he joined SAIL as chairman in 1985 it was a loss-making company. He realized that the company had tremendous talent in its employees which was not being harnessed. He initiated a project called priority for action where he got all the managers involved to diagnose SAIL's problems and find ways to resolve them. He changed the performance appraisal system, conducted a series of action workshops, and turned around SAIL within his five years there.

Problem-solving

One is likely to face difficulties in any job. To set up a company one has to cross many hurdles. In carrying out one's own job there are always issues, some created by employees, others by infrastructure inadequacies (power failure, inadequate facilities like roads, transport, materials, etc.), employee unions, strikes, rising prices, consumer movements, share price fluctuations, bureaucratic processes, corruption of others, etc. To be an effective manager one needs to manage things. In fact a manager's life may be best described as continuous problem-solving. Therefore, the capacity to solve problems becomes an important part of his or her effectiveness. Our sense of efficacy is strongly connected to our perceptions of ourselves as either problem solvers or avoiders.

In the early 1980s, Kiran Bedi was in charge of traffic police in Delhi. She found that the congestion caused in the city was largely due to vehicles being parked in unauthorized places. The Delhi traffic police, however, didn't have enough cranes to lift these illegally parked vehicles. Bedi summoned private crane operators and created an incentive system where the crane operators could also make money by collecting a fee from the car owners. She was named 'Crane Bedi' because of this initiative.

HOW EFFICACY IS ACQUIRED AND HOW IT CAN BE DEVELOPED

Our sense of efficacy is acquired from early childhood. Parents, teachers, our surroundings, friends, and the community, all have a role to play. Here is Shantanu Prakash again on how he developed his goal-oriented, proactive approach to life:

> Whenever my dad used to travel, he used to buy me books. In fact I don't remember getting other presents except books. And so I used to read voraciously. And probably that unlocked something in my mind. Big thinking, big horizon, and so on. Secondly, when my dad retired and wanted to come and settle down in Delhi, he found that he didn't have enough money to buy even a DDA flat. Right! So somewhere at the back on my mind I thought that if I need to make money, then working in a job is probably not going to do it for me. (Bansal 2008: 20)

Studies by David McClelland (1961) quoted in his famous book *The Achieving Society* indicate that the way in which children are brought up in their early years influence personality formation, in particular achievement motivation or a drive to do things well and accomplish higher goals. A high sense of efficacy is one of the qualities of the achievement syndrome. *Mothers who are demanding and encouraging have been found to create achievement motivation in their children. Similarly reading motivational stories of great achievers helps children develop or enhance their self-worth.*

Not all of us are born in a nurturing environment and unfortunately people born in disadvantaged families or in discriminated groups may run the risk of developing a low sense of efficacy. However, research studies have also indicated that it is possible to develop a high sense of efficacy even later in life. For years Indian behavioural scientists and behavioural science trainers from other countries have been experimenting with feedback using psychometric tools, role play, classroom exercises, and motivational storytelling. These have been found to be effective tools. In the following section are some more suggestions about increasing efficacy.

HOW YOU CAN DEVELOP YOUR SENSE
OF EFFICACY

Here are some simple ways you can help increase your sense of efficacy:

▶ Internalize the four aspects of the sense of efficacy and keep writing incidents that happen in your life every day where you demonstrated one or more dimensions of this.

▶ What are your goals: short term and long term? What goal did you have for today? What is your goal for the next few months? What do you want to achieve at the end of the year? Or a few years from now? What is your career goal? Share your goals with another individual. Find a mentor and share your thoughts on your goals.

▶ What is one initiative you would like to take for the day? What did you do yesterday which indicates that you have taken initiative?

▶ How does your work affect others? What difference would you want to make for others today?

▶ Read one story a day about people who made a difference. If it is possible, interview and talk to one significant personality every month. These will help develop your confidence to be like them. They will give you the language to think and condition your thinking for higher-level goals.

▶ Attend training programmes like Vipasana, Seven Habits of Effective People, Shiv Khera's programmes and any other personal effectiveness programmes.

EFFICACY AT WORK

It has been observed that individuals with a high sense of efficacy approach their jobs and life situations differently from those with low efficacy. People with low efficacy often complain that they are not getting what they want, people around them are not being helpful, they are being exploited, etc., while those with a high sense of efficacy try to get the maximum out of each experience and continue to generate more experiences.

Consider the following responses by two of IIM graduates, both IITs toppers and IIM rank holders. Both were employed as executive assistants to the marketing director of two different organizations in two different cities. Both of them were working in similar companies. When the author visited them six months after they were employed and asked them to describe their job and how they were enjoying it, the conversation was something like this:

Person A: I am not sure what to say. I must admit that I am not at all comfortable doing what I am doing. I am not doing anything significant. When the HR head and one of the line managers came to the campus for recruitment they drew a great picture about this company and my job. I was promised a number of things and none of that has happened. I came here with the expectation that I will have an opportunity to use my talent. Being an IIT topper and IIM rank holder I came with eagerness to participate in strategy formulation, making marketing policies, influencing pricing, deciding marketing budgets, and helping the company and the director of marketing implement them. I was given a nice office next to the senior vice president (SVP). It was a good cabin and had all facilities. I was happy in the beginning but soon I was quite disillusioned to discover that my job has nothing to do with policies and strategies. I sit next to the SVP to act more like his secretary than as a manager. I am supposed to maintain his appointments though a secretary assists him, and it almost amounts to my doing the job. I am supposed to coordinate the visits of various customers and vendors. You know what that means. It means booking their hotels, arranging their transport, making their appointments, arranging their meetings, settling their bills, etc.—all clerical jobs. Then I am supposed to arrange the weekly and monthly marketing meetings for the department as well as the other departments. It means booking the meeting rooms, setting the agenda, circulating the agenda, taking down the minutes, getting them approved by the boss, ensuring that coffee and tea are served during the meetings and incurring the wrath of the boss in case of delays, etc. There is no strategy and there is nothing here to learn. I get my salary on time which is of course a great thing. However, Professor, I am wasting all my talent and keep feeling what a gap there is between what you all taught and what we are doing here. I feel that I should get out of this place after a year.

Person B: Thank you Professor. I am quite happy here and am learning a lot. I sit next to the SVP Marketing. He is a person with twenty-five years of experience and has worked in three companies before he joined here. He is not an MBA but more than an MBA in terms of his experience and thinking. However, he is not exposed to systems and I help him a lot. For example, I am required to maintain his appointments. He does not have a secretary but I help him as his executive assistant. I have developed an electronic diary on Google and after two months, began to help him to analyse the way he was spending his time. It helped him a lot. He discovered that 30 percent of his time goes into unplanned activities. He now regularly consults me and asks for my feedback on how to a make his role more effective and strategic. I have also begun to mentor some junior executives which he requested me to do after my analysis of his schedule.

I manage the customers and other visitors to this company. It was a little difficult in the first two weeks as I was new to this company but it gave me an opportunity to learn about it. I went to each HOD and asked them to give me a brief so that I could brief the customers who visit us about the various functions of the company. Now I know the company perfectly. I book the hotel accommodation and transport for the visitors and customers.

Each one has their preferences. I have explored all the hotels in the city and now have all their details, the concession they give, etc. I also know the customers' preferences of hotels and have knowledge about the taxi system and various vendors of taxi services. This task of arranging their transport and hotels gave me an opportunity to explore the city. I am supposed to book the meeting rooms and ensure that the discussions are minuted. I kept quiet and observed for the first three weeks. After the fourth meeting I pointed out to the boss that the decision taken at the meeting is problematic as the pricing they decided on ignored some variables. My boss appreciated my input and started involving me in the discussions. Now he consults me on the agenda and also relies totally on me to maintain and manage the minutes and follow-up of the decisions taken. I have also gained a lot of his confidence.

This company gives me a great opportunity to learn and use my capabilities. I am happy and am learning and almost feel that I am the SVP Marketing.

Which of them is likely to be more effective?

The answer is obvious. Person A views everything negatively and expects learning to come to his doorstep while person B takes initiative and sees an opportunity to learn in everything including administrative tasks. He is confident, takes initiative, applies his knowledge anywhere including minor issues like maintaining the schedule of his boss, booking hotel and transport for customers, and managing minutes of departmental meetings and booking meeting rooms and support services. The first one has a fixed mind and treats everything as a burden. Obviously the second person is likely to be more effective.

Udai Pareek formulated a term called 'role efficacy' (Pareek 1983) where he extended the idea of efficacy to professional roles. Role efficacy is defined as the potential effectiveness of an individual occupying a particular role in an organization. It consists of making your role the way you like (role making), feeling important and central in the organization through your position (role centring), and linking various aspects of the job to make it stronger (role linking). The various dimensions of role efficacy include:

1. Self-role integration: Where the role provides individuals with greater opportunity to use their special strengths. Integration between self and the role leads to higher role efficacy while distance between the self and the role leads to low role efficacy.

2. Proactively: Proactive behaviour (taking initiative) contributes to higher efficacy. While reactive behaviour (merely responding to the expectations of others) contributes less to efficacy. Lack of opportunity to take initiative leads to low efficacy.

3. Creativity: Opportunity for creativity and innovation increases role efficacy while performing only routine tasks becomes harmful for high role efficacy.

4. Confrontation: Confronting problems and reaching a relevant solution contributes to higher role efficacy while avoiding problems or shifting problems to others leads to low role efficacy.

5. Centrality: A person's perception of the role as central to the organization contributes to high role efficacy while a person's perception of the role as peripheral is likely to lead to low role efficacy.

6. Influence: The more influence/power a person is able to exercise in the role, the higher the efficacy.

7. Personal growth: A person's perception of the role as providing opportunity to grow and develop leads to higher role efficacy while the perception that the role does not provide the opportunity to develop contributes to low role efficacy.

8. Inter-role linkage: Linking one's role with others' increases efficacy. Joint efforts in identification of problems, problem-solving, etc., increases role efficacy.

9. Helping relationship: A person's perception that help is available when needed, leads to higher role efficacy. While the perception that respondents are hostile leads to low role efficacy.

10. Superordination: Opportunities to work for superordinate goals have the highest role efficacy while the perception that performance in a role is of value to the organization, leads to higher efficacy.

CONCLUSION

Pareek's formulation is a useful way for us to summarize the importance of efficacy in our working lives. Persons with high efficacy tend to rely on their own strengths to solve problems, use more purposeful behaviour, are active and interactive with people and the environment, persist in solving problems, show growth orientation, show attitudinal commitment, are positive in their approach and are satisfied with their jobs and role in the organization. These are the factors that make a successful manager as we will see in the following chapters. Each of these qualities are rooted in a manager's sense of efficacy or the self-image he carries with him.

REFERENCES

Bansal, Rashmi (2008). *Stay Hungry Stay Foolish*: CIIE, Ahmedabad, IIMA, (SHSF).

Cappelli, Peter, Harbir Singh, Jitendra V. Singh, and Michael Useem (2010). *The India Way: How India's Top Business Leaders are Revolutionizing Management*. Boston, MA: Harvard Business Press.

———. (2010b). 'Leadership Lessons from India', *Harvard Business Review*, March 2010, pp. 90–7.

Chary, S.N. (2002). *Business Gurus Speak*. New Delhi: Macmillan.

McClelland, David C. (1961). *The Achieving Society*. New York: Free Press, D. Van No. Strand & Co.

Pfizer, Stuart (1971). 'A Scoring Manual for Sense of Efficacy', in David C. McClelland and David G. Winter (eds), *Motivating Economic Achievement: Accelerating Economic Development through Psychological Education*. New York: Free Press, pp. 379–85.

Pota, Vikas (2010). *India Inc. How India's Top Ten Entrepreneurs are Winning Globally*. London: Nicholas Brealey.

Rao, T.V. and Raju Rao (eds). (2001). *Performance Management and 360 Degree Feedback*, Volume 1. New Delhi: Excel Publications.

APPENDIX

HOW TO MEASURE YOUR SENSE OF EFFICACY

You can get an adequate sense of your own efficacy by using the tests in the appendices.

Appendix 1 refers to a test called 'who am I?' In this test the individual is asked to write an essay about himself or herself. There are no other directions given. The story can be analysed for sense of efficacy using the criteria mentioned in the chapter. The three excerpts that opened this chapter are examples of this.

The sense of an individual's efficacy can be measured by interview questions. The questions may deal with the goals of the person, self-perceptions about their strengths and weaknesses, etc. A list of questions that can be asked in interviews is given in appendix 2.

A psychometric test called the personal effectiveness questionnaire is another test used to measure efficacy. A short version of the questionnaire along with its interpretation is given in appendix 3.

2. 1: WHO AM I?

The essays written about one's self can be scored for sense of efficacy. You may write an essay about yourself. The following instructions need to be followed in writing the essay:

Write an essay about yourself in the next 10 to 15 minutes. Write whatever you consider as significant about yourself. Please assume you are speaking about yourself through this essay. You may write whatever you like in the time period given. Alternatively you must write at least fifteen to twenty sentences about yourself. There are no other restrictions.

The essay can be scored using the manuals given by Pfizer (Pfizer 1971: 379–85). There also other systems presented by Udai Pareek in his book *Handbook of Instruments for Trainers* (2008) published by Tata McGraw-Hill. An easy way to score is to examine the strength or the extent to which the four categories mentioned above are reflected in the essay written by the person.

2.2: LIST OF QUESTIONS TO BE ASKED IN INTERVIEW FOR DETERMINING SENSE OF EFFICACY

Please describe yourself in two minutes.

- ▶ What are your current goals?
- ▶ What are your goals for the next few years?
- ▶ What are your life goals?
- ▶ Describe one or two situations you faced in the recent past which you consider as high or low points in your career or job or life and describe them in terms of what you did, felt, thought, etc.
- ▶ What do you consider as your strong points?
- ▶ What are a few areas you often think that you need to strengthen or improve?
- ▶ What are your weak areas or what qualities do you consider as hindering your effectiveness?
- ▶ What are your key strengths?
- ▶ Mention a few of the problems you have faced and tell us your story of how you approached them or solved them
- ▶ What are some of the initiatives taken by you in the recent past or at any time in your life?

2. 3: THE PERSONAL EFFECTIVENESS QUESTIONNAIRE

Rate yourself on each statement using the following 5-point rating scale.

0 = not at all characteristic of you or you normally do not do this (0 to less than 10 percent)

1 = not characteristic of you and you may do this rarely (less than 25 percent)

2 = somewhat characteristic of you and you do this sometimes (50 percent)

3 = fairly characteristic of you and you may do this most of the time (around 75 percent)

4 = highly characteristic of you and you do this almost always (90 percent and above)

☐ I am always involved in some activity or the other and find it very difficult to find any free time.

☐ I express myself openly without inhibitions.

☐ I go out of my way to seek feedback on the impact of my actions on others.

☐ I am very sensitive to the feelings of others.

☐ I spend time gathering information about various things.

☐ I have no inhibitions in talking about myself even to strangers.

☐ I make it a point to seek feedback about myself from my superiors.

☐ I can easily make out if a person with whom I am talking is not interested in what I am saying.

☐ I do not like to change my habits and methods unless it is essential.*

☐ I volunteer information about myself to others most of the time.

☐ I make it a point to seek feedback from my colleagues.

☐ I am very sensitive to the moods of my colleagues.

☐ I like to take new initiatives and play leadership roles at my workplace.

☐ In the company of strangers I can be counted upon to speak freely.

☐ I actively seek feedback from my subordinates.

☐ I am very sensitive to the feelings of my boss.

☐ I like to do different things and have variety in my work.

☐ I express my disagreement without any inhibition with my superiors.

☐ I keep trying to find out how my behaviour is being perceived by those with whom I have been interacting.

☐ I am very sensitive to the feelings even of strangers.

☐ I am not happy if I am not involved in some activity or the other all the time.

☐ I express my views and opinions freely to my colleagues.

☐ If someone criticizes me I tend to ignore and not bother than to think about it.*

☐ I am very perceptive of the non-verbal messages given by others in interpersonal conversation.

☐ I do a lot of things in my job without being afraid of making mistakes.

☐ I express my feelings even if they are not likely to be acceptable to others.

☐ I value what people have to say about my habits, style, behaviour, etc.

☐ I often find myself in situations where the other person misunderstands what I said.*

☐ I am careful in my work and prefer not to take any risks by doing new things or working in new ways.*

☐ I express my feelings frankly and openly, even if they are likely to hurt others.

☐ I am highly receptive when a colleague shares his views and opinions about me.

☐ I am quite perceptive in making out the positive or negative feelings or attitudes of people.

☐ I prefer to keep myself engaged in some activity or the other all the time.

☐ I volunteer and give feedback to others even if I am not asked.

☐ When someone gives feedback to me I receive it without hesitation.

☐ My judgement of people is mostly accurate (for example, open minded or close-minded, cooperative or uncooperative, etc.).

☐ I prefer to test myself out in various new situations and do not hesitate to take up new activities.

☐ I do not contradict anyone if I sense that it is likely to be unacceptable to the other person.*

☐ I think and reflect seriously about the feedback others give me.

☐ More often than not I can judge the integrity or character of others correctly.

SCORING SHEET

Transfer your scores on to the following sheet after reversing them for the asterisked items. So if your score on the asterisked items is 0 , make it 4; if it is 1 make it 3, if it is 3 make it 1, if it is 4 make it 0. If you have scored 2 on the asterisked item, keep it as is. The scores for the other questions are to be kept as they are. Calculate the total in the end.

Exploratory Orientation	Self-disclosure	Receptivity to Feedback	Sensitivity
Item No.	Item No.	Item No.	Item No.
1-----	2------	3-------	4-------
5-----	6------	7-------	8-------
9-----	10-----	11------	12-----
13-----	14-----	15------	16------
17-----	18-----	19------	20------
21-----	22------	23------	24------
25-----	26------	27------	28------
29-----	30------	31------	32------
33-----	34------	35-------	36-------
37------	38------	39-------	40-------
Total	Total	Total	Total

UNDERSTANDING THE TEST

Each one of us is born with tremendous potential to do a number of things. In our lifetime we are not likely to realize even a small part of it. However, some people discover and apply more of their potential while some may not be able to discover even a small part of it. The reason for our underperformance is that we are not fully aware of our inner resources, hidden potential, and inability to utilize resources. This lack of awareness about our inner resources affects our effectiveness. Our potential to perform is immense but the major hindrance of this is lack of knowledge about ourselves.

MAJOR FACTORS WHICH CONTRIBUTE TO OUR PERSONAL EFFECTIVENESS

- ▶ **Exploratory orientation**: The more you do and act the more you learn about yourself. A person scoring high on this is initiative taking, not afraid to make mistakes, can also take risks, is restless at work, enjoys high activity, and likes change.
- ▶ **Self-disclosure**: When you communicate with others, you learn more about yourself. The person scoring high on this shows a willingness to be open to others and share opinions, views, feelings, and knowledge with others.
- ▶ **Receptivity to feedback**: This refers to the feedback we receive from others, often about our blind spots. It allows us to assess the impact of our actions and learn more about our strengths and weaknesses.
- ▶ **Sensitivity**: Understanding your own feelings and being sensitive to the feelings of others is vital in our personal

effectiveness. Sensitivity is essential for exploratory orientation, self-disclosure, and receptivity to feedback. It is a basis of all three. Sensitivity helps you to strike a perfect balance between the three.

Thus, in order to be effective we need to know more about ourselves and work on areas of improvement. This test will help you to know about yourself on the various dimensions of personal effectiveness. Scores above 30 are high while below 20 can be considered as low. A high score on all the four facets makes you the ideal manager. A low score will indicate the areas you have to work on.

3

Internality

People and their attitudes can be classified in many ways. One of the determinants of what they are more or less likely to do (whether they put in their best in any given task, for example) is a way to attribute successes, failures, and other events that happen to them. Some of us attribute what happens to us to outside factors such as luck, chance, powerful others, etc., while others attribute their situation to their own ability, hard work, commitment, and activity level. Those who tend to attribute successes, failures, or events that happen to them to outside factors are called *externals* or are said to have an *external locus of control*; those who attribute them to internal factors are called *internals* or are said to have an *internal locus of control*. This chapter deals with the extent to which managers believe that they can make things happen and the extent to which they leave things to chance, luck, and other external factors. In the long run, effective managers are driven internally and attribute successes and failures to factors largely within themselves. Internality is one of the key forces in leadership—the better the manager, the more internal he/she is. Moving on from this we will look at some of the other qualities of leaders and ask what it takes to be a global leader.

LOCUS OF CONTROL

Locus of control is a term in psychology which refers to a person's belief about what causes the good or bad results in their life. The concept was developed by the American psychologist Julian B. Rotter in 1954, and has since become an important aspect of personality studies.

Locus of control refers to the extent to which individuals believe that they can control events that affect them. One's 'locus' (Latin for 'place' or 'location') can either be internal (which means the person believes that they control their life) or external (they believe that their environment, some higher power, or other people control their decisions and their life).

Individuals with a high internal locus of control believe that events result primarily from their own behaviour and actions. Those with a high external locus of control believe that powerful others, fate, or chance primarily determine events. Those with a high internal locus of control thus have better control of their behaviour, tend to exhibit more political acumen, are more active in seeking information and knowledge concerning their situation, are more likely to attempt to influence others, and are also more likely to assume that their efforts will be successful.

As an example, college students with a strong internal locus of control believe that their grades are determined by their abilities and efforts. These students believe. 'The more I study, the better grades I get'. They change their study strategies as they discover their deficiencies. They raise their expectations if they succeed and worry when they think they have no control over their assignments.

In contrast, college students with a strong external locus of control believe that their grades are the result of good or bad luck, the teacher's mood, or God's will. They are more likely to say, 'No matter how much I study, the teacher determines my grade. I just hope I'm lucky in the test'. Believing that luck essentially averages out after they do well in a test, they lower their expectations. Likewise, when they fail a test, they are optimistic they will score better in the next test. These externals are less likely to learn from past experiences, and have difficulty with persistence.

'I strongly believe performance leads to recognition, leads to respect, power. The best recipe that India has is performance, performance, performance. Then the world will respect India automatically. But I find around me many, many stimuli that tell me that not everybody buys into this. This upsets me a lot.' (Narayana Murthy, quoted in Pota: 30)

'Our company's story is of ordinary people who believed that they could do great things.' (Kiran Mazumdar-Shaw, quoted in Pota: 106)

'Believe in yourself. Have an unfailing degree of confidence in yourself. Be willing to work very hard... I have learnt a few lessons based on my experience. One is that hard work is absolutely critical to success.' Azim Premji (as told to S.N. Chary 2002: 76)

Locus of control orientation is reflected in the way a person views what happens in an organization, that is, how much control the person believes that he/she has in important organizational matters, how much is believed to be held by certain others, and to what degree the person believes that events are a matter of luck. (see appendix 3A. 1 for testing your locus of control.)

A study published in the journal *Psychosomatic Medicine* examined the health effect of childhood 'locus of control'. A total of 7,500 British adults followed from birth who had shown an internal locus of control at the age of 10 were less likely to be overweight at age 30.

CHARACTERISTICS OF INTERNALS

Internality plays an important role in human development and meaningful living. Research has shown that the following attributes are more typical of internals:

▶ Compared to externals, internals have been reported to be more sensitive to new information, are more observant, more likely to attend to cues that help resolve uncertainties, and more prone to both intentional and incidental learning.

▶ Internality is associated with various other aspects of learning such as curiosity, eagerness to obtain information, awareness of and desire to understand situations and their contexts, and the ability to process available information. For example, in order to influence or control outcomes, an internal must acquire as much information as possible.

▶ Evidence supports the assumption that an internal locus of control leads to academic achievement.

▶ Internals are more persevering, spend extra time on work, and enjoy resolving difficult and complex tasks.

▶ Internals are better at deferring gratification because they believe that their efforts lead to favourable outcomes. In contrast, externals—perceiving a lack of personal predictability and fearing that unforeseen external factors will affect outcomes—may find it more attractive to seek immediate gratification than to try to achieve distant goals.

▶ Internality has been found to be an important characteristic of people with high achievement motivation.

▶ Internality seems to be a cornerstone of the process of valuing, which includes awareness of one's own values, willingness to declare these values in public, and adherence to them and the behaviour associated with them in spite of outside pressures. This process of developing ethical norms and using them even during a crisis has also been called inner-directedness (state of being directed by one's own internalized standards, rather than by merely conforming to outside expectations, norms/pressures).

▶ Internals experience greater job satisfaction than externals, as they believe that working hard is more likely to lead to rewards and that they have more control over the way they work. Internals also prefer a participatory management style, whereas externals prefer a directive style.

▶ Supervisors with an internal orientation believe that persuasive power is the most productive approach, whereas their external counterparts rely on coercive power. Furthermore, the use of rewards, respect, and expertise is seen by internally focused supervisors as the most effective way to influence subordinates; those with an external orientation see coercion and other formal positions as most effective.

Nevertheless, the internal pays a price. Those who perceive their own abilities and actions as being solely responsible for their failures are likely to experience stress and may become self-punitive.

FORMATION OF THE LOCUS OF CONTROL

The development of one's locus of control stems largely from the individual's family and its resources, cultural stability, and early experiences where they have seen their effort in doing something lead to reward. Many internals have grown up with families who are also internal-minded. These families emphasized hard work, education, responsibility, and thinking. Parents typically gave their children rewards they had promised them.

In contrast, externals are generally associated with lower socio-economic status, because poorer people have less control over their lives. People coming from a society which faces social unrest are also more likely to feel that circumstances are out of their hands. Often low-income parents might think about their lives negatively, or lack a personal sense of power and this may affect their children. People in such societies often become more external.

Children acquire a greater locus of control as they become older, as they gain skills that give them more control over their environment. In support, psychological research has found that older children have a higher internal locus of control than younger children.

INTERNALITY/EXTERNALITY AT WORK

Each of us possess both external as well as internal tendencies. Some of us are dominated by internal tendencies, some by external ones. Try the quiz at the end of this chapter to measure the extent of your own internality/externality. In the meantime, here is a list of the ways in which internals and external perform at work.

Internals

- ▶ Take better care of equipment
- ▶ Indicate more satisfaction with job training
- ▶ Show higher rates of work tolerance
- ▶ Are more cooperative
- ▶ Are self-reliant
- ▶ Are knowledgeable about their work

- ▶ Unemployed internals exhibit more self-direction and accept more responsibility for their career development
- ▶ Are less apt to be defensive
- ▶ Tend to resort to more self-blaming behaviour
- ▶ Are more apt to express unrealistic occupational aspirations
- ▶ As supervisors, internals rely more on personal persuasion and have the ability to pick up partners who are superior or have equal ability
- ▶ Are quick to adopt innovations and new practices
- ▶ Are positively associated with indices of social and personal adjustment
- ▶ Are more achievement oriented
- ▶ Are less anxious
- ▶ Are less dogmatic
- ▶ Are more trusting

Externals

- ▶ Are less able to cope with the demands of reality
- ▶ As supervisors, externals are likely to use power and threats
- ▶ More likely to pick partners of inferior ability and are less confident of outcomes
- ▶ An extremely externalized person may blame outside factors as a defence against admitting personal inadequacies

WHY INTERNALS MAKE BETTER MANAGERS

In this book we have classified managers into four categories: Doers, Achievers, Visionaries, and Missionaries. The last three categories of managers are transformational managers. The first, transactional managers, spend a large part of their time completing the work they are assigned. They transact. On the other hand, transformational managers become leaders in some way or the other. By doing more than what is expected and by stretching goals, Achievers show leadership capabilities. By redefining or rewriting the goals or vision the Visionary also transforms something—either his own organization or a part of society. The Missionary is constantly transforming. For ease, we will refer to all transformational managers as leaders from this point on.

One thing characterizes these leaders—they all possess a sense of internality and self-confidence. Another way to describe it would be to call it the 'I can do it syndrome'. This syndrome is the consequence of early successes and the passion for achieving one's goals.

HOW TO DEVELOP INTERNALITY

- ▶ The most important starting point is to have a life or career goal or a short-term or long-term goal and keep talking about it. Sharing with others enhances your own commitment. You may even write about this in magazines, e-mails, mailgroups, social networking sites, etc.
- ▶ Read the stories of leaders and transformational managers who made a difference. There are several references at the end of this book that may help in this direction.
- ▶ Keep sharing the lessons you learnt from them. Plan a series of small steps that will give you repeated successful experiences in serve of your goal.
- ▶ Act and review, reflect, and act again. It is only repeated action that will make it a habit.
- ▶ Examine periodically how you are spending your time and using your talent.

> ▸ Have a mentor or coach.
>
> ▸ Become a part of professional bodies and attend as many meetings as you can.

THE THREE QUALITIES OF EFFECTIVE MANAGERS

We have seen that internality is a key aspect of leaders. Distilling all the characteristics of internals we can arrive at three fundamental qualities every effective manager must possess.

Perseverance: This is the ability to keep at something and not give up. Transformational managers are often obsessed by their own ideas and once they make up their mind, they stick to it. They also have the ability to ride out a rough patch. The persevering manager will not give up even when things are going downhill or they have received negative feedback. It's interesting to note that in general, Indians tend to get very defensive the moment feedback is given, which comes from insecurity. Tom Peters (1997) quoting Warren Bennis points out that one thing in common to most leaders is that they all make mistakes but bounce back from them. They use failures as building blocks. This comes from their persevering spirit.

Phanindra Sama, one of the men behind redBus, says that the early days of the company were very tough for him and his co-founders, Charan Padmaraju and Sudhakar Pasupunuri. The three friends had given up their jobs and invested their savings into redBus and as Phani says, 'Those days were full of emotional hurt. We were used to being pampered in our jobs. Moving from that environment to visiting the bus operators was a sea change. Here was a bus operator who would make you wait for hours to talk to you once. This was a real test of ego.'

Phani had always valued his personal space and lived alone in Bangalore even though all his friends lived in a shared apartment. However, as they gave up their jobs, Phani moved in with Sudhakar and Charan to save costs. One portion of the flat was converted into an office while the three of them stayed in a single bedroom. This was a period when they cut out all extra expenses like movies and looked forward to birthday treats from friends as their only source of entertainment.

Commitment and hard work: The two are spoken of together because of the readiness among types 2–4 managers to back their commitment with hard work. This is because devotion to a cause always needs to be translated into action. Commitment and hard work thus come from our sense of purpose, our personality (self-concept, sense of efficacy, locus of skills, competence) and our ambition. Hard work is not necessarily the number of hours, but the burden of responsibility you carry for the duration of work.

'Yes, if you take a normal family life, our family life was definitely not balanced… I took my first holiday 15 years after starting Mastek!' Ashank Desai of Mastek (Bansal 2008: 48).

'Obviously mine is not a very normal kind of personal life. I sort of typically get back home after 10 and leave early at 7–7.30 in the morning. I work six days a week and even on the seventh day I am on the phone half of the day.' R. Subramanian of Subhiksha, IIMA PGP '89 (Ibid.: 66).

Continuous learning: A leader has to grow constantly and increase his/her intellectual capital (this is discussed in detail in chapter 4). Listening is very important, as is the need to be alert. Your sensitivity to the world around you should be high. The more you learn and communicate, the more your value appreciates.

FROM TRANSACTIONAL TO TRANSFORMATIONAL—WHAT IT TAKES TO BE A GLOBAL LEADER

> Leaders have all the spontaneity, unpredictability, frailty, vulnerability, and potential that is possible in the human race. If we are to lead with honour, we must start with the premise that flexibility, adaptability, and wisdom are possible, that we have seeds of greatness in us, and if we care deeply about the lives of others, we can work together to accomplish worthwhile things. (Lee 1997: 265)

While every manager has to develop these three key qualities, the transformational manager has to go beyond this. There have been many studies done on leadership. A good deal of insight has been provided by the famous leadership theorist Noel Tichy from the University of Michigan—often credited as the man behind the success of GE—and Jack Welch. While perseverance, hard work, energy, and an open mind are all implied in Tichy's findings (see box), he goes one step further in his definition of the truly great leader. Leaders have to have ideas, they have to be good teachers, strong communicators, and most importantly they must have the ability to create future leaders. These have been validated by others with different emphasis. Management guru Warren Bennis defines leadership as the capacity to change the mindset or framework of another person (Tichy and Cohen 1997). Zenger and Folkman (2002) studied the 360 degree feedback of about 20,000 leaders and compared the top 10 percent of them through the eyes of their subordinates, peers, and bosses. One of the key qualities listed was their communication skills and the impact they had on others. Robin Sharma (2005), drawing from ancient wisdom, says that great leaders are always great teachers and coaches and they create a playground of ideas.

If we compress all these studies we can arrive at a list of qualities a global leader must have:

▶ Character (including integrity—or coherence between thought, word, and deeds—and commitment)
▶ Vision and global thinking (think big, entrepreneurial thinking)
▶ Value driven (have a sense of purpose, high ethical values, respect for humanity and society, etc.)
▶ Initiative and proactivity
▶ High energy and activity level
▶ Continuous learning from various sources
▶ Ability to develop juniors and build leadership competencies across the organization or department (investing in juniors, building others as leaders, coaching)
▶ Unconventionality and openness to others' ideas
▶ Risk taking and encouraging risks
▶ Creativity. They are creative problem solvers and they encourage creativity and innovation
▶ Persistence, not giving up
▶ Possess a teachable point of view (self-reflection, review and learning from mistakes, and learning from experience)
▶ Openness to change and proactively managing change (change management skills)
▶ High degree of self-awareness and focus on self-renewal (not shy of but actively seeks feedback)
▶ Result oriented and the ability to deliver results
▶ Ability to empower, reward, and recognize others continuously
▶ Has a sense of priority and purpose (good time management, respect for others' time and talent)
▶ Integrating ability (see relationship between present and

future, small elements and the whole, time perspective)
- ▶ Knows when to leave (succession planning and ability to delegate)
- ▶ Bounces back from mistakes
- ▶ Cultural sensitivity and ability to seek and manage diversity
- ▶ Communication skills
- ▶ Social skills and getting the desirable response
- ▶ Interpersonal skills and teamwork coming out of respect for others and free from biases (empathy or awareness of others' feelings, needs, and concerns)
- ▶ Strategic thinking (analytical skills, positioning, and repositioning)

Transactional competencies include: teamwork, developing subordinates, coaching and mentoring, interpersonal competence, cross-cultural sensitivity, diversity management, and openness to ideas. However, these are just the first steps to transformational competency. In order to be a truly great manager, you will need to go beyond this and develop all the qualities listed above.

The following are some of the salient points emerging from Noel Tichy's work using Jack Welch and his team at GE (Tichy and Cohen 1997).

1. Winning organizations have leadership at all levels. Winning organizations produce leaders as contrasted with others.

2. Leaders have ideas, values, energy, and edge. Ideas and values guide their decisions. Energy and edge get them implemented.

3. Without leaders organizations stagnate. They don't keep pace with changing markets. They don't add shareholder value.

4. Great leaders are great teachers. They accomplish their goals through the people they teach. They teach others to be leaders not followers. Winning leaders make teaching a priority. They consider teaching one of their primary roles. They use every opportunity to learn and to teach.

5. Winners have a teachable point of view. They have clear ideas and values based on knowledge and experience. They articulate those lessons to others. Winning leaders draw from their past. Events early in life shape lessons that they use in the future. They consciously capture these lessons and use them as guides.

6. Winning organizations are built on clear ideas. Quantum ideas set direction for everyone. Incremental ideas are about strategy, structure, and implementation.

7. Leaders make sure that ideas are current and appropriate. They assess the realities and amend the ideas as necessary. The ideas lead to significant added value. Ideas are the framework for actions at all levels. They provide the context for everyone's decision-making.

8. They motivate people towards a common goal.

9. Winning organizations have strong values. Their values define desirable behaviours. They support the organization's central goals.

10. Winning leaders live the values. Their personal conduct embodies these values. Their actions reinforce the values in others. Values are key competitive tools. They are the fabric of corporate culture. They provide instinctive grounding for smart actions.

11. Winning leaders are high-energy people. They are focused and determined. They like challenges and enjoy their work. Winning leaders create energy in others. They motivate with

their enthusiasm and actions, stretch goals and inspire ambitious effort. They turn negative energy into positive.

12. Winning leaders never take the easy way out. They face hard facts and make the tough calls. Risk and pain don't deter them. Winning leaders have the courage to see reality and act on it. They may pursue new businesses and abandon old ones. They promote risk takers and risk taking. They pursue the truth and explain to others.

13. Winning leaders portray the future in an involving way like an unfolding drama. They tell stories that engage the followers emotionally and rationally. The stories weave together ideas, values, and modes of behaviour. Winners' stories create scenarios of success. They describe a winning future. Their stories are dynamic and motivating.

14. They cast workers as protagonists who make change happen. They guide participants to identify their own roles. Winning leadership is about building for the future.

15. Leaders prepare organizations to respond to change. They create organizations that can sustain success.

16. Companies with most leaders are most agile and effective. The legacy of winning leaders is other winning leaders.

17. The best leaders know when it is time to leave. They don't hang on when it is time for the next generation to take over. They exit cleanly and let the new leaders lead.

THE INDIAN CONTEXT

Local studies on Indian business leaders have highlighted many of the characteristics listed above, with some differences, and it is worth looking at these. Udai Pareek (1994) emphasized that leaders should be institution builders while many of the other studies listing the qualities of Indian leaders included humility as a key characteristic. Research also shows that Indian managers still lack some core skills to take the leap into being transformational managers. In a study comparing the star performers with the weak performers from a single company study of twenty-five top-level managers assessed by 191 assessors in a 360 degree feedback programme, Rao and Rao (2004) found the following interesting points:

▶ Star performers do not delegate any more than the weak or average performers. Rather, they seem to do things themselves as compared to weak performers.
▶ Star performers seem to create a climate of dependency and personal loyalty besides a climate of learning, satisfaction, and empowerment.

These are confirmed by a 360 degree feedback survey of 762 senior and top-level managers from the manufacturing, services, and pharma sectors belonging to two leading business houses of India. Job knowledge was the most frequently observed strength of Indian managers as was communication, teamwork, and hard work. However, short temper and inability to build juniors were the most frequently mentioned areas in need of improvement. Vision, values, strategic thinking, decision-making skills, risk taking, innovativeness, ability to learn from mistakes, learning orientation, self-renewal efforts and cross-cultural sensitivity were also the other qualities lacking in Indian managers. These studies imply that while Indian managers clearly have abilities to be strong transactional managers, most of them lack the ability to move to the next level (Rao 2008).

CONCLUSION

In this chapter, we have looked at the qualities required to be a leader. All effective managers need to be internal-minded—they need to believe that their ability and hard work leads to success. Internals are more likely to be hard-working, persistent, and open to learning and these are the three fundamental qualities of all good managers. Transformational managers and global leaders, however, possess qualities that transcend these, including being great teachers, strong ideas people, team builders, and communicators.

REFERENCES

Bansal, Rashmi (2008). *Stay Hungry Stay Foolish*. CIIE, Ahmedabad, IIMA.

Chary, S.N. (2002). *Business Gurus Speak*. New Delhi: Macmillan Publishers.

Lee, Briane (1997). *The Power Principle: Influence with Honour*. Fireside, NY: Franklin Covey Co.

Pareek, Udai (1994, 2001). *Beyond Management*, Second Edition. New Delhi: IBH Publishing Company.

Peters, T. and R.H. Waterman, (1981). *In Search of Excellence: Lessons from America's Best Run Companies*. New York: Harper and Row.

Pota, Vikas (2010). *India Inc.: How India's Top Ten Entrepreneurs are Winning Globally*. London: Nicholas Brealey.

Rao, T.V. (2008). Global Leadership and Managerial Competencies of Indian Managers. Working paper, Ahmedabad: Indian Institute of Management.

Sharma, Robin (2003). *The Leadership Wisdom*. Mumbai: Jaico Publishers.

Tichy, Noel and Cohen Eli (1997). *The Leadership Engine: How Winning Companies Build Leaders at Every Level*. New York: HarperCollins.

Tichy, Noel and Warren Bennis (2007). *Judgement: How Winning Leaders Make Great Calls*. New York: Penguin Group Portfolio.

Zenger, John H. and Joseph Folkman (2002). *The Extraordinary Leader*. New Delhi: Tata McGraw Hill.

APPENDIX

3. 1: TESTING YOUR LOCUS OF CONTROL

There are a few tools to measure your internal and external locus of control. The following quiz is a modification of one that was developed by Rotter to test externality and internality. The respondent is required to indicate the extent to which one item is preferred over the other by distributing three points across the two items. For example, if one is preferred over the other only slightly, the marks are distributed as two to the preferred item and one to the less preferred item. If the candidate has a strong preference for one item over the other, three points may be assigned to the preferred item and zero to the least preferred item. The questionnaire consists of items dealing with everyday incidents. After you complete the test, add all your scores on the 27 (a)s and then the 27 (b)s. The (a) total is internality and the (b) total is your externality score. Your internality should be at least two to three times higher than the externality, that is, Internality scores should be above 54. If your score is above 70 it indicates that you are a highly internal person. Scores closer to 81 indicate extreme internality.

GIVEN BELOW ARE 27 PAIRS OF STATEMENTS. READ EACH PAIR CAREFULLY AND INDICATE YOUR PREFERENCE BY WRITING THE APPROPRIATE FIGURES IN THE COLUMN PROVIDED.

Some alternatives may seem equally attractive or unattractive. Nevertheless, please attempt to choose between alternatives. For each pair you have three points to distribute in any of the following combinations.

For example, in the pair of items given below.

If you prefer (a) and do not prefer (b) at all, then please assign '3' in the scoring column against (a) and '0' in the scoring column against (b) for item 1:

A. ITEM YOUR PREFERENCE

1. a. With a more responsible government, deaths due to natural calamities like earthquakes and cyclones can be reduced. 3
   b. No matter how much you try, builders will continue to cheat. 0

If you prefer (b) and do not prefer (a) at all, in your scoring column write:

1. a. With a more responsible government, deaths due to natural calamities like earthquakes and cyclones can be reduced. 0
   b. No matter how much you try, builders will continue to cheat. 3

If you have slight preference for (a) over (b) write:

1. a. With a more responsible government, deaths due to natural calamities like earthquakes and cyclones can be reduced. 2
   b. No matter how much you try, builders will continue to cheat. 1

If you have a slight preference for (b) over (a), write:

1. a. With a more responsible government, deaths due to natural calamities like earthquakes and cyclones can be reduced. 1
   b. No matter how much you try, builders will continue to cheat. 2

B. ITEM YOUR PREFERENCE

1. a. With a more responsible government, deaths due to natural calamities like earthquakes and cyclones can be reduced.
    b. No matter how much you try, builders will continue to cheat.
2. a. Competent managers get what they deserve over a period.
    b. No matter how competent you are, without higher connections you cannot get ahead.
3. a. Deserving students get what they deserve in examinations.
    b. No matter how deserving you are, circumstances or luck should favour you.
4. a. For hard-working students, there are no 'tough examinations'.
    b. No matter how hard-working you are, the nature of the examiner determines what you get.
5. a. Students get the jobs they deserve.
    b. Students are taken away by false promises at placement time.
6. a. People get the organizations they deserve to work for.
    b. It is difficult to identify a good company as all companies project only a bright picture about themselves at the time of recruitment.
7. a. My hard work and competence is the determining factor in my promotions and rewards.
    b. My boss plays a significant role in my promotions and rewards.
8. a. If you are capable, you get noticed selection tests.

    b. Most recruitment is predetermined. Selection tests are only an eyewash.

9. a. Those who have low job satisfaction do not know how to take up an appropriate job.

    b. How satisfied you are depends on what kind of organization you work for.

10. a. Capable students prosper irrespective of where they study.

    b. The college you study in determines your capabilities.

11. a. You can get to do the work you like, if you communicate to your seniors.

    b. In my case no matter how hard I try, I end up getting work that doesn't suit my interests.

12. a. For a hard-working student there is nothing like a difficult exam.

    b. The difficulty level of exam papers depends on the paper setters.

13. a. If you are careful, you can buy trouble-free electronic items from the market.

    b. There is no point wasting time looking for quality products, as most manufacturers are out to exploit you. You will get good products only if you are lucky.

14. a. Getting the best out of your boss depends upon your ability and approach.

    b. Whether your ideas are accepted or not depends on the kind of boss you have.

15. a. Capable students always find some good in their teachers.

    b. Getting good teachers to teach you is not in your hands.

16. a. Competent people can achieve results in spite of difficulties.

    b. Bad boss, poor work conditions, and unlucky situations create poor performance most of the time.

17. a. How much you sell depends on how good you are.

    b. Achieving sales targets has an element of luck in being at the right place at the right time with the right products.

18. a. Students can improve their campus culture with a little bit of effort and cooperation.

    b. Students can do very little to create a good campus culture.

19. a. If students are firm, they can prevent all political interferences.

    b. Politics plays a significant role in shaping the destiny of students in any institution.

20. a. Union problems are mostly due to ineffective handling by management.

    b. Labour unions and officers' associations will do what they want to do as they are powerful and have political backing.

21. a. Advance planning has always helped me spend my day usefully.

    b. In my case going to the office with a well-planned day has never worked out well.

22. a. Going well prepared to class always helps me learn more.

    b. There is no one preparing well as teachers do not come well prepared to class.

23. a. Students who have not succeeded have not made use of the opportunities in the modern age.

    b. Your success depends on the college in which you study.

24. a. People who communicate get things done.

     b. People who communicate land themselves into problems.

25. a. With correct information you can make correct decisions.

     b. You can never get correct information in this conservative world.

26. a. If people take care of themselves they can maintain good health.

     b. How healthy you are depends on your family history and the environment in which you live.

27. a. In the long run you get the recognition you deserve.

     b. No matter how capable you are, you should get the right break to be known.

4

Values

Throughout this book I have maintained that to be a truly great manager, one has to have strongly held values. India is largely a relationship-driven country where promises are made to please people without considering their feasibility. This creates a great many credibility issues. Integrity, as we know, is defined as the integration of thought, word, and deed. Those who speak what they think and those who do what they say are people with integrity. The issues discussed in this chapter include how managers maintain their credibility and character; what their value systems are; what they value in work and interpersonal dealings; and how values help an organization.

CHARACTER IS THE ESSENCE OF GOOD MANAGEMENT

'Everything about great leadership radiates from character,' says Dave Ulrich, the Michigan-based HR guru. Indeed, Zenger and Folkman's comprehensive 360 degree study of roughly 80,000 managers concluded that those who had gone on to become successful business leaders had shown a great deal of integrity, commitment, and strength of character. They demonstrated a remarkable amount of integration between thought, word, and deed, and established themselves as honest, transparent, and trustworthy individuals.

Key insights into the character of leaders may be gleaned from their interactions with other people. The best managers treat all others—whether peers or subordinates—with courtesy and respect. They value people for what they are rather than for their designations. Perhaps most importantly, they are quick to correct themselves when they make mistakes and bounce back, the richer for their experience of failure. Collaborative rather than competitive, they can generally be counted on to deliver results.

Character can be nurtured and built. Needless to say, ethics, family background, and education play a strong role in the development of character, as does the presence of inspiring guides and mentors at subsequent stages of one's life and career.

Zenger and Folkman suggest the following three steps to alter behaviour and build character:

1. **Always deliver**: Be cautious in the commitments you make. One of the core values of Infosys is, 'under-promise and over-deliver', rather than over-promise and under-deliver. If you know that you may not be able to deliver, then you should not commit. False commitments inconvenience others and damage their trust in you. If you have made a mistake, admit it and work on correcting it. Next time remember to be careful.

2. **Be humble**: Do not flaunt the power and authority given to you. Be willing to laugh at and correct yourself. Humility is a very commendable quality. It encourages strong relationship building.

3. **Find a mirror:** You need to be constantly aware of how others perceive you and your character. The mirror may be a good mentor, a trusted colleague, or a friend. 360 degree feedback is also helpful. The Indian Society for Applied Behavioural Science in India and the National Training Laboratories in the US conduct human process laboratories. These laboratories are five-day sessions with small groups of six to eight participants coming together. During these five days the candidates interact intensely with each other in an open atmosphere created by a trainer (known as a facilitator). Usually in this laboratory (training programme) there is no agenda. Participants discuss the impressions they make on each other and also engage with the deeper feelings that their transactions generate. The group thus works as a mirror.

SELECT QUOTES ON CHARACTER AND VALUES

'Good governance does not come from a crook. Integrity and character is essential. It can come from a Tata company. India has been unlucky in its quality of governance and the kind of people who have governed it.' Dr Verghese Kurien (quoted in Chary 2002: 186)

'I do what my conscience tells me to do. That is what I mean by integrity, total integrity.' S.B. Dangayach, Sintex, IIMA PGP '72 (quoted in Bansal SHSF 2008: 309)

'Any business that does not have values cannot endure. This is perhaps the mother of all business principles. Integrity, ethics, humility, and compassion are the primary colours that form the rainbow of business success.' Kiran Mazumdar-Shaw (S.N. Chary Foundation lecture at IIMB, p. 10)

'At Wipro we walk the talk. For example, we are not flexible about boosting our sales by securing orders the non-Wipro way... The core Wipro values include: respect for the individual, humility, integrity (individual and company), and hard work.' Azim Premji (quoted in Chary, p. 10)

'Great businesses are never built on the quicksands of opportunism. I reiterate that, if living by our values means, perhaps growing at a pace slower than we would otherwise have liked, so be it. For us, leadership lies at the heart of knowing what we stand for.' K.M. Birla (Twenty-seventh Vikram Sarabhai Memorial Lecture, Ahmedabad Management Association, September 2006)

VALUES

People with character have a strong sense of values. Having a sense of values means being guided in your thinking and actions by an inner core of standards and abstaining from what you consider as wrong. In this context we need to understand what constitutes values and what are some of the values we have, and how our values influence our behaviour and if they can be changed.

A value is the degree of worth we ascribe to a person, object, situation, or behaviour. The higher the worth or perceived worth of that object in our mind, the more we strive to get or achieve it. If we value money, we try to amass wealth. If we value relationships and people we are helpful and sociable. If we value power we may look for opportunities that give us power, and so on.

In the early part of the nineteenth century, scholars formulated what they thought were the six basic values. These were theoretical, aesthetic, spiritual, economic, political, and social.

Theoretical values represent truth and the systematic ordering of knowledge. Those with theoretical values are empirical, critical, and rational. Those with economic values focus on wealth and money. Those with aesthetic values like creativity and the arts. Those with social values have altruistic tendencies, are sympathetic to others, and like relationships. Political values orient a person towards power and politics, driving one to seek power and recognition. Religious or spiritual values drive the person towards mysticism and philosophy.

In a series of experiments conducted in the mid-1960s, people with strong values were shown nonsense words for just a fraction of a second. Although they would not have been able to read the worlds clearly, the subjects reported to have seen more words that were close to the values they held. Thus a person with social values might have seen the word 'human', while one with economic values may have seen a word like 'money'. These experiments led scientists to believe that *values influence perceptions and consequently decision-making*. Choice of profession and occupation also depends on values.

WORK VALUES

Values can be classified as work or general values and we will deal with the former as these relate to managerial life. Work-related values are the aspects of work which a person values. A stricter definition would be 'the degree of worth ascribed to a particular type of work, activity, or aspect of the work'. The term is distinct from occupational/job 'preference' because it refers to the degree of worth ascribed to it, whereas preference indicates a general attitude, values imply a stronger attitude or a positive evaluation.

What are work values? The following list presents some of the most important ones:

▶ Creativity and challenge—Work where there is scope to do new things and which challenges the employee's potential and ability
▶ Economic—Work which satisfies your financial needs
▶ Independence—Where you are given freedom to take your own decisions and are not answerable for all your activities
▶ Service—Work which gives you the opportunity to serve others
▶ Work conditions—Where the work conditions are good and all necessary facilities are provided: workstations, computers, water coolers, phones, air coolers, etc.
▶ Status—Work which gives you a good designation and is associated with prestige, authority, and the power to influence others
▶ Co-workers—Where you have good colleagues and enjoy a good relationship with them
▶ Security—Where you ensure that you will continue to have the job
▶ Academic—Work which is related to research and academics

Those who prefer academic work may be good as teachers, professors, scholars, scientists, training managers, whereas those who want to be creative might be resourceful in R&D departments. Those who prefer service may do well in public services whereas those who prefer independence should join organizations that offer autonomy and freedom. The values an individual holds about different aspects of life constantly affect their choices. Knowledge of one's own work values helps a person to choose a job that is congruent with these values and to make career decisions that reflect these work values.

Values are not just important to make employment choices, they also affect the way we work. Values influence all our choices; choices, in turn, are important in determining effectiveness because they influence outcomes. For example, the values that managers hold may influence their choice of subordinates, their likes and dislikes for given jobs, or the extent to which they involve themselves with certain tasks. A manager may value scientific and theoretical knowledge so much that he or she unconsciously may prefer a thinker or a theorizer for a routine job. Another manager's preference for a particular machine may be more a result of aesthetic values than an awareness of the efficiency of that machine. An R&D manager may try to economize unnecessarily because of personal economic values, thus limiting his or her ability to experiment with new products. Managers are likely to make better decisions if they act with an awareness of their reasons and with the knowledge of the extent to which their values direct their decisions.

USING WORK VALUES FOR TEAM SATISFACTION

Work values act as career anchors—for these are the values that the individual will not give up. Career anchors are those core competencies you possess which will make you successful in a particular career. For example, a person may always like to think and reason scientifically. He believes in science, reads science and technology books, visits technology parks, etc. He is said to have scientific and technological competencies as his career anchors. Recognition of your team's career anchors will help you keep them satisfied. Career anchors should strengthen the psychological bond between the individual and the organization.

Studies have indicated that IT professionals in India have various career anchors. Pay, interesting work content, technology, responsibility, recognition, and growth prospects were found to be important factors (with the level of priority varying in individuals). In their study of IT professionals, Agarwal and Thite (2002) found there were a lot of contradictions or mismatches in expectations. For example, while the organizations wanted their IT professionals to work on projects according to customer requirements, their own preference seemed to be working on cutting-edge technologies. While their families expected monetary advantage, their peers and they themselves valued working overseas and on the latest technology.

American Behavioural Scientist and Organizational Psychologist at MIT, Professor Edgar Schein delineated eight career anchors (Schein 1990, 1993).

1. Managerial, where the primary concern is to integrate the efforts of others and be fully accountable for total results
2. Technical/Functional, where the primary concern is to exercise their skills and talent in their area of specialization or function
3. Security/Stability, where the primary concern is to have a stabilized career one has been rewarded through promotions, etc., and to have their talent recognized
4. Autonomy and independence, where the primary concern is to have freedom and control over what work they do, the methods they use, how much to do and when to do it, and have little restriction from the organization
5. Entrepreneurial and creativity-based anchors, where the primary concern is to create something new, take risks, and have a desire for personal prominence for accomplishments

6. Service/Dedication, where the primary concern is to achieve value through helping others and making the world a better place to live in
7. Pure challenge, where the primary concern is to take on challenges, solve problems, manage tough situations and emerge a winner
8. Balance/Lifestyle integration, where the primary concern is to integrate family, career, and self-development

Rao (1983, 2002) has identified eight work values that seem to determine the career anchors of Indian managers: These include Creativity and Challenge, Economic values, Security, Work conditions, Co-workers, Service, Academic and Status. Of these, economic, work conditions, security, co-workers (relationships) are meant to be lower order values in Maslow's hierarchy and the remaining higher order values leading to self actualization. Transformational managers would have the higher values in general.

ORGANIZATION VALUES

Individuals aren't the only ones who have values—organizations also articulate what they stand for and prescribe their values. It is ultimately these values which create a firm's work culture. To aspire to be a missionary and visionary manager, you must be instrumental in creating and nurturing these values. Let us look at two cases of Indian companies that show a strong value system.

Case study 1: How Tata responded to 26/11

26/11 was the biggest crisis the Tata group has ever faced. The behaviour of their employees at the Taj Hotel and the subsequent actions of the group were an excellent display of the values the company holds.

Heroism displayed by the staff
During the actual event, all levels of staff—from janitors, waiters, directors, artisans, and captains—at the Taj Hotel displayed extraordinary courage. There were 500 emails from various guests narrating heroics of the staff and thanking them for saving their lives. The sense of duty and service among them was unprecedented. Consider some of these points:

- ▶ There was a Unilever event at the hotel on the day of the attacks. The young lady who protected and looked after the HLL guests was a management trainee. She had no instructions from any supervisor but took just three minutes to evacuate the entire team through the kitchen. Cars were organized outside the hotel according to seniority of the members. In the peak of the crisis, she stepped out into the firing and even got the right wine glass for a guest.
- ▶ Thomas George, a captain, escorted fifty-four guests from a backdoor staircase. He was the last to go out and was shot by the terrorists while trying to leave. His widow would later say that she did not know that the man she lived with for twenty-five years was so courageous.
- ▶ In a subsequent function, Ratan Tata broke down in public and sobbed saying—'the company belongs to these people'.
- ▶ When the hotel was reopened on 21 December, all employees of the hotel were paraded in front of the guests.

The Tata gesture

Some of the provisions the Tata group made were as follows:

▶ All category of employees including those who had completed even one day as casuals were treated as on duty during the time the hotel was closed.

▶ Relief and assistance was given to all those who were injured and to the kin of those killed.

▶ Relief was extended to all those who died at Chhatrapati Shivaji railway station and its surroundings, including the pav-bhaji vendor and the paan shop owners.

▶ During the time the hotel was closed, salaries were sent by money order.

▶ A psychiatric cell was established in collaboration with the Tata Institute of Social Sciences to counsel those who needed such help.

▶ Employee outreach centres were opened where all help—food, water, sanitation, first aid, and counselling—was provided. Sixteen Hundred employees were covered by this facility.

▶ Every employee was assigned to one mentor and it was that person's responsibility to act as a 'single-window' clearance for any help that the person required.

▶ Ratan Tata personally visited the families of all the eighty employees who in some manner—either through injury or getting killed—were affected.

▶ The dependants of the employees who lived outside Mumbai were flown to the city and were all accommodated in Hotel President for three weeks.

▶ Ratan Tata himself asked the families and dependants what they wanted him to do.

▶ In a record time of twenty days, a new trust was created by the Tatas for funding the victims of 26/11. Even non-Tata employees were covered in it. Each one of them was provided a subsistence allowance of Rs 10,000 per month for six months.

▶ Several lakhs were paid for the treatment of a four-year-old granddaughter of a vendor who had taken four bullets.

▶ New handcarts were provided to several vendors who lost theirs.

▶ Tata took responsibility for the life education of forty-six children of the terrorists' victims.

▶ The settlement for every deceased member ranged from Rs 36 to 85 lakh in addition to the following benefits: full last salary for life for the family and dependants; complete responsibility for education of children and dependants, anywhere in the world; full medical facility for the whole family and dependants for the rest of their life; all loans and advances were waived, irrespective of the amount; counsellor for life for each person.

The Tata DNA

How was such passion created among Tata employees? How and why did they behave the way they did? The organization is clear that it is not training and development that created such behaviour. Rather, it has to do with the DNA of the company and the Tata culture.

The organization has always told its employees that customers and guests are their top priority. They also emphasize to their employees, 'To think and act first as a citizen'. These values displayed themselves in the heroism of 26/11.

Moreover, as a business, Tata believe that family values hold them together. This can be traced to its beginnings. The hotel business was started by Jamshedji Tata when he was insulted in one of the British hotels and not allowed to stay there. He went on to create several institutions which later became icons of progress, culture, and modernity, believing that 'in a free enterprise the community is not just another stakeholder in business but is the very purpose of its existence'. Tata holds this statement very dear. It is these values that led to the extremely generous provisions the company made after the attack. The organization's attitude was that if they were going to spend several hundred crore in rebuilding the property, why not spend equally on the employees who gave their life for the hotel? (As narrated by H.N. Srinivas, HR Head of the Taj Group of Hotels at the National Institute of Personnel Management Conference held at Goa, in December 2009 and adapted from an email narration from Ravi Rajagopalan.)

The Tata Leadership programme promotes the following values: integrity, understanding, excellence, unity, and responsibility. It is included as part of the Tata Leadership programme and Tata Business Excellence model and Tata organizations are constantly evaluated using these values.

Case study 2: SAIL (Steel Authority of India)

The following is a list of SAIL values that are part of the company's appraisal system. Employees who do not follow these values don't get promoted.

1. Customer focus (internal or external as appropriate): Ability to empathize with customers. Firmly believes in and practices end-to-end customer service.
2. Concern for people: Always keeps employee interests in mind.

3. Consistent quality: Shows constant quality consciousness and designs all methods and processes to ensure quality in all aspects of work, products, and services.
4. Commitment to excellence: Shows concern for excellence.

OCTAPACE VALUES

OCTAPACE is an acronym for Openness, Collaboration, Trust, Authenticity, Proaction, Autonomy, Confrontation, and Experimentation. These values are considered important for organizations to get the best out of their employees. These are also known as HRD Values, and many organizations have been adopting them.

Openness exists where people in the organization feel free to express their ideas, views, opinions, and feelings to each other irrespective of their level, designation, etc. They are encouraged to express themselves and their views are taken seriously.

Collaboration is the culture where people are eager to help each other. Personal power is played down and people are governed by larger goals like those of the organization, country, and humanity at large. In particular, the organizational goals govern decision-making and people do not have narrow departmental or team loyalties when they are required.

The 'we' feeling refers to the feeling of team spirit. Intra-departmental loyalties don't get in the way of interdepartmental collaboration.

Trust and trustworthiness deals with a culture of people believing each other and acting on the basis of verbal messages and instructions without having to wait for written instructions or explanations. When people say that they will do something or promise to do something it is simply relied upon. There is no need for extra monitoring and controls.

Authenticity is speaking the truth fearlessly and keeping the promises once made. It is indicated by the extent to which people say what they mean and do what they say. Employees can be counted upon not to make false promises.

A *Proactive* culture is one that promotes initiative and explorations on the part of employees. A proactive culture encourages everyone to take initiative and make things happen.

Autonomy is present if everyone in the organization, irrespective of level, has some scope in his or her job to use some discretion. The discretion may be in terms of work methods, decision-making, communication, or any such area.

Confrontation is the culture of facing issues squarely. Issues are talked about and discussed. Even if people have to hurt each other the issue is faced and not put under the carpet. This culture enhances problem-solving abilities.

Experimentation is the orientation on the part of employees to try out new ways of doing things and experiment with new decisions. It characterizes a risk-taking culture in the organization.

While openness and confrontation go together, so do autonomy and collaboration. Trust and authenticity are paired together and so are proaction and experimentation. These pairs are the four cornerstones of an HRD culture. When these values are practised in an organization they become a part of life and are likely to get the best out of people.

Management studies and research have shown that strong values and the culture of an organization lay the foundation for its long-term success. Organizations with a positive culture and values win over a long period and can face temporary turbulence. Those without values are likely to lose out in the long run.

The recent scandal of Satyam in India and the earlier example of Enron in the US amply demonstrate the need for values in business.

While there are no scientific studies, a recent study of Indian organizations by H.N. Arora has demonstrated that companies that have strong values succeed in the long run. He also demonstrated when decisions not based on values are taken they create problems in productivity at some point of time or the other (Arora 2009). Cappelli and team conclude on the basis of their study of ninety-eight Indian CEOs that some values like transparency and openness get more participation and enhance employee engagement. A value like openness, for example, encourages these companies to create a participative culture. It also encourages collaboration and reduces overheads.

Examples of good OCTAPACE companies are Infosys, Larsen and Toubro, Wipro, the Tata Group, the Murugappa group in the south, the TVS group, HDFC, LIC, SBI and many other PSBs.

BUILDING VALUES INTO THE WORKPLACE: HOW EFFECTIVE MANAGERS INCULCATE VALUES INTO THEIR TEAMS

All managers, irrespective of their classification, should have a strong sense of values and try to build this into their workplace. Achievers, as they experience success, may be tempted to use short cuts in their eagerness to progress. This may also happen with vision- and mission-driven people. The risks are higher at a young age because one unethical success may lead to another until the whole thing collapses. Ramalinga Raju of Satyam is an example of this. As he said of his behaviour, 'It was like riding a tiger, not knowing how to get off without being eaten.'

Riding the Tiger: Ramalinga Raju

Dear Board members:

It is with deep regret and tremendous burden that I am carrying on my conscience, that I would like to bring the following facts to your notice:

1. The balance sheet carries as of September 30, 2008:

a. Inflated (non-existent) cash and bank balances of Rs 5,040 crore (as against Rs 5,361 crore reflected in the books);

b. An accrued interest of Rs 376 crore, which is non-existent;

c. An understated liability of Rs 1,230 crore on account of funds arranged by me;

d. An overstated debtors' position of Rs 490 crore (as against Rs 2,651 reflected in the books).

2. For the September quarter (Q2) we reported a revenue of Rs 2,700 crore and an operating margin of Rs 649 crore (24 percent of revenue) as against the actual revenues of Rs 2,112 crore and an actual operating margin of Rs 61 crore (3 percent of revenues). This has resulted in artificial cash and bank balances going up by Rs 588 crore in Q2 alone.

The gap in the balance sheet has arisen purely on account of inflated profits over several years (limited only to Satyam standalone, books of subsidiaries reflecting true performance). What started as a marginal gap between actual operating profit and the one reflected in the books of accounts continued to grow over the years. It has attained unmanageable proportions as the size of the company operations grew significantly (annualised revenue run rate of Rs 11,276 crore in the September quarter of 2008, and official reserves of Rs 8,392 crore). The differential in the real profits and the one reflected in the books was further accentuated by the fact that the company had to carry additional resources and assets to justify a higher level of operations thereby significantly increasing the costs.

Every attempt made to eliminate the gap failed. As the promoters held a small percentage of equity, the concern was that poor performance would result in the takeover, thereby exposing the gap. It was like riding a tiger, not knowing how to get off without being eaten.

The aborted Maytas acquisition deal was the last attempt to fill the fictitious assets with real ones. Maytas' investors were convinced that this is a good divestment opportunity and a strategic fit. Once Satyam's problem was solved, it was hoped that Maytas' payments could be delayed. But that was not to be. What followed in the last several days is common knowledge.

Here are some ways to build a value system into your work and in your team:

▶ Maintain consistency
▶ Keep reviewing your own values and how you are living with the help of the third party
▶ Keep talking and discussing values with your team
▶ Create personal and organizational stories about values and how they should be practised
▶ Integrate your values into the induction programme, performance appraisal, training, and other HR systems
▶ Exercise a zero-tolerance policy towards employees and team members who don't behave according to established values. Explain, regulate, understand, and ensure that they are practised.

VALUES THROUGH PERSONAL EXAMPLE

Dr P.P. Gupta, the chairman of CMC during the 1980s, was known for his value-driven management. He used to tell the employees to take leave if they needed it rather than allocate a number of leaves to them. If an employee had something important to do all they had to do was inform their manager and go. However, if they were found to be lying, they would be out of CMC the next day. Trust and trustworthiness are the values Dr Gupta attempted to promote in building CMC and it was a very successful company under his leadership. Once Dr Gupta was recruiting a candidate for his HR department. One of the candidates applied from the TVS group but during the interview he admitted that he had already left the TVS group and that he had joined another company two weeks previous. Dr Gupta gave him a long lecture on values and loyalty and how important it was for him to stick to his current company and refused to interview him further.

CONCLUSION

Values as we have seen are central to the way we operate at work. They help us determine the kind of work we should be doing and to manage our team, their talents, and expectations. Possessing larger values is vital, especially if we want to climb higher in the managerial world and be visionaries or missionaries. Moreover, organizations need values, for they create the culture of the company. As a manager it is our role not just to be values driven ourselves but also to inculcate values amongst those we work with and work towards the values of our organization. The more a manager can do this, the more effective he/she will be.

REFERENCES

Agarwal, N.M. and M. Thite, (2002). Human Resource Issues, Challenges and Strategies in India Software Service Industry, (Cited in Bandopadhyaya, P.) Indian Institute of Management, Bangalore.

Arora, H.N. (2009). 'A Study of Managing Change through Value Based

HR Practices', Unpublished Ph. D. Dissertation, Ahmedabad, Gujarat University.

Rao, T. V. (1983). 'Managerial Work Values Scale' in W. Pfeiffer, and Jones, *Annual Handbook for Group Facilitators*.

———(2002). *Work Values Scale*. Ahmedabad: T.V. Rao Learning Systems Pvt. Ltd.

Schein, E.H. (1990). 'Career Anchors Revisited: Implications of Career Development in the 21st Century'. *Academy of Management Executive*, 10(4), pp. 80–8.

——— (1978). *Career Dynamics*, Reading, MA: Addison Wesley.

———(1993). *Career Anchor: Discovering Your Real Values*. San Francisco: Jossey Bass/Pfeiffer.

Zenger, John H. and Joseph Folkman (2002). *The Extraordinary Leader*. New Delhi: Tata McGrawHill.

APPENDIX 4. 1

Given below are the profiles of four executives. Identify the profession or occupations and the nature of jobs where the person will be able to do well. Their values were assessed on a scale of 0–24 for each value. The higher the score, the stronger the value. Normally scores between 18 and 24 are considered as strong values. Scores between 0 and 8 are considered weaker values. For each candidate the scores they got on each of the eight values are presented in descending order. For example, the highest score for Mr X is 19 on service, while for Mr L the highest score is 22 on economic values. Using these scores try and predict where the candidates will be able to do well: (a) director of a social service organization, (b) manager in a financial services firm, (c) president of a hospital, (d) director of a management school, (e) manager at an event management firm, and (f) manager of a publishing house which publishes children's stories.

Mr X		Mr Y		Mr M		Mr L	
Value	Score	Value	Score	Value	Score	Value	Score
Service	19	Service	18	Service	24	Economic	22
Independence	17	Status	15	Co-workers	16	Status	17
Creativity	16	Academic	16	Academic	16	Independence	16
Academic	14	Co-workers	13	Independence	14	Creativity	16
Co-workers	13	Creativity	13	Creativity	12	Work conditions	10
Work conditions	11	Work conditions	10	Status	9	Security	9
Status	10	Independence	9	Work conditions	7	Service	7
Security	5	Economic	7	Economic	5	Co-workers	6
Economic	3	Security	7	Security	5	Academic	5

5

Creativity

Most managers and leaders who make a difference are also creative individuals. When faced with a problem they are quick in solving them. They also take initiative in implementing solutions. It is these two qualities that distinguish them from others. Initiative and creativity are the two qualities missing in our culture. While initiative is the ability to do things without being told, creativity is the ability to think fluently and in unusual ways when faced with a problem. These qualities are complementary, and both can be cultivated. We have discussed proactiveness in the chapter on efficacy. In this chapter we look at creativity and creative problem-solving abilities.

TURN PROBLEMS INTO OPPORTUNITIES

You are a manager in charge of producing a line of motorcycles. You've agreed to deliver 10,000 motorcycles to a dealer in another country by the end of the month. Today is the 25th, and your work is nearly done. The 10,000 bikes are almost ready to be delivered. There's been a slight hitch though. The rear-view mirrors for each motorcycle still need to be fitted. This takes just a few minutes per bike. The problem is that your vendor hasn't supplied all the mirrors yet. He sent 5,000 mirrors at the beginning of the month and said he could supply the rest around month-end. Now it turns out he cannot. You are running out of time fast, and are under pressure to keep your commitment to your client. What do you do?

If you are naturally non-creative, you will find yourself almost paralysed with worry and anxiety. The only solutions you'll probably be able to come up with are to keep trying to persuade your vendor to deliver and telling yourself not to place an order with him the next time. A creative mind, however, will come up with a variety of possible solutions:

▶ Consider alternative vendors who might supply rear-view mirrors on short notice
▶ Fit the 5,000 mirrors already available, and fit the rest as they arrive
▶ Negotiate with the client to deliver 5,000 complete motorcycles and ask for more time for the rest
▶ Negotiate to have the rear-view mirrors fitted at the client's facility
▶ Deliver the 10,000 motorbikes at a reduced cost, without rear-view mirrors
▶ Draw manpower and resources away from other orders that do not have a tight deadline
▶ Negotiate with the client or dealer for an extended deadline
▶ Advertise and explore if someone can make more mirrors on an emergency basis

Creativity is the ability to generate quick, alternative solutions to a given problem. It is the ability to think fast, coherently, flexibly, and perhaps unconventionally. A creative mind does not put a lid on the possible solution even before it is generated.

JOBS UNLIMITED: HOW NAUKRI.COM WAS BORN

For Sanjeev Bikchandani, the founder of naukri.com, India's largest job site, the eureka moment came when he noticed colleagues at work flipping back to front through an issue of *Business India*. The leading business magazine of the time, *Business India* carried about forty pages of job advertisements after the editorial articles. Bikchandani realized then that everybody likes to be in the know about jobs. You may not be looking *for* a job, but that won't stop you from looking *at* them. It also struck Sanjeev that week after week, headhunters called to offer jobs that weren't advertised anywhere. If there was some way of creating a database of available job opportunities, and keeping it current and live, it would certainly have many takers. Except that this was in the pre-Internet era and there was no way such a database could be compiled and made accessible to people. A chance visit to an IT exhibition at Pragati Maidan first introduced Sanjeev to the word 'Internet', and the acronym 'www'. He realized that the Internet might be just the platform for the job database idea that he had been forced to shelve. What followed was an enthusiastic and often naïve series of efforts to set up a server, find friends with some knowledge of programming who might agree to do some routine data entry work and typing out classified ads from newspapers. The rest, as they say, is history.

When naukri.com was launched in 1997, there were only 14,000 Internet accounts in India. At present Sanjeev's company, Info Edge—the flagship brand is naukri.com—has a market capitalization of over Rs 2,500 crore.

In the 1970s, I used to conduct creativity workshops for entrepreneurship development programmes in Malaysia. We used simple exercises like brainstorming sessions for improving product design. I would point the group towards simple items like a telephone, ballpoint pens, or ceiling fans and ask them to come up with new adaptations. Cellphones had not yet been invented. But even then, when asked to improve the product design of a telephone, people would come up with ideas such as:

▶ Have a phone that can be carried in the pocket
▶ Attach a timer device to the phone
▶ Have the phone include a calculator, thermometer, touch screens, and speed dialling
▶ Attach a recording machine to the phone

Most of these fanciful ideas have now become reality. *Generally, if a group of people sit and brainstorm together, there is greater commitment to the project being worked on, and collective pride taken in the solutions.* Creativity can be nurtured and developed best in a free and cordial atmosphere. When creativity is encouraged in an organization through suggestion schemes, group meetings, team problem-solving or brainstorming sessions, then creativity becomes an integral part of the organization's culture. This brings out the best in individuals and benefits the organization.

India has produced many leaders in the recent past who have turned problems into opportunities through their creative talent. For example, Dr Devi Shetty set up Narayana Hridayalya to help thousands of poor children who needed cardiac surgery. The group's creative response to provide operations at a lesser cost was by standardizing them. It now performs double the number of cardiac surgeries than the largest hospital in the US at one-tenth of the cost. Tata's invention of the Nano car at an affordable price of Rs 1 lakh is again a creative response to solve the mobility problems of small families.

Kunwer Sachdev, Founder and Managing Director of Su-Kam, is a great example of one who turns every problem into an opportunity and converts it into business through his creative talent. A graduate in Physics, and the son of a railway clerk, he now owns a Rs 500 crore company with aspirations to be a global player. He started his career selling ballpoint pens in Delhi. He wanted to do something different. He noticed people in flats and hotels using Master Antenna system and started a cable TV business that gives access to both the TV channels. When his inverter was not working he used to learn about inverters and started making inverters that work in different seasons and under different conditions. He then added remote controls. Today Su-Kam is the leading power back-up solution provider in India, with its consistent focus on technological innovation. It has attained heights unheard of, in the largely unorganized industry. Having a clear technological edge, creating new benchmarks and upgrading standards for the industry, comes naturally to Su-Kam. Today, Su-Kam is the established leader in product innovation, design sensibility, and sales distribution network. Kunwer has filed over fifty patents and continues to search for new opportunities to apply his creative genius. Hard work and commitment coupled with creativity and a penchant for innovations serves millions of people who benefit from the power back-up systems. Su-Kam products have facility for remote diagnostics where they can assess the working of the Su-Kam inverter sitting in Gurgaon. C.K. Prahalad spotted Kunwer a few years ago as a great example of Indian Innovations.

Source: Reproduced from the video on The Next Practices: Innovations from India, seminar conducted by C.K. Prahalad, Ahmedabad Management Association, 2007. For the latest story on Kunwer, also see Rashmi, Bansal, *Connect the Dots*, Ahmedabad, Eklavya Foundation, 2010.

COMPONENTS OF CREATIVITY

Creativity, though often treated as a single variable or ability, actually consists of several components; just as intelligence consists of verbal reasoning, numerical intelligence, abstract thinking, reasoning, etc. The famous psychologist from the University of Southern California, J.P. Guilford (1968), identified six components of creativity:

- ▶ Fluency
- ▶ Flexibility
- ▶ Originality
- ▶ Elaboration
- ▶ Sensitivity to problems
- ▶ Ability to redefine problems

Fluency: Fluency is the speed with which a person can produce a number of appropriate responses to a problem. For example, the number of uses of a screwdriver that a respondent can list in a five-minute period indicates his fluency. Research shows that if a person can produce several rapid responses pertinent to the given problem, he is generally quick to be able to solve the problem too. The ideas required may range from simple (suggesting an appropriate word) to complex (quickly outlining a possible business plan or course of action).

Flexibility: Flexibility in thought is the ability to change focus and shift gears rapidly. Your response to a given problem demonstrates both the spontaneity of your thinking and how adaptive you are. Your spontaneous flexibility is usually evinced by the number of categories of use/purposes that you are able to list. For instance, when asked to list the uses of cotton, you may suggest such things as making carpets, bedcovers, pillow covers, etc. These points represent the use of cotton only as a fabric. Therefore, you may show yourself to be considerably less flexible than someone who suggests that cotton may be used for surgical purposes, for making fabric, making wicks for kerosene lamps, for cosmetic purposes, etc. Adaptive flexibility is the ability to see different solutions to the same problem. It is said that when a schoolboy sent a particularly vexing problem in geometry to Einstein, the scientist responded with eight different solutions to the problem.

Originality: Originality is perhaps the most basic ingredient of creativity. It implies a response or a solution that is both novel and useful. In psychological research, originality is demonstrated by an acceptable response that is statistically infrequent. For example, three individuals are asked to list the possible uses of a fan. All three indicate cooling a room; two indicate drying a wet floor and drying clothes; and only one indicates creating a visual display by attaching coloured paper or balloons to the fan blades. The last response would be considered the most original because it is infrequent but appropriate.

Elaboration: Elaboration is the ability to follow through on a general idea. It means you can think through, step by step, how an idea may be implemented. Many imaginative people are ultimately unable to bring their ideas to fruition because they cannot elaborate on their initial thoughts. The capacity to elaborate may be judged by the level of detail in which each step in the plan is described.

Sensitivity to problems: A creative person tends to be unusually sensitive to the problems and possibilities involved in whatever he/she encounters. He/She is unusually aware of the gaps in knowledge, the problems that remain unsolved, and of missing or contradictory elements. To measure sensitivity to problems, typically, individuals are exposed to a situation, say, a picture of children playing an unknown game. They are then asked to list the questions that come to their mind that cannot be answered with the information available in the picture. Those who raise a high number of pertinent questions score higher in terms of their sensitivity to problems.

Redefining problems: This is the ability to redefine a problem in the clearest and simplest possible manner, often breaking the problem into its constituent parts, so that it becomes easier to arrive at a solution.

INDICATORS OF CREATIVITY

The following are accepted indicators of creativity and innovativeness. These criteria are used in performance appraisals and in creating innovation-centric organizational cultures.

▶ Coming up with numerous ideas and solutions when faced with a problem
▶ Looking for new ways of doing things
▶ Demonstrating original thinking. Thinking in a creative and unconventional way
▶ Being quick in adopting and approving innovations
▶ Appreciating others' ideas
▶ Translating creative ideas into workable solutions
▶ Showing enough flexibility and willingness to revise one's earlier views
▶ Being able to elaborate on a project with relevant details

THE LOOT

With over a 100 stores opening within four years, The Loot is the fastest growing chain of multi-brand discount stores. While still an undergraduate, Jay began to think about setting up a business of his own. Watching branded retail take off in India in late 1996, Jay felt that this was a business area that could be profitably tapped. Sitting behind a desk at a retail franchise outlet in Mumbai, he noticed that the store had a lot of potential customers but very few of them actually bought anything. He decided that he'd have to come up with a creative idea that allowed the average Mumbaikar to bridge the gap between wanting to own a brand and actually agreeing to spend on it. Thus, The Loot was born.

In order to attract buyers, The Loot introduced merchandise priced between Rs 99 and Rs 149, and offered schemes such as 'Buy 1 Get 1 free'. It also introduced its own private labels—'Eccentrics' and 'Bus Stop'—to fight the lack of availability of the sizes in greatest demand. The franchisee arrangement also worked to Jay's benefit as he believes that 'Franchisees are more entrepreneurial in nature than company-owned store managers.'

The Loot has won a series of awards—for its contribution to Indian retail and innovative start-up ideas—in a short span of time including being nominated 'The Most Admired Retailer of the Year' by India Retail Forum in 2007. Jay describes his own entrepreneurial journey as 'an adrenalin rush', and adds that 'seeing the company grow at a fast pace and watching content, satisfied customers increases this drive.'

DEVELOPING CREATIVE THINKING

As discussed in chapter 3, a manager needs to make decisions on a variety of matters. The quality and impact of his decisions will be particularly high if he can think of innovative methods and solutions to problems. A manager's creative abilities are, therefore, always an asset to his organization. It was commonly believed that creativity was an inborn talent, but recent sociological research and experiments have shown that this is not necessarily true. Social scientists have found that most people have certain inherent creative abilities, but these tend to be killed off by socialization, indoctrination, and instituted systems of reward and punishment. Special training and HR programmes are often designed to help people revive or develop their creative skills by first helping them understand the factors that have impeded their ability to think innovatively.

Creativity can be developed in a number of ways. Most importantly, though, it needs to be practised constantly. As a manager or subordinate do not hesitate to try and come up with innovative solutions. Many of your suggestions may ultimately be rejected, but what's important is to keep thinking and build a reputation as a creative thinker. It certainly helps if you read about the lives of creative individuals and business innovators. Additionally, try to engage in the following:

▶ Brainstorming: An exercise where, given a problem, you list all the possible solutions you can think of. While listing the solutions, you ought to suspend your faculty of judgement (what is right, wrong, acceptable or unacceptable to others). Allow your thoughts to flow freely and generate as many ideas as possible.

▶ Making project plans: As practical exercises, prepare project plans from time to time, and share your original ideas with others.

▶ Assessing yourself: If possible, participate in self-assessment or psychometric tests and relevant questionnaires (such as those pertaining to personal 'blocks') which your HR department may be using. Filling in these questionnaires provides you detailed and structured feedback, whose implications you may not have hitherto appreciated or fully understood.

▶ Using force field analysis: Learning and using techniques such as the 'force field analysis'. This technique is based on the assumption that any given problem is a consequence of two sets of factors. The first set is called 'facilitating factors' and the second 'inhibiting factors'. You need to identify these two sets of factors, develop strategies to weaken the inhibiting factors and strengthen or add new facilitating factors. You would have to begin by clearly stating the given problem, and then state the ideal situation you want to achieve, that is, the situation at which you want to arrive after satisfactorily solving the problem. Now, identify the current situation in detail. List all the factors that would help shift the current situation towards the desired one. These are your facilitating factors. Then list all the inhibiting factors. Rank each of your facilitating and inhibiting factors by giving it a value (1 = lowest intensity, 5 = highest intensity). Brainstorm and identify how you could lessen the aggregate score of the inhibiting factors and strengthen the score of the facilitating factors. In this process, you might find yourself able to add more facilitating factors to your list. By weakening the inhibiting factors and/or by strengthening the facilitating factorss, you increase your chances of moving towards the desired state.

Rekha Shetty, in her recent book *Innovate: 90 Days to Transform Your Business* has put together a 90-day habit of innovation in thought and action. Her book illustrates how to use innovative thinking tools in different business activities, from planning strategies to customer focus, and presents real-life success stories. A sample of the ideas presented in her book is given below:

1. Create a problem bank by using Post-it slips. Do it when you are well.
2. Teamwork drives innovation. Challenge each other when working together as a team.
3. Create a steering committee for steering innovations and innovative problem-solving. Use suggestion schemes. Naina Kidwai, CEO of HSBC Bank, has used a programme called 'Magic Ideas'. The best ideas received awards and others were acknowledged. In 2005 she created 134 task forces to look for ways to make the bank a better place to work. (pp. 79–82)
4. Create incubators for innovation like Harsh Mariwala of Marico does. (p. 23 in Shetty)
5. As Albert Einstein said 'problems cannot be solved by thinking within the framework in which the problem was created'. Change your thinking.
6. Create action teams like what Ramaswamy Seshasayee, CEO of Ashok Leyland, did by putting a youth organization with its own website to share ideas. (p. 30)
7. Encourage communication. Practise listening.
8. Encourage failures and use them to get solutions and learning.
9. Transform spectators into participants like what Muthuraman did in Tata Steel, Jamshedpur. Every week workers from different departments got together for a three-hour meeting with no one from the management. Thoughts from them were exhibited in an exhibition. They saved Rs 700 crore in a single year through various initiatives like this. (p. 74)

10. Use thinking tools like: Turn it Upside Down; Tent Thinking versus Marble Palace Thinking; Attribute Matching; Five Senses Exercise; Analogies; Metaphors; Bug-list Technique; Turn Coats; Caps; Excursion; Force Field Analysis (explained above); Wildest Idea Technique; Brain Writing; etc. (a number of these explained in detail in her book).

IMPEDIMENTS TO CREATIVITY

Often, the process of socialization stifles one's natural creative abilities. As a manager, there are certain traits for which you need to be on your guard. If you think you possess any of the following qualities, you would do well to try and work your way around them over time, and give them up as you would a bad habit. Consciously make yourself a more adaptive, flexible, and tolerant person—this greatly increases your worth and efficiency as a manager.

▶ Intolerance for ambiguity and unwillingness to try anything new; a tendency to avoid unfamiliar situations or to feel anxious the moment one faces suspense or when the outcome of an event is pending; an aversion to a lack of structure and definiteness.

▶ An overwhelming desire for conformity—either adhering to certain sanctions and norms yourself, or always expecting your team members to do so as well.

▶ A tendency to stereotype another person, event, or situation on the basis of one set of inputs, one experience, or one trait. For example, the tendency to think that people from X communities make good tenants, people from Y community lack cleanliness, people from Z community are exploiters, etc.

These snap judgements prevent a manager from understanding a person or situation fully and thus impedes his creativity.

▶ A fear of failure might cause you to approach any task with pessimism. A fear-oriented attitude will prevent you from trying anything new.

▶ Resource myopia is the inability to see what is available around you when faced with difficulties or problems. Sometimes you become so paralysed by the difficulty of a given situation that you forget the strengths and resources you may well be able to utilize.

▶ The tendency to feel easily upset in the event of negative feedback. If you're a touchy person, the quality of your interaction with others will suffer. If you seek only positive feedback, then your touchiness may inhibit creativity.

▶ For a detailed discussion on creativity, creative problem-solving techniques and on methods to develop creativity, read Khandwalla 2004, 1988 and De Bono, 1992, 1967. Both these authors have written extensively on this theme. Khandwalla describes a number of creative problem-solving methods in his book *The Fourth Eye*.

IMPLICATIONS FOR MANAGERS

In order to encourage creativity and creative problem-solving in their teams, managers must necessarily be out-of-the-box thinkers themselves. You might introspect and strategize about how to overcome the impediments to creativity that both you and your team members or subordinates habitually encounter. Create a friendly and stimulating atmosphere in your department that encourages your subordinates as they experiment with their own mechanisms of solving problems. Support them and be flexible enough to encourage experimentation.

Doers are unlikely to adopt a creative approach. They usually look to their seniors to implement unconventional solutions and wait for their suggestions. Doers prefer to follow manuals and codified guidelines, without quite realizing that their inherent creativity is hampered when they are blindly manual driven. Thrusters tend to work more intelligently, and use some creativity to achieve efficiencies of time and cost. The cleverness of their solutions or suggestions often makes them stand out in an organization. As they gradually develop more and more teams and units to implement their ideas, they are accepted as visionaries. Visionaries and missionaries are the most creative managers—they actively look to find interesting solutions to the business problems they encounter and try to set newer goals for their companies. Mission-driven managers tend to be the most effective at inspiring large numbers of people to explore creative solutions. We shall now look at two innovators and how they created new business ideas.

Case study 1: Sam Pitroda—The telecom sector's creative genius

Throughout the late 1960s and early 1970s, US-based Sam Pitroda was involved in cutting-edge research in telecommunications and handheld computing. He established himself as a leading thinker in the field when he introduced microprocessors into telephone switches, causing the early wave in digital switching. In 1974, Pitroda and two other entrepreneurs founded Westcom Switching, Inc. His invention of the electronic diary in 1975 is regarded as one of the earliest examples of handheld computing. Five years later, they sold out to Rockwell International, and Pitroda became one of the few NRI multimillionaires in those days.

Despite his wealth and success, Pitroda was plagued by a sense of guilt at having 'walked out on India'. He began to dream of a resurgent India, and became increasingly convinced that telecom connectivity was needed for nation building. Understanding the need for innovative technological solutions in order to make India 'telecomable', Pitroda developed a new digital switching system for a fraction of the estimated cost. Within a period of only thirty-six months, and with the help of 300 enthusiastic young recruits, he completed his project at the Centre for the Development of Telematics (C-DOT). C-DOT opened its offices at Delhi and Bangalore with a staff whose average age was twenty-five.

Pitroda's innovations were not just technological but social as well. He set seemingly impossible targets and cheered people on in a good-natured manner. He knew from first-hand experience that Indian employees in the US did very well and so he tried to create an 'American' work environment. Laying great emphasis on action, teamwork, risk taking, flexibility, simplicity, and openness, he was almost brutal in his determination to root out hierarchy and bureaucracy. He once created a massive scene, screaming at the typists to stop leaping to their feet each time a manager entered their workspace to use one of the office's two telephones.

Pitroda tried his best to shield young engineers from bureaucrats, politicians, and business interests. At the same time, he opened the doors to the media who responded with excitement, optimism, and the kind of hero worship that Pitroda hoped would attract more young people to careers in technology. By 1986, C-DOT had sprawling, chaotic offices, 425 employees—the average age remained twenty-five—and all the drive, activity, and high spirits of a US presidential campaign.

Pitroda's management methods were highly unconventional for India and were very unpopular with much of the old guard, but within C-DOT they had accomplished wonders. As the head of the Telecom Commission, he installed one rural telephone exchange in the country every day in 1989. By 1993, the figures had moved up to twenty-five exchanges being installed daily. Not long afterwards, Pitroda met his seemingly impossible target of connecting all of India's 600,000 villages by telephone.

Case study 2: Nirmal Jain—India Info Line

Nirmal comes from a family of risk takers. His forefathers, who were commodity traders in Rajasthan, had made huge profits and then become nearly bankrupt in the late 1970s when silver prices spiked and then crashed. It was not much of a surprise when he decided to strike out on his own rather than take up a job.

After doing his MBA at IIMA, he started work with Hindustan Lever but quit a couple of years later to set up an equity research unit, Inquire-Indian Equity Research. His work set new standards for equity research in India. But like most entrepreneurs, Jain was itching for bigger, better things.

In 1995, he decided to fill the gap in the market for research and information services and set up Probity, an equity research firm which sold company reports for Rs 20,000 and sector research for Rs 10,000. They were the first company to introduce a report on the IT sector, which was very well received. The key strategy was to think differently. Jain wanted to have a portal that could tell the layperson everything he or she needed to know about the Indian economy.

In 1999, Jain decided to put all his research online—his thinking was that the Internet would help him increase his reach for a fraction of the price. Instead of only 250 people seeing his reports, now 2.5 million could buy them.

India Info Line was the biggest gamble Jain took. The company was giving free access to brokering and reports and many people thought he was crazy to make such large volumes of research data freely accessible. Convinced that it was a foolish move, many of his core team members quit. He may have been considered crazy, but India Info Line went on to become hugely successful in the online brokerage business.

Jain continued to show creativity and risk taking in his business when in 2000, he launched 5paisa.com. Brokerage rates used to be 130 basis points but he cut them down to five. The logic was that the Internet would allow him to cut out the costs of communication such as telephone, courier, etc. Today, more or less all brokers use the concept but back then nobody had thought of it. It was a paradigm shift and revolutionary at that point.

CONCLUSION

Creativity is a key component among effective managers. In the world of work, creativity refers to how fluently a manager solves problems. Despite our preconceptions, it is neither an abstract force nor a predetermined character trait. It can be broken up into various components and we can all improve our ability to think out of the box. Ultimately, the quality of a manager is judged by the quality of his ideas. Creative managers should be able to see something that no one else has seen. Their fortunes rest on their ability to capitalize on this and convince the world about it. Visionary and missionary managers are able to inspire and lead their teams into uncharted territory as we have seen in the examples of Sam Pitroda and Nirmal Jain.

REFERENCES

Bansal, Rashmi (2010). *Connect the Dots: The Inspiring Stories of 20 Entrepreneurs without an MBA Who Dared to Find Their Own Path.* Ahmedabad: Eklavya Education Foundation.

De Bono, Edward (1992). *Serious Creativity: Using the Power of Lateral Thinking to Create New Ideas.* New Delhi: Indus Publications.

——— (1967). *The Use of Lateral Thinking.* Harmondsworth, Middlesex: Penguin.

Guilford, J.P. (1968). *Intelligence, Creativity, and Their Educational Implications.* San Diego: Robert R. Knapp.

Khandwalla, Pradip N. (2004). *Lifelong Creativity: An Unending Quest.* New Delhi: Tata McGraw-Hill.

——— (1988). *The Fourth Eye.* Mumbai: A.H. Wheeler.

Shetty, Rekha (2010). *Innovate: 90 Days to Transform Your Business.* New Delhi: Penguin Books.

6

Interpersonal Engagement

This chapter deals with the interpersonal competence of managers—or, in short, their dealings with their employees and colleagues in discussing and resolving issues fairly and clearly, mentoring them, and building trust. Effective managers have strong interpersonal skills. They operate mostly without ego and are flexible enough to manage their juniors, seniors, colleagues, and customers. Interpersonal competence begins with self-respect—or self-efficacy as we discussed in the first chapter—and flowing out of that, a respect for others. The key to being a good manager is to treat every human being as a source of ideas and thus carry out our transactions with them in a befitting manner.

Our interpersonal skills are vital to our roles as good managers and to our professional success. 'Everyone in organizational life is constantly being watched and evaluated by bosses, clients, vendors, peers, subordinates, and other significant people. Every day, with every bit of human interaction you engage in, some member of this crowd forms an opinion about you,' writes David F. D'Alessandro, CEO of John Hancock and author of *Career Warfare*. This collective opinion will determine whether or not you will conquer the vertical space or be conquered by it.

INTERPERSONAL ENGAGEMENT

Ajay Godbole (Vice President [VP] of Sales) and Janak Parikh (VP, Commercial) are both VPs for a carpet manufacturing company. Recently, when a 360 degree feedback was conducted, Godbole got very low ratings on the way he inspires and develops his juniors. Even his colleagues did not have many positive things to say about him. Godbole is a good taskmaster and gets results. However, he is coercive, loses his temper and rarely appreciates his staff. Most of his juniors say they are most happy when he is on tour and prefer to avoid him for fear of being reprimanded. He does have a couple of admirers among the fifteen or so employees who report to him. On the other hand, Janak is rated as one of the most pleasant people to work with in the company. He is informal, smiles, and is polite with everyone. The juniors of both these VPs stay late on certain days to complete work. Janak's staff stay voluntarily to complete their work, as they believe that if they don't, the department will get a bad name and the company will lose face in compliance. Godbole's team, on the other hand, stays back mostly with resentment.

Each manager develops, over a period of time, their own equation with people by virtue of their qualities, style, mannerisms, attitudes, beliefs, and so on. These create the manager's chemistry, which determines how much he can get out of those who work for him. *Interpersonal engagement is the extent to which a manager can get an employee engaged in doing what is mutually beneficial, or the extent to which the manager can get the other person committed to do what they want and feel it is being done for the junoir's own self.* The higher our interpersonal skills, the stronger our interpersonal engagement with our colleagues. (See appendix 6.1 for an interpersonal engagement questionnaire.)

DEALING WITH EMPLOYEES

As a manager, most of our interpersonal skills are tested by our dealings with our juniors or employees. The main duties of managers towards their juniors are:

- ▶ Goal setting
- ▶ Providing information and support required to do their jobs
- ▶ Managing conflicts
- ▶ Recognizing and rewarding good work
- ▶ Listening to grievances and solving problems
- ▶ Career guidance and coaching
- ▶ Inspiring them with ideas and assisting them to develop

While most of us will agree with these points in principle, almost all of us will find it hard to put them into practice. Consider the dealings of three managers: Gupta, Punjabi and Sen.

Manager Gupta

Mr Gupta is the manager of the cost accounting department of a large company manufacturing road transport equipment. Mr Anand is one of his supervisory employees. Anand has been with the company for three years and has been doing highly satisfactory work. He has sent all his reports on time and with good, efficient analysis. He seems to create a lot of free time for himself by doing whatever has been assigned to him well. Gupta often feels that if Anand took a little more initiative he could have done many other things in the department. In addition, Gupta has never noticed Anand assisting others in the department nor taking any responsibility beyond his prescribed duties. He thinks that Anand wastes a good deal of time socializing. Gupta feels that while Anand's performance is satisfactory in terms of meeting targets, he needs to improve his ability to contribute to the team spirit and to the development of his subordinates. Gupta calls Anand into his office for a discussion of his performance to motivate him to do better.

Gupta: Hello! Anand, please come and have a seat. I called you in to talk about your performance.

Anand: Thank you, sir. What about my performance?

Gupta: Please sit and relax; we shall talk about it.

(As Anand sits down, Gupta keeps signing some papers. He completes signing, calls his secretary, passes on the files and asks her to bring in the letters he dictated in the morning as soon as she has completed them.)

Gupta: Yes, Mr Anand. I am a little concerned about one or two things relating to your job. I see you quite often spending time with Satish and Chander of the other department and taking long coffee breaks with them. I have also received complaints from Satish and Chander's boss that they are not to be found in their seats most of the time.

Anand: Well, I am sorry, sir, if you got this impression. I thought you were going to say something positive about my job. I am not wasting my time with Satish and Chander. You know that a couple of years back both of them were in this department and did a good job. Recently I have been having some problems both at home and here at work. I was discussing this with them...

Gupta: If you are having problems, they are not the people to talk to just because they did a good job two years ago. You must talk to me rather than waste your time and theirs and get a bad name in the bargain.

Anand: I am not wasting anyone's time here, sir. In fact, I don't want to waste your time, either. Recently, I faced a particular problem and I knew a similar situation had come up a couple of years ago and that they had both handled it very well. I have been going to them to discuss this issue. In fact, the new costing methodology that I've suggested for our project is one given by them.

Gupta: Oh, I see! They are responsible for your target achievement. Another thing I would like to mention before I forget is that I am not sure to what extent you are helping your subordinates to take more responsibility and develop to perform managerial roles of higher levels. This is another quality you must develop. You must work with them like a team leader and build them...

Anand: I have given enough freedom to my subordinates and responsibility, too. In fact, I leave them to do their own thing most of the time.

Gupta: Is that how you get enough time to spend with Satish and the other fellow? I would not like to see you...

(The telephone rings and Gupta picks it up. The phone call is from another officer at Anand's level.)

Gupta: Yes Mr Sampat... I am not busy... You can come over. You've done an excellent job... I know I can always rely on you. Come immediately. (keeps the phone down.)

Gupta: (to Anand) Yes, I was saying that hereafter I would like to see you doing much better than you have done so far and not taking long coffee breaks and not spending too much time with your friends, okay? I would like to see you grow and develop. You should aspire to be a better performer, okay? I am your well-wisher. Now go and look after your work.

Anand: Thank you, sir. I only wish you had some more time to discuss the issues at length.

Gupta: I am going to see Sampat now to discuss some urgent issues. As long as you keep the points I am telling you in mind, we can discuss matters any time. Come to me if you need any help, okay? See you. Before I forget, I am nominating you for the team building programme. It costs Rs 80,000. Hope you will enjoy this and it adds to your bio-data.

Anand: Thank you. (leaves the room)

Analysis

The above case amply demonstrates the insensitivity of the manager to the junior. Gupta has done all that is possible to demotivate Anand. His intention was good but the way in which he proceeded resulted in a poor outcome. First, Gupta started with the assumption that Anand was wasting his time. He had a golden opportunity to compliment his employee on his good work, timely submission of reports and analysis of data, etc. Instead, he focused on what Anand has not been doing or on how he is wasting his time. He did not listen and was not open to correct his views. As a result the conversation ended up as a one-way communication.

Good managers take pains to understand their juniors and colleagues well. One way to understand this is by asking open questions and listening to them. Open questions allow the other person to speak and thus help us get facts and make judgements based on them. For example, if Gupta had complimented Anand and asked him to discuss his concerns, Anand may have expressed his dilemmas and aspirations more. This could have led him to appeal for better utilization of his colleague's time. Gupta was too eager to share his negative observations and did not even provide an opportunity to listen to Anand.

Materials manager Punjabi

Mr Punjabi is a materials manager in charge of a centralized material control department. Mr Gulati is one of the four engineers working in his department and is attached to the purchasing section. Six months ago Punjabi asked Gulati to take charge of two more items independently and ensure that there were no stock-outs or inventory mount-ups. Punjabi also assigned him the role of meeting all the suppliers as he did not have time to speak to them himself. After six months, Punjabi was getting an increasing number of complaints from each department and he had to intervene frequently to calm the irate suppliers. He called Gulati for a review and to counsel him to improve things.

Punjabi: Mr Gulati, I have received twenty-six complaints in the last six months, four about inspection, and ten about payment and twelve about change in delivery schedules. What the hell is the matter?

Gulati: You know that I've never had so many complaints in the past. I am terribly unhappy about my job now. I have to run around a lot to organize the transport to get materials on time. Often I have to work outdoors, particularly in the rainy season. I have many problems at home, too. My children are sick and my landlord is asking me to vacate the house.

Punjabi: I see. (pause) What can we do to reduce the complaints? I am getting fed up having to pacify people every day.

Gulati: Besides these problems, I do not see much opportunity for my growth in the purchasing section. You have given me independent charge of some more items. I have to supervise and maintain so many records. You know, when your mind is being pulled in so many directions, at home and here, you cannot attend to everything perfectly...

Punjabi: (interrupting Gulati) Now look, we all have problems and we all have limitations. Now, I do not want to spend my time dealing with irate suppliers. What can we do concretely to minimize these complaints?

Gulati: Oh, the suppliers! They keep on saying things, you know. I am very much overworked here. On top of it you expect me to send every bill and every note to you. I have to be meticulous. That takes a hell of a lot of time.

Punjabi: My dear Gulati, I understand all that. I know in this company people have to work very hard if they want to survive. Now, let us see what we can do about reducing the complaints....

Gulati: ... (continues)

Analysis

Punjabi initiated the conversation with good intentions but his starting point was wrong. He could have begun by trying to understand the cause of the problem. Without understanding the problem, you cannot solve it. To understand the problem means to understand it through Gulati's eyes. The doer, in this case Gulati, always has more information about realities on the ground. Unless a supervisor's manager understands these realities they cannot help their junior solve such problems. Gulati mentions family issues as a reason and it must also be kept in mind that every employee comes to work as a whole person. He cannot be expected to leave his personal problems outside.

Punjabi made the second error of obsessing with the problem but not attempting to analyse it with Gulati. He cannot improve Gulati's performance unless he gets Gulati to understand the problem. Diagnoses of problems in such situations are mutual. Joint diagnosis leads to joint commitment and thus paves the way for resolution.

Thus, if Punjabi had been more sympathetic and presented the problem for Gulati to diagnose himself, he would have ended up with a more motivated employee.

Contrasted with the above two cases, consider how Manager Sen deals with his executive secretary.

General Manager Sen

Mr Puri is Executive Secretary to Mr Sen, who is General Manager (GM) of (Marketing) in a multinational company. Puri's job requires him to be accurate in preparing reports, drafting letters on the basis of direction from the GM, organizing customer meets, and keeping electronic records of Sen's various correspondence files and data. As Sen cannot spend a lot of time going through every report he signs, he would like to have his Executive Secretary do a good job of his correspondence and reports. He would also like to have his data and files maintained properly. Recently, he has been finding a number of mistakes in the reports indicating that Puri is not paying full attention to their quality—so much so that one of his clients commented that he had received a report from Sen with the word 'urinal' in place of 'union'. Sen is very concerned about the drop in Puri's accuracy. He decides to talk to Puri about it.

Sen: Puri, can you come in for a little while for a personal discussion?

Puri: Yes sir.

Sen: Come in. Please have a seat.

Puri: Thank you, sir. (sits down)

Sen: How are things with you?

Puri: Fine, sir. Thank you. I am preparing for my MBA examinations, for which I am appearing privately. That keeps me a little tied up.

Sen: Oh, I see. You are doing the evening course for which we sponsored you? I forgot about it. How do you find the course?

Puri: Quite interesting, sir. I am learning many things. It is a very useful programme and keeps me quite occupied with various assignments. I keep talking about the things

I learned in that school to visitors who come to see you while they wait for you. That reinforces my learning.

Sen: Oh, you are keeping them busy and you also find yourself busy, don't you?

Puri: Yes sir, certainly and I must thank you again for sponsoring me for this course.

Sen: So, you are enjoying the MBA course and you are tied up with your exams. Do you think this overload is causing you some anxiety?

Puri: No, sir. Not at all. Though I have to prepare a lot for the exams and struggle for time to do concentrated work. But I am managing, sir.

Sen: Oh, I see. You have to struggle for time to concentrate. Do you think this is affecting your office work in any way?

Puri: I don't think so, sir. I do not see any issues. Any problem, sir?

Sen: Well, as of late, the number of mistakes in the reports we are sending have increased. I am a little concerned about that. I wonder if that has something to do with your having to work under pressure. You also seem to have missed reminding me of some of the deadlines in sending the reports. For example, the other day there was a call from the MD's office about a report that was not sent and apparently they left a message to call them back. I did not even know about it. I have one or two other instances but I hope there are no other calls you missed noting and informing me about.

Puri: Well, sir, thank you for pointing this out. I am sorry that the mistakes have increased. I shall try to be more careful. Maybe I am trying to save time by doing things in a hurry. Have I committed any serious mistakes?

Sen: Well, you know that I do not go through all the reports we send out with my signature. In one of the reports, 'union' was typed as 'urinal' and the client was joking about it at a party. I was embarrassed.

Puri:	Oh my God! I am extremely sorry, sir. How could that happen? What a shame! This could be due to the spellcheck in the computer. Has that created too much of a problem? I always try to read the reports line by line before we send them out. Recently I have been slipping up on that. I am extremely sorry. May I write an apology letter to the party concerned?
Sen:	No, don't worry. Fortunately, it is a friend. I am glad you realize the importance of being extra careful before you dispatch the reports or even send them for my signature. Hereafter, you may like to follow the procedures of reading letters twice before you send them out. That would certainly require some more time. Can we do something to reduce any other workload you have?
Puri:	Regarding the call from the MD's office, sir, they wanted some information to be passed on to the Public Relations Officer about the contents of our annual report under preparation. I had promptly given that information directly to the PRO. I did not want to bother you by informing you about what I have done. Is there anything else I missed, sir? I will be more careful next time.
Sen:	There were some calls from our customers. I will tell you once I remember. They may not be that important but I wanted to make sure that there is no goofing up with our clients.
Puri:	Yes, sir. Please tell me. I will be careful and leave all information and messages on your table. I will also make sure to read reports twice before sending them to dispatch. If part of the routine filing can be taken care of by your personal secretary, it will help me a good deal, sir.
Sen:	How much filing work would he have. You can use him for an hour every day. Is that okay? I will talk to him.
Puri:	Yes sir. Thank you for this... (continues)

Analysis

Sen had every reason to share many negative things relating to the drop in Puri's performance. However, he chose to first understand the situation. He started the conversation with open questions 'How are things with you?' and continued the conversation on matters of significance to Puri—his MBA and keeping the visitors busy. He also showed his empathy by paraphrasing what he understood Puri was saying (Oh, you are keeping them busy and you also find yourself busy; You have to struggle for time to concentrate, etc.). *Paraphrasing a statement gives an opportunity to communicate your understanding of the other person and also the significance you attach to what the other person is saying. It also gives you an opportunity to clarify if you have not correctly understood the other person.* By using empathy, understanding through open questions and paraphrasing, Sen has been able to jointly diagnose the issue with Puri. Sen also worked towards an action plan to change the situation and resolved it by providing assistance. Since the action plan came from Puri himself, after understanding the implications of his declining performance, things are likely to be better. Puri feels that he works for an understanding and supportive boss.

HOW TO BUILD INTERPERSONAL COMPETENCE

We can build our interpersonal relationships with our teams in the following ways.

Empowering transactions

An empowering transaction is one in which both parties feel more powerful or confident and positive of each other after the transaction. In cases of senior and junior or boss–subordinate transactions, an empowering transaction is one in which the junior or the subordinate feels more powerful or confident and motivated to do better than before. Effective managers build their juniors through empowering transactions. The Sen case is a good example of how such empowering transactions can be initiated and managed. The following attitudes are required to generate such empowering transactions:

▶ A positive view of people and a desire to use their competencies for the common good or organizational effectiveness
▶ An attitude to play win-win games or an attitude where the manager understands that one plus one can be more than two if both understand and support each other
▶ An empathetic attitude or an ability to frequently put oneself into the shoes of the other
▶ Respect for oneself leading to respect for others. This is the heart of good management and it results in emotional self-control, humility, and the desire to be good to the other: I will treat you as I like to be treated or I too have weaknesses and therefore I can understand and tolerate yours
▶ A desire to play on each other's strengths

Mentoring

When a young person joins an organization he needs a senior to help him adjust. Many organizations assign seniors to guide the young person. Such a relationship is called a mentor–protégé relationship and the process is called mentoring. By mentoring someone, you don't just focus on their work or help them learn a skill, but offer support and advice on any aspect of their life. The benefits of mentoring for your junior is that it will help them develop confidence, learn more effectively and acquire new perspectives. As a mentor, your ways of working with people will improve and it will satisfy your desire to help others.

Narayana Murthy set a great example for mentoring by designating himself as Chief Mentor of Infosys after he decided to pass on executive responsibilities to others. Mahendra Patel, MD of Mamata Group in Ahmedabad, is a good example of a manager who has made mentoring a part of his work and the work of others. Over the years, he has created a strong sense of loyalty among his employees and there are many people in the Mamata Group who started their career and retired from there. Mahendra Patel follows a very simple strategy for retaining employees. He believes if an employee has served in one position for two to three years, it is time for their relocation and promotion. This holds good for employees at all levels. You can find people who joined Mamata as peons and are now purchase officers, accountants, or junior cashiers. The first peon who joined the company is now chief accountant in the group's travel agency.

The Neyveli Lignite Corporation in south India has a good mentoring programme in which seniors with experience are assigned to mentor new recruits. Many organizations like the Aditya Birla Group have had successful experiments with mentoring programmes.

Interpersonal feedback

The reason Punjabi and Gulati didn't handle their interactions with their juniors well was due to the way they managed their conversations. *The key to giving an effective appraisal, or indeed any feedback, is to control the communication.* Udai Pareek, former professor at the IIMA, has given the following hints for making feedback effective—as long as the person giving it (counsellor) is sure of it:

1. is descriptive and not evaluative
2. is focused on the behaviour of the person and not on the person himself
3. is data based and specific and not impressionistic
4. reinforces positive, new behaviour
5. is suggestive and not prescriptive
6. is continuous
7. is mostly personal, giving data from one's own experience
8. is need based and solicited
9. is intended to help
10. is focused on modifiable behaviour
11. satisfies the needs of both the giver of the feedback and the one who receives the feedback
12. is checked and verified
13. is well timed
14. contributes to mutuality and relationship building.

Here are a few examples of ineffective feedback and what could be a better way of phrasing it:

1. **Evaluative**: Your reports are not good.
   Descriptive: You sent the reports well before the deadline. The totals in three of the seven tables do not tally with the figures.
2. **Focused on the person**: I am not happy with you. Because of you our department is getting a bad name. You must change yourself.
   Focused on the behaviour: In the last fifteen days you came late five times and every time you were late by more than an hour. I am very unhappy with your latecoming. I expect you to set a good example for others rather than continuing this way.

3. **Impressionistic**: I understand that you are not cooperative.

   Data based: You refused to take the indent from the production supervisor as he was late by ten minutes. They did not have the material this morning and we lost ten units of production.

4. **Focusing on the negative:** So you find time to supply information to the marketing department even when you are not required to do so. How about showing some more initiative in supplying information to your own boss?

   Reinforces positive behaviour: You took initiative and supplied the figures to the marketing department. I am very pleased with this. We value such initiative here.

5. **Prescriptive**: Don't waste the company's money talking on your cellphone with friends. Besides, you also waste the company's resources with last-minute changes in your travel plans and hotel bookings and frequent emails marking copies to all.

   Suggestive: Would you like to think about ways of avoiding last-minute changes in your travel plans? Our travel cancellation charges have gone up by 70 percent over the last three months.

6. **Based on what others say**: It looks like the higher-ups are not happy with your performance. The boss wants you to change.

   Based on your views: I think you can do better on this KPA. I'd like to see you make a mark in the next three months.

7. **Focused on behaviour that is difficult to change**: You need to learn some communication skills. You stutter a lot and people lose confidence in you.

   Focused on modifiable behaviour: You are making mistakes repeatedly every time you face such (specify) problems.

> Would you like to attend a training programme to get more insights into (specify relevant systems like inventory control, etc.)

If we apply these principles to our three managers above, we can see how and why Gupta and Punjabi went wrong. One of the most effective ways in which you can manage your interpersonal engagements is to follow these rules.

From the perspective of the feedback recipient, it is important that the reaction is not defensive. Try to avoid the following:

1. Denying feedback as opposed to owning up responsibility for behaviour
2. **Rationalization** (explaining away feedback by giving excuses) as opposed to self-analysis to identify the reasons for such behaviour
3. **Projection** (attributing negative feelings to the other person) as opposed to empathy (trying to understand the point of view of the other person)
4. **Displacement** (expressing negative feelings towards someone who may not fight back) as opposed to exploration (taking the help of the other person in knowing more about the feedback which has been given)
5. Quick **acceptance** without exploration as opposed to collecting more information and data to understand behaviour
6. Aggression towards the person giving feedback as opposed to seeking his help in understanding the feedback
7. Humour and wit as opposed to concern for improvement
8. Counter **dependence** (rejecting the authority) as opposed to listening carefully
9. **Cynicism** (general, strong scepticism that things cannot

improve) as opposed to a positive critical attitude which accepts some points and questions others

10. **Generalization** (explaining things in a general way) as opposed to experimenting

---

THE 20 SECRETS OF INTERPERSONAL EFFECTIVENESS

Here are the 20 secrets of interpersonal effectiveness outlined by Bacon (1996):

1. Act friendly, smile
2. Make people feel important
3. Share the credit
4. Be interested in people and disclose yourself to them
5. Remember people's names
6. Remember facts about people's lives and enquire about them now and then
7. Do the right thing even if it is not convenient
8. Be honest and straightforward to everyone
9. Give and receive feedback graciously
10. Be a good listener
11. Let people save face
12. Admit it if you are wrong
13. Be encouraging, involved, and enthusiastic
14. Be there for people when they need you
15. Don't be negative
16. Resist saying you should do this or that, etc.
17. Don't be abrasive
18. Don't use foul language
19. Don't overreact to stress or bad news
20. Don't make jokes at anyone's expense

TOOLS TO BUILD INTERPERSONAL COMPETENCE

Earlier we provided a simple overview about ways to become aware of your own interactions and manage them but there are also professional tools that you can use. Transactional analysis is one method that has helped people to become more competent interpersonally by analysing their transactions. Emotional intelligence is another very useful concept. Most of us have performance review discussions (PRDs) or assessments at work—this provides an excellent way to build on one's interpersonal competence.

Transactional analysis

Transactional analysis is a framework offered by Eric Berne (1961). This theory attempts to explain the dynamics of human behaviour in terms of transactions between people. According to this theory, the personality consists of three ego states. These three are known as parent (P), adult (A), and child (C) and we are constantly operating from them. The parent ego state consists of a set of feelings, attitudes, and behaviour patterns which resemble those of parents; the adult ego state reflects the current reality of the individual; while the child ego state contains the relics of the individual's own childhood.

The parent ego state is either nurturing or controlling. Its main function is to focus on values and norms. In this ego state, the parent gives instructions to others in detail on what should be done, how it should be done and controls the behaviour of others through approval, punishment, etc. The nurturing parent, conversely, provides needed support.

The adult ego state functions as collecting and processing information in the present. It responds to reality. In this ego state the person acts on the basis of information without values and emotions.

The child ego state can be divided into three parts. These include the natural child characterized by curiosity and fun-loving and playful behaviour. The adaptive child ego state is one in which the child is influenced by the parent, while the third is rebellious, represented essentially by revolting against authority.

Most of our interpersonal communication consists of sending and receiving messages. When the first person sends a message to a second person who receives the message and responds to it, one transaction is complete. The first person may send a prescriptive message to the second person in which they may be admonishing or reprimanding them. In such a case, the first person is said to be operating from the controlling parent ego state. The second person may respond by seeking information from the first person indicating that they're operating from an adult ego state. Alternatively, the second person may also admonish the first person. In this case they are also operating from a controlling parent ego state. Alternatively, the second person may admit a mistake in which case they are operating from the adapted child ego state.

Every message you send to the receiver from one ego state may be received by the receiver from the same ego state or from a different one. If the response is from the same ego state as the one from which it was received, it is called a parallel transaction. Such transactions are complementary and satisfying. When a response comes from a different ego state from which it was received, it is called cross-transaction.

Since the time it was invented, transaction analysis has become a very popular approach in understanding and managing interpersonal exchanges. For example, this approach can be applied to the transactions between Gupta and Anand, Punjabi and Gulati, or Sen and Puri in the cases mentioned earlier. This analysis helps us identify, for example, that Gupta is mostly operating from a controlling parent ego state. Sen and Puri have mostly operated from adult-to-adult ego states. The transactions of Gupta and Anand were crossed while those of Sen and Puri were complementary. Transaction analysis as language has helped many people in controlling their behaviour and managing interpersonal competence. It has helped sales and marketing people to increase their sales by interacting with the customers using the right kind of transactions.

Emotional intelligence

Emotional intelligence as a concept has its roots in the concept of social intelligence formulated by E.L. Thorndike in 1920 (Pareek 2007). Thorndike defined social intelligence as the ability to understand and manage people to act wisely in human relations.

Emotional intelligence is a type of social intelligence that involves the ability to monitor one's own and others' emotions, to discriminate among them, and to use the information to guide one's thinking and actions. Thus, emotional intelligence involves the following five domains:

▶ Self-awareness (observing yourself and recognizing a feeling as it happens)
▶ Managing emotions (handling feelings so that they are appropriate, realizing what is behind a feeling, finding ways to handle fears and anxieties, anger and sadness)
▶ Motivating oneself (channelling emotions in the service of the goal, emotional self-control or delaying gratification and stifling impulses)

- ► Empathy (sensitivity to others' feelings and concerns and taking their perspective, initiating the differences in how people feel about things)
- ► Handling relationships (managing emotions in others, social competence and social skills).

Emotional Intelligence is a very important ability to develop. A lot of training programmes are available for developing these abilities. For example, the Indian Society for Applied Behavioral Sciences (ISABS) conducts a programme called the Basic Human Process Laboratory (BHPL). In this laboratory the candidate interacts for five days with groups of strangers to discover themselves, their emotions, and the way they appear to others. Emotional self-control is not an easy thing to attain, however. It requires a lot of practise and deeper understanding and control. Many methods such as meditation, vipasana, etc., have been found to help attain emotional self-control.

Performance review discussion (PRD)

PRD or coaching has become an integral part of performance management systems or appraisal exercises in most organizations. These discussions of performance between bosses and their juniors are conducted one on one, every six months or quarterly.

The main objective of PRD is building mutuality and empowering a relationship so that both the boss and the junior understand each other's expectations, difficulties, learn from each other, and prepare themselves to do better than before.

During the discussion the appraiser should: (i) compliment the appraisee for his accomplishments and good qualities; (ii) understand and appreciate his difficulties and make action plans for the future with a view to help him; (iii) understand the appraiser's perceptions of the situation and make corrections if necessary; (iv) help him to recognize his strong and weak points; (v) communicate the appraiser's expectations from the appraisee; (vi) identify developmental needs of the appraisee and chalk out a course of action for meeting these needs.

Such a discussion should bring the appraisee and appraiser closer. Therefore, it should be conducted in a congenial atmosphere and the appraiser should focus on two-way communication. Bear the following points in mind:

▶ Every annual review discussion, if properly conducted, will require about three to four hours. Short review discussions show a lack of respect on the part of the appraiser for the appraisee or lack of commitment of the organization to development-oriented appraisals.

▶ It is also necessary for organizations to conduct separate appraisal meetings/discussions. Employees should be given the freedom to use the company guest house or any other place that is convenient for such review discussions. Some organizations have the practice of declaring a particular month or fortnight as appraisal month/fortnight and expect the appraisers to conduct their reviews during this period. If an employee is not at work on any day during that month, it is assumed that he is busy with his appraisal and review discussions.

Please keep in mind the section on interpersonal feedback during assessments.

THE IMPORTANCE OF TRUST IN MANAGEMENT

Trust is a vital component of life, particularly in the world of work. It has been found that trusting employees leads to reduced overheads, increased happiness and creation of a trusting corporation. It is the role of the manager to create trust by trusting others and demonstrating his trustworthiness. It is an essential element in our interpersonal engagement with others.

In the modern world, are effective managers trusting or suspicious? Do they follow up a lot or do they trust and leave people to carry out their promises. How do they deal with cheating or lack of trustworthiness? Effective managers have been found to have trust as their core value and they believe in creating a trusting society.

Imagine a person who does not trust strangers, salespeople, doctors, newspaper reports, teachers, examinations, politicians, government, drivers, his office, etc. What will he be doing? He will be cautious all the time. He will check and recheck each issue and spend an enormous amount of time collecting information until he knows beyond doubt that the person is trustworthy. The time spent on collecting such information forms a part of what is called as 'overhead time' or 'wasted time'.

Consider the case of production manager Mr Mathew. He is in charge of the manufacturing of bottling machines. He works with a company that has an annual turnover of $500 million. The machines are largely exported. He needs to use many components for his machines. His company developed some local vendors and a few other global vendors. Mathew needs a particular component to be procured by next month which is critical. The purchase procedure requires him to send an indent form giving details of the component required and indicative costs, etc. He fills the indent form and gives it to his assistant to send to the materials department at 11 a.m. At 12 he reminds his assistant to make sure that the form is sent. The next day it occurs to him that the form may have been sent from his office but may not have been received by the materials chief. He calls his assistant to check with the head of materials division to find out if they have received the indent. After a few days it occurs to him that there may be a delay in the materials department in sending the specifications to the vendor. He again calls the materials department. A few days later he enquires about the status. Finally, the material arrives on time and as per specifications. However, he made at least a dozen calls to check and recheck. Each time he makes a call, the other person is either getting annoyed or saying to himself let him call for the second time or third time and then I will act. Thus, the consequence of not trusting people is either that they behave according to your expectations or you get into interpersonal issues. Mistrust has thus been found to be very expensive. In fact, studies conducted in various countries have indicated that trusting countries are more efficient and develop faster than less trusting countries.

Researchers have recognized that interpersonal trust between employees helps in the development of social capital within organizations. Social capital refers to the value of social networks in modern life and it is linked (in the corporate world) with sustained competitive advantage, reduced transaction costs, organizational learning, knowledge sharing, innovation, and better financial performance. This is because coordinated action for these is only possible when interdependent employees effectively work together through trust (McAllistar 1995). *So trust can facilitate better relationships and attitudes among employees which impact an organization's bottom line.*

Trust is also an extremely important ingredient in the institution-building processes. According to Tyler and Degoey (1996), managers play a crucial role in the development of trust since they control the flow of information by either sharing or not sharing key information. The degree of trust within an organization depends somewhat on managerial philosophy, organizational actions and structures, and employees' expectations of reciprocity. However, studies that focus on a 'trust in management' perspective often ignore trust relationships at the co-worker level. This may be an unfortunate oversight as according to Laurence and Cohen, (2001) investing in social capital requires the development of trust both within and between management layers.

TRUST

The literature of trust is extensive. Many have defined it in terms of a person's evaluation and expectation of the other. Some contend that 'trust pertains to whether or not one individual is able to value what another is up to and demonstrate respect for him or her particularly when the individual's needs and those of the person taking the action momentarily compete' (Gulbert and McDonough 1986: 175). Others argue that trust is the expectation of just and ethical behaviour between parties (Carnevale and Wechsler 1992).

Trust has also been defined in terms of perception. Cook and Wall (1980: 39) suggest trust is 'the extent to which one is willing to ascribe good intentions to and have confidence in the words and actions of other people'. Mishra (1996: 265) argues that trust is one party's willingness to be vulnerable to another party based on their belief that the latter party is honourable and effective. Other authors have proposed that trust is a 'risk taking behaviour' or the 'willingness to engage in such behaviour' (Cummings and Bromiley 1996, Zand 1972).

Finally, trust is contingent to a certain context and tends to be based not only on personal information but also on non-personal (situational) information that either serves to enhance or to inhibit the development of that trust (Morris and Moberg 1994). According to Lewicki and Bunker (1996), trust is based on expectations that go beyond the characteristics or intentions of those involved, also including considerations about the situation and the risks associated with acting on such expectations.

Based on these considerations, trust can be defined as a state of mind that:

- ▶ Manifests itself in our behaviour towards others
- ▶ Is based on our expectation of their behaviour, and on our perceptions of their motives and intentions
- ▶ If negative, could jeopardize our relationship with them

In this definition, trust is viewed as an attitude held by an individual in relation to another individual or group of individuals and it is applicable to work relationships in team contexts.

BUILDING TRUST AS A CORE MANAGEMENT VALUE

The best way to build trust is by both trusting others and becoming more trustworthy oneself. Trust begets trust is a good principle to follow. A manager who is trusted is a manager who is regarded by others as possessing integrity. Integrity means the integration of thought, word, and action. Speaking fearlessly of what one feels (not having one thing in mind and speaking another thing or speaking different things to different people to please them or to gain some kind of advantage), attempting to keep promises or verbal commitments or what is popularly termed as 'walking the talk' are indications of integrity and trust.

A trustworthy manager thus:

▶ Speaks fearlessly of what he feels
▶ Does not keep one thing in mind and speak other things to different people to please them or gain some kind of advantage
▶ Keeps verbal promises
▶ Does what he/she says
▶ Says what he/she intends to do
▶ Maintains coherence between thought, word, and deed
▶ Does not play games with facts to win a point
▶ Presents the correct picture even if it is not pleasing to the other party
▶ Does not manipulate figures in financial dealings and goes out of his/her way to ensure correct figures are entered and correct claims are made
▶ Presents and claims allowances, perks, bills, etc. that are due to him/ her as per rules
▶ Does not change rules to suit him/herself
▶ Does not favour self or others close to him/her

The indicators of untrustworthiness are:

▶ Makes promises without thinking
▶ Does not make attempts to honour his/her word
▶ Tries to please people somehow and ends up making commitments that cannot be fulfilled
▶ Does not speak his/her mind—says different things to different people
▶ Is inconsistent
▶ Is not honest and sincere in financial matters

- ▶ Interprets rules and regulations to suit him/herself or favoured employees
- ▶ Manipulates data
- ▶ Presents financial interpretations and figures to suit his/her convenience

See appendices 6.2 and 6.3 to assess how trustworthy and trusting you are.

CO-WORKER TRUST

Co-worker trust involves workers feeling confident that colleagues are competent and will act in a fair, reliable and ethical manner. It assumes that co-workers will support their peers and will not take advantage of them by withholding information. Co-worker trust will also lead employees to act on the basis that they have faith in the words and actions of their peers. When developing an instrument that measured trust in management and their peers, Cook and Wall (1980) found that job satisfaction had a positive relationship with trust at the peer level, as did organizational identification and organizational involvement.

Negative consequences of high interpersonal trust are:
- ▶ Gullibility—you may get cheated more frequently
- ▶ Dependency
- ▶ Blind faith

Positive consequences of high interpersonal trusts are:
- ▶ Security
- ▶ Mental peace
- ▶ Self-confidence
- ▶ Risk taking

TRUST AND DELEGATION

Managers who trust their juniors tend to delegate more. In fact, trust can be built through delegation. If delegation has to be used as a trust-building tool, those who delegate should assume the role of trainers and should be willing to spend more time with their juniors to ensure that they have the required skills to perform what has been delegated to them. In the initial stages, therefore, delegation involves more work for seniors who delegate. Achievers have been found to have difficulties delegating. They tend to take personal responsibility for everything and would like to do things themselves. In such circumstances, juniors do not learn. If achiever managers learn to trust and delegate to their juniors they create the space for themselves for doing higher-level tasks. Normally, visionaries are good at delegation.

CONCLUSION

Our interpersonal skills are vital to our role as a manager. As a boss we have to learn to get the most out of our employees and we can do so by empowering them, respecting their opinions and listening to them. The way in which we frame questions, give and receive feedback, critique and praise is central to this enterprise. Trust is also another key element—the more we trust, and the more we can be trusted, the better our relationships will be and the more we can get out of our employees and juniors. While it is possible to be an efficient manager who achieves all his tasks like Godbole, the truly effective manager is one who is liked, trusted, and respected.

APPENDIX 6.1: INTERPERSONAL ENGAGEMENT QUESTIONNAIRE

Interpersonal engagement can be measured by administering a simple questionnaire to all those who have working relations with a manager. These may include boss or bosses, juniors or subordinates, colleagues, internal customers, suppliers, and customers and all others who matter. The questionnaire may simply ask questions like: To what extent to do you enjoy working with this person? Or feel happy working with him? Or feel energized when you work with him or interact with him in relation to your work? You can use a 5 point scale or a percentage scale. The sum of all the ratings (genuinely given by them) divided by the number responding will give you the interpersonal engagement score.

For example, here are the interpersonal engagement scores of Godbole and Janak. To what extent do you feel happy working with this person or feel energized when you work with this person? The responses are given below.

	Godbole	Janak
Boss (1)	4	4
Boss (2)	3	4
Junior (1)	2	4
Junior (2)	3	5
Junior (3)	1	4
Junior (4)	2	5
Junior (5)	1	3
Junior (6)	2	5

Junior (7)	1	4
Junior (8)	4	3
Junior (9)	2	4
Junior (10)	2	5
Junior (11)	5	5
Junior (12)	1	5
Junior (13)		1
Junior (14)		4
Colleague (1)	3	4
Colleague (2)	2	3
Colleague (3)	4	5
Total	44	78
Average and percentage engagement score	42/17 = 2.47 (49%)	78/19 = 3.89 (78%)

APPENDIX 6.2: HOW TRUSTWORTHY ARE YOU?

Answer the following statements by using the 5-point rating scale given below:

5 = Strongly agree
4 = Mildly agree
3 = Neither agree nor disagree
2 = Mildly disagree
1 = Strongly disagree

☐ I never say things that I do not really wish to carry out
☐ Once I make a commitment, I stick to it
☐ I'm normally punctual for meetings
☐ I'm known to meet deadlines
☐ If I give time to someone, I'm 100 percent sure to be there on time
☐ If I agree to do a thing, I don't need to be reminded even once
☐ I have always honoured my financial commitments
☐ I frequently change my deadlines if I get new ideas or data
☐ Most people with whom I have dealings rely on what I say
☐ I never make promises I cannot keep

Add your scores on all the ten items. If your scores are less than 50 you are not completely trustworthy. This means there are occasions when you may be making promises that you don't mean or not keeping your promises or commitments, etc. While no one is a perfect human being, we must try our best to be trustworthy all the time. It is the trustworthiness or talk of it on our part that makes others trust or mistrust us. Even if you are trustworthy 90 out of 100 times, you will be regarded as untrustworthy.

APPENDIX 6.3: HOW TRUSTING ARE YOU?

Answer the following statements by using the 5-point rating scale given below:

5 = Strongly agree
4 = Mildly agree
3 = Neither agree nor disagree
2 = Mildly disagree
1 = Strongly disagree

☐ Most teachers speak the truth

☐ I feel quite comfortable leaving the house when a plumber is doing repair work

☐ Most salespersons can be trusted to give correct information about the products

☐ I would trust a teacher's judgement in place of examinations

☐ Today's newspapers are full of gossip and wrong information

☐ In dealing with strangers one is better off being cautious until they have proved to be trustworthy

☐ Politicians can be relied upon to keep their promises

☐ Most students will not cheat in competitive examinations even if an invigilator is not present

☐ Most people can be counted on to do what they say they will do

☐ The judiciary is a place where we can all get unbiased treatment

Add your scores on the ten items. If your scores are anywhere below 30, your general interpersonal trust level can be considered on the lower side. If your scores are above 45 then you are a highly trusting person. If your scores are between 41 and 45 you are highly trusting and scores between 35 and 40 are indicative of reasonably high trust.

REFERENCES

Albrecht, S. (2001). 'Trust in Senior Management'. Unpublished doctoral dissertation.

Albrecht, S. and A. Travaglione (2003). 'Trust in Public Sector Senior Management During Times of Turbulent Change', *International Journal of Human Resource Management*, 14(2), pp. 1–17.

Anderson, L.M. and T.S. Bateman (1997). 'Cynicism in the Workplace: Some Causes and Effects', *Journal of Organizational Behaviour*, vol. 18, pp. 449–546.

Bacon, Terry R. and McKinsey and Company Inc. (1996). *Interpersonal and Interactive Skills*. Durango, CO: Lore International Institute.

Berne, Eric (1961). *Transactional Analysis in Psychotherapy*. New York: Grover Press.

Carnevale, D.G. and B. Weschler (1992). 'Trust in the Public Sector: Individual and Organizational Determinants', *Administration and Society*, 23(4), pp. 471–94.

Castelfranchi, Cristiano and Rino Falcone 'Socio-Cognitive Theory of Trust'. National Research Council, Institute of Psychology. Viale Marx 15, 00137 Rome, Italy.

Cook, J. and T. Wall (1980). 'New York Attitude Measures of Trust, Organizational Commitment, and Personal Need Non-Fulfilment', *Journal of Occupational Psychology*, vol. 53, pp. 39–52.

Cristina Costa, Ana 'The Role of Trust for the Functioning of Teams in

Organizations'. Department of Product Innovation and Management, Landbergstraat. 15, 2628 CE Delft, The Netherlands.

Crossman, Alf 'Exploring the Dynamics of the Psychological Contract'. University of Surrey.

Cummings and Bromiley (1996). *Journal of Managerial Psychology*, 21(4): (Download date: 28 March 09). http://books.google.com/books?id =Z0Cu18xlqj4C&pg=PA1987&lpg=PA1987&dq=cummings+%26+ bromiley,+1996+trust+is+a+risk+taking+behaviour&source=bl&o ts=ZGCU3c1APv&sig=qpc8oRqDwUwrJnaGPhCSzia9X7Q&hl=en &ei=6cjNSbToOcGJkQWx0NXWCQ&sa=X&oi=book_result&resn um=3&ct=result#PPA1988,M1

Currall, S. and T. Judge (1995). 'Measuring Trust between Organizational Boundary Role Persons', *Organizational Behaviour and Human Decision Processes*, vol. 64, pp. 151–70. (Download date: 28 Mar. 09)

D'Alessandro, David F. and Michele Owens (2004). *Career Warfare: 10 Rules for Building a Successful Personal Brand and Fighting to Keep It.* New Delhi: Tata McGraw-Hill.

'Empowerment', *Public Administration Quarterly*, vol. 10, pp. 171–88. (also see for various definitions of Trust: http://www.instituteforpr. org/files/uploads/2004_Watson.pdf)

Ferres, Natalie, Julia Connell, and Anthony Travaglione. 'Co-worker Trust: A Social Lubricant for Positive Workplace: Attitudes and Perceptions of Support'. University of Adelaide, University of Newcastle.

Gambetta, D. (ed.) (1988). *Trust: Making and Breaking Cooperative Relations.* New York: Blackwell.

Gulbert, S.A. and J.J. McDonough (1986). 'The Politics of Trust and Organizational
http://findarticles.com/p/articles/mi_qa5427/is_200001/ai_n21464956

Lewicki, R.J. and B.B. Bunker (1996). 'Developing and Maintaining Trust in Work Relationships', in R. Kraner and T.R. Tyler (eds), *Trust in Organizations.* Thousand Oaks, CA: Sage Publications, pp. 117–39.

Mayer, R.C. and J.H. Davis (1999). 'The Effect of the Performance Appraisal System on Trust for Management: A Quasi-Field Experiment', *Journal of Applied Psychology*, vol. 84, pp. 123–36. (Download date: 28 March 2009).

McAllister, D. (1995). 'Affect- and Cognition-based Trust as Foundations for Interpersonal Cooperation in Organizations', *Academy of Management Journal*, 38(1), pp. 24–59. (Download date: 28 March 2009).

McLain, D.L. and K. Hackman (1999). 'Trust, Risk and Decision-Making in Organizational Change,' *Public Administration Quarterly*, 23(2), pp. 152–76.

Mishra (1996). 'Organizational Trust: What it Means, why it Matters'. (Download date: 28 March 2009).

Morris, J. and D. Moberg (1994). 'Work Organizations as Contexts for Trust and Betrayal.

Pareek, Udai (2002). *Training Instruments in HTD & OD*. Second Edition. New Delhi: Tata Mc Graw-Hill Publishing Company Limited.

———(2007). *Understanding Organizational Behavior*. Second Edition. Oxford University Press.

Pelligra, Vittorio (2002). 'Trust Responsiveness: Theory and Experiments'. University of Cagliari, September.

Prusak, Laurence and Don Cohen (2001). 'How to Invest in Social Capital,' *Harvard Business Review*, 79 (6), pp. 86–97.

Rotter, J.B. (1971). 'Generalized Expectancies for Interpersonal Trust', *American Psychologist*, vol. 26, pp. 443–52.

Rousseau, D.M. and S.A. Tijoriwala (1999). 'What's a Good Reason to Change? Motivated Reasoning and Social Accounts in Promoting Organizational Change', *Journal of Applied Psychology*, vol. 84, pp. 514–28.

Silvera, D.M. (1988). *Human Resources Development: The Indian Experience*. New Delhi: News India Publication.

Tan, H.H. and C.S.F. Tan (2000). 'Toward the Differentiation of Trust in Supervisor and Trust in Organization', *Genetic, Social, and General Psychology Monographs*, 126 (2), pp. 241–60.

Tyler, T.R. and P. Degoey (1996). 'Trust in Organizational Authorities: The Influence of Motive Attributions and the Willingness to Accept Decisions, in R.M. Kramer and T. Tyler (eds), *Trust in Organizations: Frontiers of Theory and Research*, Thousand Oaks, CA: Sage Publications, pp. 331–56.

Zand, D. E. (1972). 'Trust and Managerial Problem Solving', *Administrative Science Quarterly*, vol. 17, pp. 229–39 (Download date: 28 March 2009).

7

Team Building

Managers always work in many contexts. First there is a global context, next is the country in which the person works, lives in or comes from. Third in line is the organization for which they work and fourth the team to which they belongs. There are other contexts, particularly in India, of family, region, caste, community and so on, but these four are shared by managers around the world. *The most important of all these contexts is the immediate work group which may be a project team or a department or another form of work unit.*

As organizations grow there is division of work and there are boundaries, norms, and expectations set. If the teams don't perform well the organization does not do well and if most organizations don't do well the economy of the nation is affected, which in turn affects individuals and their growth, quality of life, etc. There are managers who forget this context and believe they're working in isolation and for themselves. This is a mistake. We are always interdependent. Effective managers seem to understand these interdependencies well. Most of them, while working as individuals, keep the group or the organizational goals in mind. Their actions are directed to the extent to which they work for larger group goals.

An effective manager has to have strong interpersonal skills and build a team. In this chapter we will look in greater detail at the importance of team building and the exercises by which we can create these. If a manager wants to be a visionary, they have to keep in mind the larger goals of their work.

SMALLER IDENTITY VS THE LARGER IDENTITY

In the late 1980s, CII invited Sieji Yamamoto, at that time director of their leadership centre Pegasus, and director of Mobil to address a group of Indian CEOs. Yamamoto talked about how he had been able to build his company which has offices all over the world. At the end of his speech one of the participants asked him a question: 'Sir, after World War II both your country and my country started with the same resources and problems. However, your country in a matter of two decades made a mark and stood out as one of the best developed countries in the world. We still seem to remain where we were. What is the secret behind your success?'

The CEO replied:

I am sorry I don't know much about your country. I have some manufacturing units here and I visit once in a while. I can't tell you much. However, I can tell you one thing about my country. In my country if a house is on fire, every neighbour gives a glass of water to put the fire out. They do this without thinking, not bothering about the effect of a single glass of water. I am told, and I may not be right in saying, that in your country if the neighbour's house is on fire, the person with a jug of water waits for the person with a pot of water to put off the fire, and the person with a pot of water is waiting for his neighbour with several pots of water to empty his pots first and so on. As a result the fire never gets put out. I don't understand how so many industries here have no concern for their neighbours who live in poverty and dirt and can't afford to educate their children. I have seen a lot of poverty around the industrial units and little done by them to put out the fire. [As narrated to me by Anil Sachdeva, an active member of CII at that time]

This anecdote is indicative of how some cultures have been able to promote teamwork and an idea of the larger good. In countries where people worked for the larger good or common good by making personal sacrifices, progress has come more easily. In India and some other Asian countries, the moment you assign a group identity, the 'we' feeling gets restricted to the group. The assumption begins in the mind, perhaps even unconsciously, that if you have to win someone else has to lose. Hence the mindset is to play a win-lose game than a win-win game.

This is also true for organizations. The organizations where there is more collaboration and acceptance of common goals and work towards those goals, development has been faster. As a corollary to this, it can be said that managers who make a difference as well as higher-level mangers exhibit the following characteristics:

1. They give priority to group goals and team goals over their individual goals.
2. They are aware that their individual goals are linked to those of the group and as individuals they can achieve only limited things without the support of others in their team or organization.
3. They respect their team members and work towards empowering them to do their jobs well. They extend a helping hand whenever required.
4. They think beyond themselves and think of larger goals.
5. They are ready to sacrifice or postpone their individual goals for the sake of the group and their small group goals for the sake of the larger organization, community, country, or humanity at large.

In other words they are good team workers and exhibit a collaborative spirit. They sacrifice smaller identities for the larger one.

WIN AS MUCH AS YOU CAN

In many MBA and training programmes, behavioural scientists play a game called 'win as much as you can'. This game has to be played by a minimum of four individuals and preferably in four teams. Each individual or team is given a name—A, B, C, and D, or blue, red, yellow, and green, etc. The groups/individuals are given the following instructions: You are about to play a game called 'win as much as you can'. In this game you will have about ten rounds. Each team is seated in one corner of the room and will be given ten slips of paper. On each slip is marked your team's name. The slips are also marked round one, round two, etc. For each round your team is required to choose an 'X' or a 'Y' secretly without the knowledge of the other groups. All teams will then display the letter they have chosen. Depending on the configuration (of the number of Xs and Ys), each team will win or lose certain points. Keep making a note of the points you get at the end of each round. The aim is to try to win as much as you can.

The points for each round are as follows:

▶ If there are two Xs and two Ys, the teams that have chosen 'X' will get +2 points and the 'Y' teams will get −2 (i.e., they lose 2 points).
▶ If there are three Xs and one Y, then the teams that marked 'Y' will get −3 and the teams that marked 'X' will get +1.
▶ If there are three Ys and one X, then the 'X' teams will get +3 and the teams that marked 'Y' will get −1 each.

- ▶ If there are four Xs then each of the teams will get −1.
- ▶ If there are four Ys then each of the teams will get +1.

Some rounds will be held as bonus rounds. In these, whatever score you get will be multiplied by a number as announced before the round begins. For example, if the bonus is five times the points you earn, your positive or negative score will be multiplied by five. So in the first case where there are two Xs and two Ys, the X teams will make +10 and the Y teams will make −10.

There are also opportunities provided between some of the rounds (fifth round on) for the groups' representatives to meet. In the final round all the groups are given the opportunity to meet and discuss.

WHAT THE GAME REVEALS

A study of the game indicates interesting possibilities. There is only one way all the teams can win and that is by marking a Y. However, in most cases at least one team starts with the belief that X will lead to victory. They normally do not bother to see that all the teams can win and that is the only way they can also win. Sometimes those who participated in this game for the second time or third time are ignored by their teams when they explain this rationale. Most of the time all the teams end up losing or scoring zero.

The game highlights the tendency of people to play against each other than to play with each other. The moment a team was given a label (A, red, etc.), they saw the other team as an adversary and worked for narrow interests. It is extremely rare to find a team that interprets 'we' as the totality of all the four teams. I have used this game hundreds of times in my career and have come across only one instance when the groups interpreted 'we' as the total team and started playing win-win. Even in this group, by the fourth attempt, one team decided to go it alone. Sadly, once the trust was breached by that party it never returned. I still remember an occasion when an army officer trying his best to convince his team to play a win-win game failed to do so and started crying. The overall score of his group went up but he was very upset to see the groups behaving in a divisive way.

It is the rare set of teams who have the vision and courage to play a win-win game that will succeed. The same is true with managers. Managers who make a difference prefer playing win-win games rather than win-lose games. They seem to have a philosophy that there should be place for everyone in the universe and one cannot win or keep on winning at the expense of others. These managers use education, communication, and empowerment as tools for creating such an atmosphere. They are integrating rather than divisive individuals.

DIVISIVE AND INTEGRATING MINDS

A divisive person assigns to him/herself or other people, a group identity (caste, community, linguistic, professional, occupational, cultural, social, batch, national, etc.) and behaves and makes decisions on the basis of such identity. He/She constantly divides people into smaller groups and uses the groups for decision-making and various other purposes. A university faculty opposing the allocation of resources or blocking the growth of another department because it is growing out of proportion is an outcome of a divisive mindset. The divisive mind always sees the benefits to a part and often ignores the benefits to a larger community.

To integrate, on the other hand, means to combine parts into a whole. It also means to make someone accepted within a group. The integrative personality strives towards inclusion, cooperation, putting an emphasis on the whole and benefiting a larger group. The integrative personality always gives importance to the whole over the parts and thinks of larger goals and society at large. Conscious effort and an emphasis on superordinate goals help in the creation of an integrative personality.

In fact *the more visionary the manager, the more integrative the personality*. In my view the physicist and founder of ISRO (Indian Space Research Organisation), Vikram Sarabhai, and Ravi Matthai, the founder of IIMA, are two great integrative personalities. Sarabhai built a number of institutions in different fields, most importantly in space and management. Ravi Matthai promoted his belief of professionalizing management and actively demonstrated in his own life how management should enter all sectors.

The institutions were associated with speaking for their integrative mind. Take IIMA. The symbols that differentiate people and communicate that you work for a team or group are minimal here. Every faculty member gets the same-sized room and each one, irrespective of their designation, shares the same secretary and privileges. You charge the same consulting fee irrespective of the designation. You are addressed as professor, irrespective of whether you are a professor or assistant professor. There are no departments and there are only areas. The term 'area' signifies a broad categorization. You may be a member of more than one area, group, or centre. You may also change areas. All these are organizational mechanisms to create a larger identity and bring down the overheads or transaction costs associated with management of the system.

THE INDIAN CASE

In India, we are taught from childhood to be divisive. It is, in fact, a cultural phenomenon, as the Japanese CEO pointed out; for we are brought up to define ourselves through caste, and subcaste or gotra, community, religious affiliation, language, regional affiliation, etc.

A few years ago I was working in Indonesia as a USAID consultant to the Ministry of Health. As part of my work I had to take a group of doctors on field trips to teach them Task Analysis, a technique we introduced to bring more professionalism in the management of health services in the country. Whenever I asked the team to choose a health centre for fieldwork, they would talk among themselves and within five minutes come up with a proposal. Their decision was always unanimous. I was amazed at the teamwork and one of the doctors told me this story when I complimented them:

> Professor Rao, I agree that we in Indonesia work like a team. We care for each other and respect each other. There is a lot of sharing that takes place. I also agree that it should strike you as an important part of our culture as I believe that your country which taught us a lot at one time lacks this. I would like to tell you a story about this.
>
> A few months ago I went to a meeting of UNFPA in Bangkok which was attended by participants from various countries such as Sri Lanka, Pakistan, Malaysia, Singapore, Bangladesh, the Philippines, Japan, India, etc. Whenever a Pakistani said something about his country, his colleague supported it. Similarly, when a Bangladeshi spoke about his country, his colleague from another department supported it. All the countries worked like this. However, whenever an Indian spoke, another Indian always contradicted him saying, what my colleague said is true in his state [Tamil Nadu] but the situation is different in my state [Uttar Pradesh]. Another Indian would get up then and present a third

story. Sometimes these disagreements would even lead to fights. We found that by the fourth day the Indian delegates were even staying at different places and coming at different times to the conference. So I understand that in your country teamwork is difficult, as every Indian seems to differentiate himself, unlike other countries. We on the other hand are an integrating nation and we help each other.

The IIMA example cited above shows that it is possible to institute structural mechanisms to promote integrative tendencies even in India. An integrative personality can be developed as we will see in the following sections.

HOW DIVISIVENESS WORKS IN ORGANIZATIONS

Organizations have several forms of divisiveness. Divisiveness by hierarchies or levels, by roles and designations, and by departmentation and other forms of identities. Organizations need to have roles identified (like Finance Manager, Sales Manager, HR Manager, Personnel Manager, Training Manager, IT Manager, Marketing Manager, etc.). Such role-based assignments are necessary to communicate to the incumbent as well as to the outside world the broad areas of work responsibility or specialization of the individual. The creation of departments also serves the same purpose.

Every senior manager in the hierarchy is supposed to perform integrating functions. If HR and IT managers report to the Vice President (VP), Finance, the latter is expected to integrate and make the services of the three functions (HR, IT, and Finance) available to the rest of the organization. A divisive mind performs this role in ways that are dysfunctional to the organization by unconsciously or consciously favouring one or more of the functions. For example, he may use IT mainly to develop a management information system (MIS) for finance and neglect the rest of the organization like the production, materials, HR, etc. A senior manager needs to be extra cautious and careful in performing his integrative roles. He has to develop conscious and formal mechanisms of sharing, communication, and integration. In their absence, overheads go up and the company may suffer.

Divisiveness is also expressed through the 'this is not my job' syndrome or role-boundedness. In one national travel agency which I consulted for, the employees were divided into those who worked for individuals and those who handled group travel. As the work for both was seasonal, the group travel team were overstretched in certain months and the individual tours teams in others. Though sitting under the same roof and belonging to the same organization, employees working in these two teams did not help each other in their respective peak periods. When asked why, one of the groups said that they were paid lower salaries than the other group and thus would not help them. The second group said they didn't help the first group as the first never helped them when asked.

Asian cultures, particularly Indian cultures, as I've already observed, seem to be either role-bound or rule-bound.

TEAM BUILDING

The first aim of an effective manager is to create a cohesive team where members collaborate with each other. From this point on I will be focusing on the micro-picture of team building, but it is worth noting here that the same behaviours of collaboration that build teams also help in larger groups. The basic building blocks of organizations are teams and one of the basic building blocks of organization development is team building. The more integrative the manager, the more collaboration needs to be encouraged from the micro to the macro level.

Collaboration depends upon the extent to which people in teams have shared goals, values, perceptions and cooperative attitudes. In addition, the extent to which they trust each other and the history of trust are important. Collaborative tactics include getting information, giving information, seeking clarifications, giving clarifications, summarizing, consensus testing, appealing to the superordinate or higher-level goals, socializing, exchanging, etc. The following are the characteristics that promote teamwork:

1. Listening to each other
2. Communicating transparently and freely
3. Willingness to share
4. Building on each others' ideas
5. Seeking and giving feedback
6. Focusing on maintaining group morale and motivation
7. Supportive attitudes of each other
8. Committing to larger goals

LOST IN THE MOON OR DESERT SURVIVAL EXERCISE

There are a number of exercises behavioural scientists play to demonstrate effective group behaviour. Some of the best known of them are the Moon Landing Exercise or Desert Survival or Lost at Sea in the Forest. In all these exercises, you are to act as a member of a team of seven or eight people who are separated from the mother ship or are lost in the desert or forest, etc. and are trying to get back to their destination safely.

The team is told they have managed to salvage ten or fifteen items like a pistol, a knife, a map, magnetic compass, water, etc. Their job is to rank these in order of their importance. First, each member ranks them solo and then they discuss their rankings as a group for about half an hour or forty-five minutes and come to a consensus. There is a correct order of ranking of the objects and the facilitator notes the solo rankings and the group rankings and scores it against this.

In every group there is someone who has the most error-free score. He is perhaps knowledgeable about most items and hence scores like an expert. But he/she does not know that their score is good. Similarly, the individual who has the highest number of errors also does not know that he has a lot of misinformation.

Once the groups have handed over their rankings, everyone is given their individual scores and team scores. One expects the group scores to be better than the average of individual scores as a result of the group's discussion. However, this does not happen always. Sometimes as a result of the group discussion the group's errors increase because someone with the most misinformation may have influenced the group.

Those groups that have listened to and reasoned with each other usually perform well. In these cases the average of each individual's scores will be far lower than the group scores or the errors of an individual as averaged out will be higher than the group's average scores. In some extraordinary cases the groups do even better than the best individual.

TEAMS: THE STRATEGIC UNITS OF AN ORGANIZATION

We can arrive at an important conclusion from these discussions. Individuals learn all the time but the impact of their learning can be varied. But if teams learn, they become a microcosm for learning throughout the organization. Insights gained are put into action. Skills developed can be propagated to other individuals and to other teams. Teams can become the means for change, a means for individual growth, and a means for organizational learning. The team's accomplishment can set the tone and establish a standard of learning together for a larger organization.

> **WHAT IS A TEAM?**
>
> A team is a small number of people with complementary skills who are committed to a common purpose, set of performance goals and approach for which they hold themselves mutually accountable.

There are certain underlying reasons why organizations have wanted to establish and promote teams. First, there is a belief that productivity will increase when staff are involved in local problem-solving and decision-making. Second, involving employees both in local and strategic planning will aid implementation. Finally, there is an increased value of personal and professional learning, with the team being viewed as a place to share knowledge, learn new skills, and take risks.

▶ The specific goals to be achieved by teams differ from team to team and organization to organization. Here are the benefits teams bring to a corporation:

▶ **Innovation:** Bringing together people with a variety of experience and expertise to address a common problem or task increases creative thinking.

▶ **Speed:** In addition to introducing new ideas, teams can also reduce the time required for product development, customer service and other required functions.

▶ **Cost:** Like many organizations, reducing costs and responding more quickly to customers is extremely critical. Teams can enable this.

▶ **Quality:** Maintaining and increasing quality is a primary goal of work teams.

It is through these interlocking groups that the work of the organization gets done. The key reality seems to be that individuals in organizations function not so much as individuals alone but as members of groups or teams. For an individual to function effectively, the prerequisite usually is that the team must function effectively.

DIFFERENCE BETWEEN A GROUP AND A TEAM

Group	Team
A group is a number of persons, usually reporting to a common superior and with some face-to-face interaction, who have some degree of interdependence in carrying out tasks for the purpose of achieving the organizational goals	A team is a form of group, but has some characteristics in greater degree than an ordinary group, including a higher commitment to common goals and greater interdependency and interaction
A group is assembled	A teams is built
A groups usually has a designated leader	Team leadership will be shared or rotated
Effectiveness is measured by the influence a group has on business	A team Implies a sense of shared mission and collective responsibility to a common purpose and performance goals

PRINCIPLES OF TEAMWORK

Principle 1: Teamwork implies that members provide feedback and accept it from one another. For teamwork to be effective, team members must feel free to provide feedback; the climate within the group must be such that neither status nor power stands as an obstacle to team members providing this. Effective teams engage in tasks with an awareness of their strengths and weaknesses. When team leaders show the ability to accept constructive criticism, they establish a norm that this type of criticism is appropriate.

Principle 2: Teamwork implies the willingness, preparedness, and proclivity to back fellow members up during operations. Better teams are distinguishable from poorer teams by their willingness to jump in and help when they are needed. They also accept help without fear of being perceived as weak. Team members must compete not only in their own particular areas but also in the areas of other team members with whom they interact directly.

Principle 3: Teamwork involves group members collectively viewing themselves as a group whose success depends on their interaction. Team members must have high awareness of themselves as a team. Each member sees the team's success as taking precedence over individual performance. Members of effective teams view themselves as connected team members, not as isolated individuals working with other isolated individuals. Effective teams consist of individuals who recognize that their effectiveness is the team's effectiveness, which depends on the sum total of all team members' performance.

Principle 4: Teamwork means fostering team interdependence. Fostering team interdependence means the team adopts the value that is not only appropriate but also essential for each team member (regardless of status within the team) to depend on every other team member to carry out the team's mission. Contrary to what may take place in the rest of the organization, interdependence is seen as a virtue—as an essential characteristic of team performance—not as a weakness.

Principle 5: Team leaders have to serve as models for their fellow team members. If the leaders openly engage in teamwork—that is, provide and accept feedback and supportive behaviours—other team members are likely to do the same. Team leaders are vital and have tremendous influence on teams, and when team leaders are poor, so are the teams.

CHARACTERISTICS OF EFFECTIVE TEAMS

1. The atmosphere tends to be relaxed, comfortable, and informal
2. The group's task is well understood and accepted by team members
3. The members listen well to each other; there is a lot of task-relevant discussion in which most members participate
4. People express both their feelings and ideas
5. Conflict and disagreement are present but are centred around ideas and methods, not personalities and people
6. The group is self-conscious about its own operation
7. Decisions are usually based on consensus, not majority vote
8. When actions are decided upon, clear assignments are made and accepted by the members

---

9. There is a clear purpose of the aim to be accomplished
10. The members are informal and frank with each other for better effectiveness
11. There is a high level of participation at all levels
12. Leadership is shared and everyone is given an opportunity to stand
13. The diversity of styles in the team helps them to get a variety of exposure and deliver better quality

Role making

Normally in designing teams, in most organizations, roles are most often assumed rather than prescribed. The most usual roles prescribed are that of the leader and at best the secretary or coordinator. Normally the leader is required to look after setting the direction, reviewing, reminding the members of tasks and processes, and maintaining the morale of the group. The leader also performs the role of summarizing outcomes and communicating results to respective agencies. The better defined and delegated the roles of the other members within a team are, the more effective it is.

Some members are particularly good at performing certain roles. For example, some members are very good at conflict resolution. They are humorous, have a high degree of empathy, and hence make sure that there is periodic tension release. It is, therefore, recommended that periodically the roles performed by various groups and their members be reviewed and the absence of any significant role be identified and feedback given to the group.

Games and sports are good ways of learning about the various roles members can play in teams. Cricket, football, hockey, baseball, kho-kho, etc., all offer opportunities to identify and learn about teamwork. The following are the most essential roles in any team:

▶ **Input providing roles:** These include information-giving roles where members provide information needed to complete or perform a task.

▶ **Information-seeking roles:** These include asking for information to perform a task.

▶ **Summarizing or consolidating roles:** These deal with summarizing the progress and providing milestones for members to reiterate their progress.

▶ **Empowering roles**: These deal with providing sanctions required to legitimize or energize participation. These include acknowledging the contributions of other members, building on the ideas of other members, complimenting, etc. These also include resolving conflicts when they occur, asking for breaks, designing morale-building activities, etc.

▶ **Consensus-building roles:** These include ensuring that every member gives his/her input, involving those who didn't participate in the consensus building, etc.

TASKS OF A TEAM

1. Setting culture and norms
2. Converting the larger goal into specific tasks and assigning these to various members (division of labour, assigning specialist duties, etc.)
3. Conflict resolution
4. Ensuring participation of all members
5. Driving to consensus

---

6. Summarizing and reviewing progress
7. Documentation
8. Humour and releasing tension
9. Supplying information and other resources
10. Logistics management
11. Closing and reconvening
12. Communicating decisions to others

Team dynamics at Starbank

Starbank is fifty years old and one of the largest PSBs in India. The average age profile of the bank in 1990 was 49 years. The bank found itself enmeshed in bureaucratic procedures and as a result customers found it difficult to get decisions made fast.

Earlier a businessman submitted his project proposal to the branch from where it went up to the region, then to the zone, and finally to the state. At the state level, the proposal was screened by the head of credit and passed on to the deputy MD and then finally to the MD. The MD would take the final decision but when in doubt could go to the state-level governing board. Most often the process from the branch to the CEO took six months with everyone asking the client a few more questions and then sending the file to the next level.

With many private banks from developed countries coming into India, Starbank had to speed up its decision-making and customer service. It appointed an MNC with experience in banking sector-fortune consulting. The fortune consultants concluded that Starbank lost nearly 70 percent of potential business to its competitors because of this system. They also warned the bank that it would soon be losing even more as the FIIs were fast decision makers and high risk takers.

They recommended that State banks should improve their customer service by speeding up their decisions, moving closer to customers, and removing bureaucracy. In order to do so, they suggested a 'Committee Based Credit Team (CBCT)' to take decisions fast. The committees existed in each zone (ZCBCT) and as well as in each state.

All proposals are to come to the:

1. Zonal Credit Officer (ZCO) (of the ZCBCT) or state CO (SCO) depending on the amount
2. The ZCO or SCO circulates proposals and collects questions to be answered by the client within one week of receiving the project proposal
3. The ZCO or SCO gives comments and asks for a fresh or modified proposal to be submitted within two weeks
4. Once this is over a ZCBCT or a State CBCT meeting is convened

These meetings are mandatory every fifteen days. The proposal is discussed and a collective decision is made. The decision has to have a consensus. Even if one person dissents the project is not sanctioned to ensure that all members are a party to the decision. If a proposal is not sanctioned within four weeks after submitting the final project, it is returned with regrets.

The fortune consultants felt that through this process the following advantages would be achieved:

1. The proposal is processed in six weeks instead of six months
2. There is collective responsibility so that no single individual is penalized for any risk exposure and wrong decisions

3. Quality of decisions improves due to four persons examining and deciding as a team
4. Costs will be saved due to speed and the image of the bank improves
5. Members share their knowledge and the bank becomes wiser

The outcome

How do you think this will work? What problems do you see in the recommendations of the fortune consultants? What positive things do you see in the approach of the consultants?

This initiative was a major failure at Starbank in the initial years when it was introduced for the following reasons.

Starbank had a high culture of hierarchy. The deputy CEOs didn't oppose the CEO and the SCOs or ZCOs didn't open their mouths in meetings once the CEO's views were known out of respect or fear of authority. What was intended as decision-making by consensus became the decision of the CEO by virtue of others merely agreeing with him. The speed of decisions went up and so did the rejections.

However, when the teams were trained subsequently through a series of workshops on decision-making by consensus with focus on how to behave as non-hierarchical teams in a hierarchical culture, the quality of decisions improved. Speed combined with quality brought some of the states closer to the customer.

Tools for making teams effective

When teams don't work, sometimes it is because their roles are not clear, or are overlapping resulting in conflicts, or are badly designed, or some are overloaded and others are underloaded, etc. Some role holders become dysfunctional when they have no work or limited challenges. Role ambiguity, role overload, role conflict, lack of challenge, lack of binding mechanisms, etc. are some of the reasons teams fail to work.

There are many other types of activities like outward-bound training programmes, sensitivity training, interdependency exercises, team-building workshops, and so on. The focus, broadly, is on the process to enhance the awareness of individual roles, the impact created by the individual on the team, and the shift or clarity needed for strengthening team performance. The effectiveness of team-building activities is determined by many organizational factors like the support and encouragement of top management, available resources, ability to understand the need and cope with the necessary actions, and above all, a willingness to change. The following are some of the techniques used.

ROLE ANALYSIS TECHNIQUE

In organizations, individuals have specialized roles. This division of labour and function facilitates organizational performance. Often, however, the role incumbent may not have a clear idea of expected behaviour or what others can do to help the incumbent fulfil the role. Ishwar Dayal and John M. Thomas developed a technique to clarify roles. *This is particularly applicable for new teams, but can also be used for established teams where role ambiguity or confusion exists.*

In the role analysis technique, role incumbents, in conjunction with team members, define and delineate role requirements. The role being defined is called the focal role. Upon the conclusion of this step, the focal role person assumes responsibility for making a written summary of the role as it has been defined. This is called a role profile and is derived from detailed discussions.

This intervention can be a non-threatening activity with a high payoff. Often the mutual demands, expectations, and obligations of interdependent team members are not publicly examined. Each role incumbent wonders why 'those other people' are 'not doing what they are supposed to do', while in reality all the incumbents are performing as they think they are supposed to. Collaborative role analysis and definition by the entire work group not only clarifies who is to do what but ensures commitment to the role once it has been clarified.

RESPONSIBILITY CHARTING

In teams, decisions are made, tasks are assigned, and individuals and small groups accomplish these. This is easily described on paper, but in reality a decision to have someone do something is somewhat more complex than it appears because there are in fact multiple actors involved. There is the person who does the work, one or more people who may approve or veto the work, and the persons who may contribute in some way to the work while not being responsible for it. The issue is, who is to do what, with what kind of involvement by others. A technique called responsibility charting helps to clarify who is responsible for what on various decisions and actions. It is a simple, relevant and very effective technique for improving team functionality.

> **Step 1:** Construct a grid. The types of decisions and classes of actions that need to be taken in the total area of work under discussion are listed along the left-hand side of the grid and the actors who might play some part in decision-

making on those issues are identified across the top of the grid.

Step 2: The process then is of assigning the behaviour to each of the actors opposite each of the issues. The four classes of behaviour are:

(a) Responsibility **(R)**—the responsibility to initiate action to ensure that the decision is carried out. For example, it would be a department head's responsibility (R) to initiate the departmental budget

(b) Approval required **(A-V)**—the person who reviews the action to either veto or approve it

(c) Support **(S)**—providing logistical support and resources for the particular item

(d) Inform **(I)**—must be informed and by inference, cannot influence

Task Decision Responsibility Grid

Actors → Decisions ↓							

FORCE FIELD ANALYSIS

This is a device for understanding a problematic situation and planning corrective actions.

▶ **Step 1:** Decide upon a problematic situation that needs to be improved and carefully describe the current condition. The need is to understand the current state and why there is a need to change.

▶ **Step 2:** There needs to be a careful, complete, and clear description of the desired conditions.

▶ **Step 3:** Identify the driving and the restraining forces towards and against the desired conditions.

▶ **Step 4:** There needs to be close examination of these forces, in particular looking at those factors that are controllable and those that are not.

▶ **Step 5:** Look at strategies for moving equilibrium from the current condition to the desired state through increasing driving forces and reducing restraining factors. With this methodology, the desired condition can be arrived at and action plans can be worked out to maintain the state.

ROLE NEGOTIATION EXERCISES

Sometimes the cause of a team's ineffectiveness is based on the fact that one person is unwilling to change their behaviour because it would mean a loss of power or influence. In these situations, role negotiation is a great tool. It directly intervenes in the relationships of power, authority, and influence within the group. But the change is directed at the work relationships among members and thus avoids probing into the likes and dislikes of members for one another.

This technique takes at least one day to conduct. A two-day session with a follow-up meeting a month later is best. The steps are:

Contract setting: The focus is on work behaviours and not on feelings about people. There has to be complete clarity on what needs to happen, what needs to stop happening, and what needs to continue being done.

Issue diagnosis: Individuals think about how their own effectiveness can be improved if others change their work behaviour. Then each person fills out an issue diagnosis form for every other person in the group. On this form the individual states what he or she would like the other to do more or less of and the things they should not change.

Influence trade: Two individuals discuss the most important behaviour changes they want from the other and the changes they are willing to make themselves. The negotiation ends when all parties are satisfied that they will receive a reasonable return for whatever they are agreeing to give in written. It is best to have a follow-up meeting to determine whether the contracts have been honoured and to assess the effects of the contracts on effectiveness.

DOON SCHOOL

In the early 1990s, parents started putting more pressure on Doon School to change the curriculum and prepare students more rigorously to find a place in medical, engineering, and other professional schools. A section of teachers in the school maintained that the school was meant to develop the all-round personality of the student through a variety of educational experiences. They argued that it was because of this that the school had produced leaders in various fields, not just doctors and engineers. Another segment of the faculty held a different view—namely, that the school should change with the times and focus on preparing students for competitive examinations. Interestingly, it is the older faculty who wanted change while the younger faculty didn't.

A three-day workshop was held for the groups to come together, evolve a common agenda and work towards it. The common agenda was created by holding a visioning exercise and a role negotiation exercise. Those who opposed extracurricular activities were required to give some of their time towards these; those opposing the preparation for competitive exams had to volunteer as counsellors for assisting students who wanted to give them.

The role negotiation and visioning exercises thus helped both groups come together. Subsequently, there was more collaboration between the teachers. Such exercises are good tools to foster collaboration and team-work.

I conducted a similar excercise in the State Bank of Travancore under the leadership of the then MD Vepa Kamesam. These exercises got the unions and management to work harmoniously together.

TOOLS TO ENABLE TEAM COMPATIBILITY

The members of your team will most likely be very different from each other. One of the ways to ensure that this doesn't result in conflict is to make your team aware of their own and their teammates' personalities through some simple tests.

Fundamental Interpersonal Relationships Orientation–Behaviour (FIRO-B)

There is a tool called FIRO-B, based on the construct that there are three fundamental needs with which people operate—inclusion, affection, and control.

The theory further assumes that there are two sides of each need—the expressed side and the wanted side. The expressed side deals with the individual's desire to include others, show affection to, and control others. The wanted side deals with the need to be included by others, to receive affection from, and be controlled by others. A person can have any combination of these needs. The person with a high need to be included (expressed) and be included (wanted) gives parties, forms groups, invites others and also likes to be invited by others. The person with high expressed and low wanted control, desires to control other people's thinking, but would not like others to exert the same influence over him.

Now imagine a person, A, who has a high need for expressed inclusion and a low need for wanted inclusion and wanted control. Consider his colleague, B, with a high need for wanted inclusion and a high need for expressed control and a low need for wanted control. A is inviting B to parties. B goes to parties reluctantly but once he is there he tries to dominate A. A dislikes being controlled by B but likes B to attend his parties. Thus their teaming is not a perfect match. If one's desire to include and the desire to be included of another is high, there is compatibility. If they have a similar profile, that is, both have a need for expressed control and a low need for wanted control there is conflict.

Now extend the logic to a team. In the team, if there are five to six people with different interpersonal needs, some may be complementary with others and some may not. Conflicts, lack of synergy, friendships and tensions, subgroup formation, etc. are natural. For effective functioning of the teams, such heterogeneity needs to be recognized and appreciated.

Myers Briggs Type Indicator (MBTI)

The MBTI is a psychometric tool that deals with the differences between team members. It provides a self-report and tries to explain differences in behaviour between two or more people. The MBTI takes four aspects of a person—their energy orientation, decision-making, information gathering, and lifestyle—and offers them a choice of two opposing behaviours within that category.

1. Energy orientation—Extraversion and introversion

Extraversion—Indicated by **E**, this points at a preference to focus attention on the outer world of things and people, act on them, influence and be influenced in turn. Extroverts are those with a strong preference for extraversion.

Introversion—Indicated by **I**, this points at a preference to focus attention on the inner world of thoughts and ideas, impressions, for example, introverts.

The orientation of energy for extroverts is outside while for the introverts it is inside.

2. Information gathering—Sensing and intuition

Sensing—Indicated by **S**, there is a preference to focus on tangible, concrete things and information gathered from the five senses. Attention is on the here and now.

Intuition—Indicated by **N**, there is a preference to focus on the future or on possibilities through linkages or patterns identified in information taken in.

The sensing person doesn't process his/her information beyond the fact, the intuitive person links it to some other thought or idea. This is the reason why an apple reminds some of Adam and Eve while others just perceive it as a fruit or think about its taste, colour, etc.

3. Decision-making—Thinking and feeling

Thinking—Indicated by **T**, is a preference to base decisions on logic and on the objective analysis of cause and effect.

Feeling—Indicated by **F,** is a preference to make decisions that are person centred and based on values and subjective reasoning.

This is the classic head versus heart classification.

4. Lifestyle—Judging and perceiving

Judging—Indicated by **J**, is a preference to have a planned and organized approach to life and work, to settle things before moving on to others, a preference for boundaries, guidelines.

Perceiving—Indicated by **P**, is a preference for flexibility and a spontaneous approach, having all options open. Uncomfortable with borders and deadlines.

Lifestyle is the way individuals prefer to be perceived and function in the outer world.

Depending on our choices each one of us is a four-letter type like ENTJ, ENFJ, ESTP, ENFP, etc. There is a possible combination of sixteen such different types.

Using the MTBI test

There are sixteen personality types according to the MTBI test and a summary of these can be found in books and online. Apart from the MTBI test being an interesting tool for learning more about ourselves, we can also use it to make a team more effective.

▶ You can use type preferences to better understand yourself and what you can contribute to a team. For example, an individual with sensing type would do better by avoiding tasks that require creativity, design, or generating new alternatives, while an individual with intuition could contribute to the team by pointing out future implications, providing alternative solutions, and sharing insights with the team.

▶ You can also use this tool to better understand your team mates and their contributions. For example, understanding that thinking-type individuals are often objective in decision-making and need not be stereotyped as being 'harsh' or 'without feelings'; respecting the private space of introverted individuals without judging them as being non-participative or silent members; and allocating organizing, planning, recording tasks to individuals with judging-type preference since they are strong in such areas.

▶ Finally, you can use this test at the team level by analysing the collective personality preferences of all team members, akin to allotting a type preference score to the whole team and treating the group as a virtual individual. You can also assess the working of your team by looking at the individual psychological types. Consider the following:

  ▶ The more similar types there are in a team, the faster there will be mutual understanding; the more different the types in the team, the slower the understanding and acceptance between the team members.

  ▶ Groups with similar types are prone to reach decisions quickly, but are likely to make more errors or suffer on the quality side, due to low representation of all viewpoints.

  ▶ Groups with varied types reach decisions more slowly (and painfully), but may reach better decisions since more viewpoints have been covered.

  ▶ Teams that appreciate and use type preferences experience less conflict and tend to work faster, covering a large number of bases.

  ▶ The person who is the only representative of a particular type may be seen as 'different' by other team members.

  ▶ Leadership roles may shift depending on tasks, as each may require skills of different types on the team.

▶ Teams that are one-sided, that is, have more similar types and very few different types, will succeed if they use different types outside the team as resources. One-sided teams may fail if they overlook aspects of problems that other types would have pointed out or if they stay 'rigidly true to type' and fail to use other resources.

Please note: Trained facilitators are needed to administer this test and educate the participants before the first use.

CONCLUSION

Teams are the building blocks of any organization and one of the primary functions of an effective manager is to create teams that are collaborative and work harmoniously. Such teams listen to each other and work consensually and are conscious and content in being part of a team. But the most visionary and missionary managers don't just build a good team, they also work towards integrating themselves and their team into the larger organization, and eventually into society at large.

REFERENCE

Dayal, I. and J. Thomas (1968). 'Operation KPE: Developing a New Organization', *Journal of Applied Behavioural Science*, 4(4): 473–506.

8

Time and Talent Management

Time is money. It is our biggest resource. If you don't have time you can't do anything. The next biggest resource is our competence, which is our knowledge and experience. Competence can be extended from an individual to a team to an organization as a whole, and then to the nation or society. This is how the youth becomes the biggest resource for a country, or an organization for that matter. They have long careers ahead, and if their competency is increased by developing appropriate skills, they will be the capital to cash in on.

People bring time and talent to their organization. Organizations pay for the application of talent to provide various services. Managers who make a difference are aware that the two most important resources they have are their talent and time. Talent consists of the knowledge, attitudes, skills, etc. they have acquired over a period of time. Time is what they get to apply this talent. Unfortunately, organizations are sometimes unaware that they suppress the talent of their employees by assigning tasks that do not use their strengths. As a result the individual may get frustrated and may not be able to stay with the organization long. Even if they stay, they are likely to be an expensive resource, especially because the organization is paying them and not using their talent.

In this section we will look at tools to help you prioritize your time and then look more closely at utilizing intellectual capital.

WHERE DOES YOUR TIME GO?

Effective managers are conscious of their own and others' time. There are only 365 days in a year and some of us are given just a year or two to make a mark in our company, particularly if in a senior position. This means that as a manager you have only about 3,000 hours to make a difference. How do we arrive at this? Consider the following calculation.

Fifty-two days of the 365 are Sundays. You need to use this time to spend with your family and give enough relaxation to your body and mind. Then take out thirteen days for festivals, holidays, etc., which leave you with only 300 solid days. Every day gives you, at best, ten hours of productive time.

If you have to travel to your office and live in a city like Mumbai or Delhi, it will most likely take you a minimum of thirty to sixty minutes to get to work one way and therefore about sixty minutes to 120 minutes of travelling time each day. Your daily exercise, yoga, and other morning preparations for the office will take another 120 minutes. You may at best have about ten productive hours if you begin your work at 8 a.m. and can go on till 8 p.m.

Of these twelve hours, you have two hours for travelling, lunch, tea, and chats with others. Thus you have ten precious hours and a total of about 250 hours a month. For an ordinary executive we normally put this cap at 2,000 hours per year. Thus, 3,000 hours is a very realistic estimate for a senior manager.

Now, you have to make a difference in using these 2,000–3,000 hours to do the following especially if you are a CEO or unit head:

- ▶ Manage current operations of your company or department or section and make sure they run smoothly
- ▶ Travel to other cities or countries to negotiate major business deals or meet key customers or suppliers
- ▶ Keep yourself informed of the various critical events and things happening in your company
- ▶ Manage meetings with your staff or attend meetings
- ▶ Plan and monitor the performance of your top team or key individuals or role holders
- ▶ Learn about changing markets, competition, competitor experiences and practices, etc.
- ▶ Articulate vision and plans for the future of your organization
- ▶ Manage and announce monthly, quarterly, half-yearly, and annual performance reports
- ▶ Conduct quarterly, bi-annual and annual appraisals and budgets
- ▶ Manage the finances of your company
- ▶ Deal with any crisis occurring in the company/department or section
- ▶ Read and learn about new developments
- ▶ Attend conferences, seminars, and meetings where you get an opportunity to meet other CEOs and industrialists or professional specialists
- ▶ Meet visitors and other people of interest who come to add value or get value from your company
- ▶ Attend to telephone calls, dictate letters, correct drafts, oversee the upkeep of your office and see if it is aesthetically organized (housekeeping jobs)

A large part of your time may be going in meetings and other tasks, which you may not even be aware of. In the case of one unit head that I worked with, we found that he spent as much as 60 percent of his time in meetings. Every day he would have a meeting with all his heads which took two hours on an average. He found he was discussing the same problems over and over again with all of them every day. And most of the time he was doing the talking in the meetings. This was followed by weekly meetings, monthly seminars, and other unscheduled meetings with the head office. It is not too difficult to conclude that this unit head was obsessed with day-to-day activities and micro managing. Everyone wanted him to take decisions and create an agenda for the next meeting. This was an enormous wastage of human talent.

All managers, particularly CEOs and SBU heads, need to manage their time well and enable others to manage their time. Given below is a simple way of calculating the cost of time (TVRLS has evolved a time cost methodology for organizations © TVRLS which is described below).

THE COST OF YOUR TIME

We all know that we have to manage our time. But how do we do so and what is to be prioritized? At TVRLS, my HR consulting firm, we have come up with a useful tool to measure the cost of our time as managers.

To measure the performance of employees at senior levels objectively has always posed a problem to most organizations. Comparing the return on the investment (ROI) on each senior employee has not been an easy task, particularly as managers work in different departments with their own levels of assessment. For example, how do you compare the output of a production manager or maintenance manager with that of a personnel manager or finance manager or a manager incharge of security or town administration, etc?

The TVRLS method assesses the input costs (i.e., investment made by the company) of managers that can be compared with a reasonable degree of objectivity. The individual's cost to the company (CTC) is taken as the investment on that individual employee or manager and almost all organizations today calculate this very accurately. Thus, if a general manager recieves a salary of Rs 6 lakh per annum, excluding living costs, other benefits and community facilities, his CTC may come to be Rs 10 to 12 lakh.

KTR International Ltd (KTRIL) is a construction company involved in infrastructure projects. Its current turnover is Rs 1,000 crore and it intends to multiply five times in the next three years. Its people cost is estimated at Rs 100 crore. The general manager heading the cement unit carries a CTC of Rs10 lakh. There are eight HODs, who are deputy general managers(DGMs), reporting to him and looking after Materials, Quality, Maintenance, Marketing, Personnel, Finance, IT and Logistics and Planning. Each DGM is in the salary bracket of Rs 60 crore and their CTC is around Rs 8 lakh each. The company prescribed 2,000 working hours to be put in by each employee in a year as all the managers follow a five-day week. Every manager gets twenty-five days off in a year if he puts in 2,000 hours of work in that year. Now consider the following:

▶ The opportunity cost of a one-hour meeting of the GM with all HODs to discuss even something as trivial as whether tea should be served on the table or at another place would be Rs 37,000 or more; and that of a fifteen-minute telephone conversation between the GM and his DGM (Marketing) would be Rs 2,250.

- ▶ If the GM has a habit of coming even half an hour late for a meeting he is wasting Rs 1,600 of the company's money and an opportunity cost of Rs 16,000.
- ▶ The annual cost of interactions between two GMs for an hour a day is Rs 2 lakh and opportunity cost is Rs 20 lakh!
- ▶ If two HODs do not get along and send notes to each other even on trivial matters, often the GM has to intervene. In one year it has been found that there were 800 such email transactions recorded between them. Assuming that on average, each mail takes fifteen minutes to compose and send, it costs Rs 80,000 in a year with an opportunity cost of Rs 8 lakh.
- ▶ The GM and DGM (HR) felt that two of their HODs (DGM Marketing and DGM Production) would benefit if both attended a programme on conflict management together. If both of them are to be sponsored to attend a training programme in conflict management at one of the IIMs for five days, the fee would be Rs 20,000 and the travel cost for each of them Rs 10,000. After how many weeks does the company start getting its return on training, investment or costs, assuming that the conflict is reduced by 50 percent after the programme? (Returns will begin after the costs are recovered.)
- ▶ What is the opportunity cost of the daily production meetings if the plant has a record of meeting every day on an average for ninety minutes and the plant is shut down every year only for two weeks for annual maintenance, during which period the production meetings are not held?

HOW TO CALCULATE YOUR COST OF TIME

Step 1: Calculate your CTC. This should include all direct costs in terms of salary and perks + indirect costs incurred by the company for your salary, your maintenance, socialization, guidance, and development + investments made or likely to be made to enable you to perform your current role or possible future roles as well. Let this be figure X (sum of X1 + X2 + X3)

Step 2: Estimate the number of hours you are expected to work or you normally work in a year.

This is:

The number of working days (after deducting the number of holidays and leaves you are eligible for annually) x number of hours per day on an average you are likely to work (excluding your travel time to and from work).

This may range between 2,000 and 2,400 hours. Let this figure be T.

Step 3: Find the real cost per hour of your time (R-COT). You can get this by dividing X by T = X/T

Step 4: Now find the opportunity cost factor (OCF) for the company: Opportunity Cost is the returns each employee is expected to give to the company as a result of investments on time or CTC. While these vary from job to job and expectations may hike them up, there is a decent way to calculate (ROI):

Take the annual turnover of the company as targeted for the current year (AT). Also find out the annual estimated people costs (APCTC = salaries + perks + all other people costs including welfare costs, etc.). Your HR or finance department can give you an approximate figure. The previous year's balance sheet will also give you some idea.

Now divide the annual turnover (top line targeted) by the company by the annual people costs estimated for the year. This is the OCF.

So OCF = AT/APCTC

Usually in a manufacturing set-up the OCF varies from eight to ten. In IT firms and consulting companies it may be around three to four.

Step 5: Your opportunity cost of time (O-COT) is arrived at by multiplying your R-COT by the OCF, that is if your R-COT is Rs 1,000 per hour and the OCF is 3, your opportunity cost for the company is Rs 3,000 per hour or if the OCF is 10, your O-COT is Rs 10,000 per hour.

Note: R-COT and O-COT are always expressed in terms of rupee costs per hour.

Here are some examples:

1. Position: Senior Vice President HR is working in an IT firm
CTC: Rs 25 lakh.
Hours of work per year: 2,000 hours (250 days x 8 hours)
R-COT: 25,00,000/2,000 = Rs 1,250 per hour and per day cost, therefore Rs 10,000 if the employee is expected to work for about eight hours a day and 250 days in a year.
OCF: 3 (People cost is 33 percent of the annual revenue and hence the OCF is 3)
O-COT: Rs 3,750 per hour or Rs 30,000 per day.
2. Position: Senior Vice-President in manufacturing set-up
CTC: Rs 24 lakhs
Hours of work per month: 200 hours (or yearly = 12 months x 200 hours = 2,400 hours)

R-COT: 24,00,000/2,400 = Rs 1,000 per hour
OCF: 8
O-COT: Rs 8,000 per hour (i.e., the Senior VP's cost of time is Rs 8,000 per hour or by paying him Rs 1,000 per hour the company expects to generate a revenue of Rs 8,000 per hour)

USING O-COT AT WORK

O-COT is a useful tool to measure all kinds of work situations and assess how necessary they are. Consider the following scenarios.

Scenario 1: An Executive Vice President of Operations of a machine tools company holds weekly meetings with all HODs. Each meeting lasts for two hours. There are six HODs who attend the meeting. Two of the HODs (VP Manufacturing and VP Systems) come from two different plants located outside the head office (HO). Their travel time is one hour from the HO. Four others sit in the same building as the Executive VP (EVP) of Operations. The R-COTs of various HODs is given below.

The O-COT of the meeting is as follows:

EVP, Operations (R-COT = Rs 2,000)
VP, HR (R-COT = Rs 1,000)
VP, Marketing and Corporate Affairs (R-COT = Rs 1,250)
VP, Logistics and Systems (R-COT = Rs 1,500)
VP, Manufacturing (R-COT = Rs 1,250)
VP, Finance (R-COT = Rs 1,000)
VP, Sales and Distribution (R-COT = Rs 1,500)

The R-COT of the meeting = Rs 9,500 + 2,750 (additional time taken by VP of Systems and Manufacturing to attend the meeting) × 2 hours (duration of meeting) = Rs 24,500.

If the OCF of the company is 8, the O-COT = Rs 1.96 lakh.

Knowing the time cost of an event, how would you plan the agenda and the priorities of the meeting differently? Try the exercise at the end of the chapter.

Scenario 2: Recently, I attended a meeting to plan a World Conference on Ancient Wisdom in Management. The conference was to be organized by a person with many media connections. The CEO of a large company was chosen to be the chairman of the conference. The CEO is also well connected and genuinely believed that this conference would help Indian managers save investing on foreign consultants and also bring Indian values to the notice of worldwide management experts. As a result he also donated a large sum of money towards this.

About forty people attended the meeting. They were CEOs, management gurus, and most of the who's who of management. The meeting was in Mumbai and about 50 percent of them were from the city. It lasted three hours (180 minutes) and closed with lunch. Of the 180 minutes, the chairman spoke for forty to fifty minutes, which I have calculated to be nearly 40 percent of the time if you account for the time used for pleasantries, tea breaks, introductions of members, etc. It appeared as though the chairman had called all the luminaries to listen to his ideas rather than get ideas from them. I got barely three minutes to speak. So did most of the other invitees. If you simply divide the effective time of about 120 minutes out of these 180 minutes by 40 it works out to be about three minutes. If you are a demanding speaker you may get about three to four transactions and about seven to eight minutes. But it will be four to five minutes on an average.

I spent my own money to attend this meeting as the CEO is a close friend. I paid nearly Rs 6,000 on air travel and on a conservative estimate, my time is valued at Rs 10,000 per day (a very conservative consulting fee). All this to make a three-minute speech and to listen to my CEO friend! The conclusion of the discussion was to appoint another conference committee to work out the agenda and identify speakers for the conference. I was asked to be the adviser for this conference, which I politely declined.

Now calculate how much on an average each person who attended this meeting for half a day would have cost their respective companies. On a very conservative estimate every single individual in the group drew more salary than me and would have cost to his company Rs 10,000. If half of them paid their airfare, at again a conservative cost of Rs 5,000 each, and only twenty of them travelled to reach Mumbai, it is another Rs 1 lakh.

Thus my estimate of this large meeting cost is:

Salary costs: 40 x Rs 10,000 = Rs 4 lakh (opportunity cost of the time for these people will be at least three to four times that = Rs 16 lakh)
Travel costs of 20 persons x 5,000= Rs 1 lakh

So the meeting cost is at least Rs 5 lakhs, and the opportunity cost is Rs 16 lakh. Who paid for this? If all of us in the team donated a half to full day by offering it to an executive development programme, we could have offered twenty 'one-day programmes' in Mumbai on ancient wisdom and got in each programme Rs 5 lakhs if appropriately priced and earned Rs 1 crore with a capable organizer. That is the opportunity cost of planning a conference with large participation.

Scenario 3: A consultant is asked to take a prepaid taxi from the airport to visit the company he/she are working for. The consultant costs Rs 12,000 per hour assuming an eight-hour work day, which means the company pays Rs 2,000 per minute. Now if this consultant stands in a queue at Delhi airport for fifteen minutes to get a prepaid taxi and another five minutes for the taxi driver to pull out his car, the total loss is Rs 4,000. Add to this the time taken to organize the reimbursement. The cost of hiring a private taxi may be Rs 1,000. The company has lost Rs 4,000 of the consultant's time.

Each time you make a decision to do something—from attending a conference, to prioritizing certain roles—you can use this tool to answer the following questions.

▶ How much am I spending?
▶ Whose money is it?
▶ For what purpose am I spending it?
▶ Who is the beneficiary?
▶ Can the same thing be done with low cost and with the same or even better effects?

This formula is used mainly to sensitize ourselves to the value of time. Employees forget quite often that the organizations that employ them are paying for their time and application of talent. Employee value is determined by both time and talent.

Employee value = Use of talent x Use of time.

If we waste any of them we are also wasting an opportunity to build our own intellectual capital.

HOW MUCH DOES IT COST TO ACCOMPANY YOUR WIFE TO BUY VEGETABLES?

It is worth being cautious in applying the above calculations. A friend of mine used to accompany his wife to buy vegetables twice a week, on Wednesdays and Saturdays. After I explained the concept of O-COT to him, he started to calculate the cost of this. The vegetable market is about five kilometres from his residence. Next to his apartment was a supermarket which had all the fresh vegetables they needed. His wife, however, preferred the open vegetable market to the supermarket as she found the prices to be 10 percent lower. They normally bought vegetables worth about Rs 200 each time and saved Rs 20 per trip. My friend always felt uncomfortable accompanying his wife for vegetable shopping as he had to return from the office a little early on Wednesday and had to spend almost two hours with her for the trip. So he calculated the cost of his time and mentioned to her that for saving Rs 20 she was using up Rs 500 of his time and another Rs 40 for petrol. She reluctantly agreed to go alone the next time. But over the next two months, my friend started feeling lonely and left out. By the third month they started having fights on trivial issues like the choice of curry she had made, whether to attend a party in the neighbourhood, and so on. Finally, his wife got fed up of arguing with him and left for her home town on a two-month vacation. My colleague had to cook for himself for the next two months. My friend did not connect the buying of vegetables with the family happiness. Can you estimate how much it cost the professor to save Rs 500 a week?

WAYS OF MANAGING YOUR TIME

There is only thing you need to manage your time—and that is to be aware of how you are spending it. Listed below are useful ways to increase your awareness and help redesign your schedule.

Become more productive

You can be much more time productive by following the simple steps outlined below.

1. First of all, be aware of where your time is going. Assess the way you are spending your time (use appendix 8A.2 to assess this).
2. Use your secretary or an executive assistant to do this for you. You could even hire an MBA for a couple of months to do this job or use management trainees (see the case study given in the conclusion of chapter 1).
3. Now put a cost on your time.
4. Delegate. Decide the critical areas where you are needed and select others who can do the less crucial jobs at a lower cost, equally or more effectively.
5. Determine the priorities for your stage of the company. Some companies may need a lot of PR in particular periods and some others may need internal management and housekeeping time. You need to be sensitive to the changing needs of your company.
6. Discuss with your colleagues or top team about your use of time and seek suggestions from them.
7. Sensitize yourself and others to the cost of time.

Analyse the time you have spent

Managers typically spend their time at work in five ways. Look at these in detail.

1. Visitors?
    (a) If yes, what kind? And how much of your time goes for this?
    (b) Friends?
    (c) Business magazines and other media people?
    (d) Your own employees?
    (e) Family members? Relatives?
    (f) Casual visitors?
    (g) Customers?
    (h) Suppliers?
    (i) Investors and other financiers or stakeholders?
    (j) Consultants and salespeople?

2. Travel?
    (a) If yes, how much time? What kind of travel? What purpose? What is the amount of time you spend travelling, waiting, etc. How do you use that time?
    (b) Travel to the office?
    (c) Travel to visit customers? Suppliers? Competitors?
    (d) Travel for business? Collecting benchmarking information?
    (e) Professional travel for training and own learning?
    (f) Travel for monitoring of the company?
    (g) Communication travel (i. e., travel to communicate and enthuse employees or customers.)

3. Meetings?
    (a) If yes, what kind of meetings? How many of these need

your personal attention? Is it enough to look at the minutes? Can you join the meeting at the end if you have a habit of talking all the time in the meetings? Hear first what the group has to say when you join them at the end and then give your comments, or use a strategy of starting the meeting and then joining them at the end?

(b) To what extent are these meetings operation matters related? Future related? Resource related? Planning related? Problem-solving or crisis related? Get your executive assistant to analyse these meetings and give you feedback on the man-hours spent.

(c) Two-person meetings?

(d) Group meetings?

(e) Planned and predictable meetings?

(f) Unplanned meetings?

(g) Time spent on meetings can be analysed by the source and some kind of cost–benefit analysis could be done.

4. Telephone calls?

(a) From where do you get most of your calls?

(b) Are they routed through your office?

(c) How efficient is your office? Have you briefed them adequately? Are they aligned with your priorities?

(d) Is there an escape window in the event of mistakes? (for example, if your office refuses to connect a call to you thinking that they are likely to waste your time and later you discover it is a potential client, supplier, or a VVIP?)

(e) Dealing with habitual callers and time wasters?

(f) Does your office have a system of analysing how your calls are taking time, and give you feedback?

5. Individual work?
    (a) Decision-making?
    (b) Reading?
    (c) Listening?
    (d) Making decisions?
    (e) Internet surfing?
    (f) Dictating letters or writing personal emails? Some CEOs prefer to answer their own emails and in the process they accumulate a lot of mails and also give emotional responses. They also may take time in typing these. Some other CEOs are never satisfied with their drafts and they need a lot of time to check and recheck or draft and redraft.
    (g) Making self-initiated telephone calls?

TEN AREAS TO SPEND TIME ON FOR MANAGERS AT DIFFERENT LEVELS INCLUDING CEOs

We have said this before but it's worth repeating. Be aware of what your role in the company is. You have to not just work on everyday tasks, but focus on the bigger picture.

1. MIS and systems
    (a) Daily or weekly performance monitoring and review
    (b) Planning and implementing systems
    (c) Learning about events in the company
    (d) Giving instructions
    (e) Problem-solving

2. People management
    (a) Allocating tasks

- (b) Monitoring performance
- (c) Listening to complaints
- (d) Appraisals
- (e) Communication
- (f) Incentives, rewards, and recognition
- (g) Recruitment
- (h) Development and review
- (i) Coaching
- (j) Directing, reprimanding

3. Visioning and strategizing
    - (a) Sharing ideas
    - (b) Listening to ideas
    - (c) Testing out ideas
    - (d) Visiting benchmark companies
    - (e) Developing strategies
    - (f) Collecting competitor information or assimilating information
    - (g) Internal SWOT studies
    - (h) Consultant reports, task forces and seminars, training programmes
    - (i) Reading and strategizing, discussions about strategies
    - (j) Systems development for converting strategies into operational plans

4. Planning and goal setting
    - (a) Short-term and long-term goal setting
    - (b) Task forces—listening to them and appointing and monitoring their work

5. Customer management

6. Stakeholder management
   (a) Investor management

7. Financial management
   (a) Financial planning
   (b) Funds management
   (c) Monitoring finances
   (d) Legal aspects and ensuring statutory obligations

8. Board management
   (a) Board meetings
   (a) Quarterly reviews

9. Public relations and brand-building activities
   (a) Ceremonial roles
   (b) Presentations about the company to visitors and other dignitaries
   (c) Socializing and networking
   (d) Media
   (e) Internal communications
   (f) Ceremonial meetings and parties

10. Actual execution (especially important for small and medium enterprises)
   (a) R&D activities
   (b) Online work
   (c) Solving problems using technical expertise
   (d) Making calculations on the computer
   (e) Taking over someone else's functions, carrying out quality checks, for example

PEOPLE ARE THE ULTIMATE RESOURCE

The resources a manager and his organization have at their disposal are money, materials, technology, systems, discipline, etc. Each of these resources is vital to a company's fortunes at different periods. Initially, organizations that had access to technology produced many products in large quantities and thus made money in the 1960, 1970s, and 1980s—for example, automobiles, televisions, etc. Later, technology became easily available to anyone who had money. Many Indian companies like BPL had collaborations and even developed their own—Tata Motors in the last decade, for example. As supply and access to money increased due to financial instruments and globalization, its value as a strategic resource receded in importance. The way many Indian business houses and pharma companies were able to acquire resources from other countries indicated the availability of capital. Systems, quality standards like ISO, CMM, etc., then came into existence to regulate the quality of products. As the systems became available through books, programmes, assessors, etc., this too has become less important. Now the resource we value the most in our workplace is human talent.

We are living in a knowledge society. One indication of this is the way salaries have skyrocketed in the last decade. As talent becomes scarce, it gets costlier. This is why managers change jobs much more often than they would have a generation ago. Mobility is caused by shortage of talent as well as the rising price of talent. It is because of this rising price of talent that we need to calculate, by the minute, how much each organization is spending on its employees.

Managerial success is enhanced if you are at the right place to do the right things at the right time. In choosing a job, a manager makes the choice mostly on the basis of what can be got and not so often on the basis of what can be given or what is expected to be given. When there is a mismatch between what an individual is able to give and what the organization expects them to give, problems begin. Who is responsible? Largely, the person himself. Managers are often not clear about what they are meant to give. Often the organization itself is hazy about the matter and many Indian companies do not systematically assess people.

COMPETENCY MAPPING

Competency mapping is a simple tool to assess the suitability of managers. It consists of breaking a given role or job into its constituent tasks or activities and identifying the competencies (technical, managerial, behavioural, conceptual knowledge, attitudes, skills, etc.) needed to perform it successfully.

The process of competency mapping is not very complex. Some of the methods are as follows:

1. Simply ask each person who is currently performing the role to list the tasks to be performed one by one, and identify the knowledge, attitudes, and skills required to perform each of these.
2. Consolidate the list.
3. Present it to a group or a special task force constituted for that role.
4. Edit and finalize.

Note: The task force should consist of some current incumbents of that role who are performing it well, the reporting and reviewing officers of that role, and some of the past incumbents who have performed successfully in that role. Make sure that the task force consists of at least one or more members who have some understanding of competencies and the nature of competencies. Most professional managers with MBA degrees should have this competence. If they do not it is easy to acquire it by reading a few books. I recently spent two hours introducing competency mapping to MBA students (all with experience of more than two years) at the Indian School of Business at a course I taught there. By the end of the class they had mastered the skill and done a great job in their exercises. Professional HR firms and consultants can also do this for you, if you so decide.

WHAT IS COMPETENCY?

Any underlying characteristic that requires performing a given task, activity, or role successfully can be considered as competency. Competency may take the following forms:

- ▶ Knowledge
- ▶ Attitude
- ▶ Skills
- ▶ Other characteristics of an individual
- ▶ Motives
- ▶ Values
- ▶ Concept of self

Competencies may be grouped into various areas. In a classic article published a few decades ago in the *Harvard Business Review*, Daniel Katz grouped these into three areas which were later expanded by Indian management professors into the following four:

- ▶ Technical: dealing with technology or know-how associated with the function, role, task (now also referred to by some as functional)
- ▶ Managerial/Organizational: dealing with managerial aspects, organizing, planning, mobilizing resources, monitoring, systems use, etc.
- ▶ Human/Behavioural: including personal, interpersonal, and team related
- ▶ Conceptual/Theoretical: including visualizations, model building, etc.

The following box gives an illustrative list of competencies for a marketing manager in a dairy firm.

COMPETENCIES REQUIRED FOR BRANCH MANAGER OF SALES OF MILK AND MILK PRODUCTS OF A DAIRY INDUSTRY

Goal: To monitor daily sales activities, management of the branch office and ensure achievement of sales targets at the beginning of the year

Technical/Functional competencies
- ▶ Thorough understanding of the milk business and latest developments in the industry
- ▶ Knowledge of the sales and marketing process
- ▶ Knowledge of market research and research tools
- ▶ Knowledge of MIS reports and their interpretation
- ▶ Working knowledge of computers (PowerPoint, Excel, Word and email management)

Managerial competencies

- ► Vision
- ► Decision making
- ► Cost consciousness
- ► Target orientation
- ► Planning and organizing skills
- ► Knowledge of supermarkets and other outlets
- ► Knowledge of consumer preferences and profiles
- ► Knowledge of pricing
- ► Resource mobilization skills

Behavioural competencies

- ► Negotiation skills
- ► Problem-solving
- ► Drive to achieve
- ► Quick thinking
- ► Assertiveness
- ► Ability to work under pressure
- ► Motivating/Inspiring others
- ► Team management
- ► Clearly articulating the vision of the company down the line
- ► Customer orientation
- ► Fast learner

This is a general classification and a given competency may fall into one or more areas. Just as we manage our time to bring out the best of our competencies, we should also manage our team's competencies. Competency mapping is an essential exercise for this (see box). Every well-managed firm should

- ▶ Have a clear organizational structure
- ▶ Have well-defined roles in terms of the KPAs or tasks and activities associated with each role
- ▶ Map the competencies required for each role
- ▶ Identify the generic competencies for each set of roles or levels of management
- ▶ And use them for recruitment, performance management, promotion decisions, placement, and training needs identification

COMPETENCY BUILDING LEADS TO CREATION OF INTELLECTUAL CAPITAL

'Intellectual Capital is Intellectual Material-Knowledge, Information, Intellectual Property, and Experience—that can be put to use to create wealth.' Thomas Stewart, *Fortune* 1994.

The reason we need to manage our time is so that we can use it to good purpose. And the most important thing we can do with time is to use it to learn new skills and knowledge. In short, we build our competencies and it adds to our intellectual capital. When the competencies of employees are built the value of that company goes up for the expertise it posseses. This enhances the intellectual capital of the company. We introduced the concept of R-COT and O-COT because it is a useful way for us to change our attitudes about the way we spend our time at work. Similarly, the concept of intellectual capital is a useful way to look at the kind of activities we engage in: are they adding value to the company we work for and building value for self?

The intellectual capital of the individual includes: (a) human capital, primarily consisting of his internal strengths in terms of knowledge, skills and other forms of talent or competencies (attitudes, styles, traits, habits, practices, beliefs, values, motivations, self-concept etc.); (b) structural capital in terms of his employment history, accomplishments, experience, inventions, and everything else that determines his market value and image; and (c) image capital the individual has as a professional in the institution or the agency, or as an individual in society or the community.

Converting and executing intellectual capital to economic capital becomes an important part in today's context. For example, many fresh MBAs are willing to join PSBs to acquire banking knowledge even though they are paid lower salaries; then after acquiring this knowledge they are able to get jobs at two to three times their salaries. Similarly, consulting companies that recruit young managers have high attrition rates because intellectual capital added by them drives the employee's market value upwards. Some people have a high amount of intellectual capital. Unfortunately they do not put it to use. Sometimes they themselves are not aware of what they have. See the exercise at the end of this chapter on ways to assess your intellectual capital.

Here are ways in which effective managers build on their intellectual capital.

- ▶ Clear objectives in life and articulated thoughts about what they want to do and how they like to enrich their internal strengths, structural capital, and image
- ▶ High activity level that enables them to put to use intellectual capital or acquire more of it
- ▶ Focused work in terms of putting to use the intellectual capital already acquired
- ▶ Good professional and social networks, and partnerships including professional co-workers, loyal customers or clients, students, and others who like to be in a networking relationship with them

The demand for retired managers is a great illustration of the value of intellectual capital. Many Indian organizations (for example, Reliance) employ retired government officers for their knowledge on dealing with government. Dr Kaza Gandhi is a good example of how intellectual capital gained in one's lifetime can be put to use even after retirement.

Dr Gandhi was the former director of the Andhra Pradesh Police Academy's Forensic Science Laboratories. After he retired, Dr Gandhi set up Truth Laboratories to deal mainly with white-collar crimes such as forgery, embezzlement, cheating, and cyber fraud. Now, based on demand, Truth Labs has expanded from its headquarters in Hyderabad to New Delhi and Chennai in less than two years and will launch operations in Bangalore soon. Similarly Samuel Paul, former director of IIMA, at eighty years of age is continuing to do great service to society by setting up the Public Affairs Institute in Bangalore. This institute is an NGO set up to measure the satisfaction levels of public with various public service agencies and give them feedback on their performance. The institute helps improve the efficiency of agencies that supply water, electricity, education, transport, communication, infrastructure, etc. to the public at large.

CONCLUSION

To be an effective manager you need to manage the two most essential commodities in your working life: time and talent. In this chapter we've discussed the value and cost of time and given you tools with which you can assess the way you use your time at work. The key to time management is to allow yourself to use your competencies and to delegate those tasks that others can do at a lower cost. In today's working environment, humans are the most precious resource and their competencies thus need to be properly utilized. The more one develops one's competencies, the more one creates intellectual capital and an effective manager is one who manages his time and competencies while growing his intellectual capital.

HR INTERVENTIONS IN INTELLECTUAL CAPITAL BUILDING

Not all activities may result in intellectual capital formation but planning work, understanding the work of others, understanding effective strategies are all ways of building it. If you understand this, you will be able to see the importance of HR tools in building one's intellectual capital.

When a manager sits with a junior to plan his work, the manager is building his own intellectual capital and also helping the junior increase his own intellectual capital. Knowledge of the work done by one's juniors or seniors, knowledge of the processes used in carrying out various activities, review of the activities and processes, which of them work and which of them do not work, are all parts of intellectual capital formation.

Imagine a territory manager of a FMCG company supervising about twenty-five sales officers in different areas or branches. If there are quarterly meetings with each sales officer and at each meeting the manager listens to each of them for half an hour, many things can be learned about customer preferences, business opportunities, competitor strategies, pricing, and so on. Using the performance review discussion he also builds his experience and expertise as an area supervisor. In addition, the manager can use the information gathered to monitor the performance of sales officers and gain experience as an area manager. This is intellectual capital building.

Performance planning and review or any performance management system is a way to build intellectual capital. I wish more line managers would realize this. Here are some other HR processes that help increase our intellectual capital formation (in order of importance).

▶ Job rotation adds to knowledge and skills in new areas and is a direct contribution to intellectual capital formation.
▶ 360 degree feedback enhances our intellectual capital formation through enhanced self-awareness and our recognition of our strengths and weaknesses.
▶ Feedback from assessment and development centres adds to intellectual capital formation.
▶ Training programmes and other learning opportunities provided by our organizations are intellectual capital formation.

A manager who learns to use PMS as an opportunity for intellectual capital building will be less bothered about whether his performance appraisal resulted in annual increments or incentives. It is only those who fail to learn from others who will seek incentives for planning their performance and rating to assess how they translated their intellectual capital during the year to other forms of capital for the company.

APPENDIX 8.1

An Executive Vice-President of Operations of a machine tools company holds weekly meetings of all his HODs. Each meeting lasts for two hours. There are six HODs who attend the meeting. Two of the HODs (VP Manufacturing and VP Systems) come from two different plants located outside the HO. Their travel time is one hour from the HO. Four others sit in the same building as the EVP of operations. The CTC of various HODs is given below. Calculate the opportunity R-COT and O-COT for the meeting and give your rating of the appropriateness of each of the following agenda items given in Table 8.1.

EVP, Operations (R-COT = Rs 2,000)
VP, HR (R-COT = Rs 1,000)
VP, Marketing and Corporate Affairs (R-COT = Rs 1,250)
VP, Logistics and Systems (R-COT = Rs 1,500)
VP, Manufacturing (R-COT = Rs 1,250)
VP, Finance (R-COT = Rs 1,000)
VP, Sales and Distribution (R-COT = Rs 1,500)

Evaluate which of the agenda items are worth taking up in this meeting:
Use the following scale:
4 = Very appropriate, take it up
3 = Useful, take it up
2 = Can be postponed or someone else can take it
1 = Not appropriate, drop it from this meeting and use other methods like delegation, etc.

TABLE 8.1.

Agenda item	Approximate time in minutes allocated	Points for discussion and decision	Your evaluation of appropriate-ness
Appointment of dealers	15	15 new dealers to be appointed all over India. Biodata enclosed	
Shortage of raw material x-type bridges for the new machines ordered by German client	15	Substitute material and vendors to be discussed	
Resignation letter of GM Production	15	Experienced GM for last 15 years. Joining competitors. Arrangements if accepted or rejected	
Complaints from an old customer	10	5 percent contributing a few years ago and 2 percent this year	

Item	Value	Remarks
ISO certification	20	Audit team arriving and departments are not prepared
New performance appraisal system	15	Consultants suggested. Seminar held. Needs ratification
New incentive system—Consultants report	45	Report to be discussed. Consultant called in to present
Restructuring of the SBU-5 for doubling annual turnover	30	SBU 5 is being separated from SBU 4. New structure needs discussion. Roles to be clarified. Turnover of SBU 5 is 1 percent potential high
Change of lunch menu and canteen timings	10	Widespread demand for including new items and changed timings. May affect production in factories
Membership of clubs—change of eligibility	10	Proposed membership for newly created cadre of AGMs
Operational problems and issues in SAP implementation	25	People are trained, still resulting in many mistakes

Shortage of raw materials anticipated	20	Shortage of certain imported materials expected
Change in requirements for machines from Nigeria	15	Parties have changed their requirements for 100 machines placed earlier and the new requirements reduce margins
Should coffee be served on the tables	10	Request from a group of senior executives to serve tea on their tables to save time
Purchase of laptops for Regional Managers, Sales (25 in number)	10	Regional Managers, Sales, are asking for replacement of their old laptops
CII delegation to China	15	Nominations to be finalized. 15-day tour. Cost per member is Rs 5 lakh
Assessment centres for senior executives	15	Succession planning and potential appraisal
KPAs not completed by most departments	10	KPAs need to be completed as a part of the appraisal

Press conference in Mumbai	20	PRO has organized a press meet on the occasion of 25th anniversary of company
Face lift of office and change of logo	10	New logo to be done by NID

Answer: R-COT of the meeting = (Rs 9,500 + 2,750) x 2 = Rs 24,500

If the OCF of the company is 8, the O-COT = Rs 1.96 lakh

APPENDIX 8.2

The following table is a useful tool to assess how you are spending your time. It can be filled in by you or an executive secretary.

TABLE 8.2.1

Managerial tasks or roles	Number of hours spent in a month out of the total 200 hours with the cost of time					
	Travel	Visitors	Meetings Group and two person	Telephone calls	Individual work	Total
Visioning and strategizing						
MIS and systems						
Execution						
Planning and goal setting						

People management					
Public relations and ceremonial roles					
Customer management					
Other stakeholder management					
Financial management					
Board management					
Others					
Total					

APPENDIX 8. 3: COST OF TIME

The following table is an example of an HOD/CEO's cost of time calculated at 2,400 hours per year or 200 hours a month

TABLE 8.3.1

Annual salary/CTC of the employee	Cost of time		Opportunity cost of time		
	Per minute	Per hour	Per minute IT companies C = 3 times	Per minute Manufacturing and others C = 8 times Rs 10	Opportunity cost of a five-minute telephone call Range*
Rs 1.2 lakh	Re 1 rounded off	Rs 50	Rs 3	Rs 8	Rs 15 to Rs 40
Rs 2.5 lakh	Rs 2 rounded	Rs 104	Rs 6	Rs 16	Rs 30 to Rs 80

Rs 5 lakh	Rs 3.5	Rs 208	Rs 10	Rs 28	Rs 50 to Rs 140
Rs 10 lakh	Rs 7	Rs 417	Rs. 21	Rs 56	Rs 105 to Rs 280
Rs 15 lakhs	Rs 10	Rs 625	Rs 30	Rs 80	Rs 150 to Rs 400
Rs 20 lakhs	Rs 14	Rs 833	Rs 42	Rs 112	Rs 210 to Rs 560
Rs 25 lakhs	Rs 17	Rs 1,042	Rs 51	Rs 136	Rs 255 to Rs 680
Rs 50 lakhs	Rs 35	Rs 2,083	Rs 105	Rs 280	Rs 525 to Rs 1,400
Rs 1 crore	Rs 69	Rs 4,167	Rs 207	Rs 552	Rs 1,035 to Rs 2,760

* Excludes other person's opportunity cost. If the telephone is internal add the opportunity cost of the other side or simply double the cost shown here.

APPENDIX 8.4: MEASURE YOUR INTELLECTUAL CAPITAL

WHAT IS YOUR INTELLECTUAL CAPITAL?

Assess or at least document your own intellectual capital using the following guidelines. You will need several days to complete this. Once completed, keep updating it. Take the help of your close friends, boss, juniors, seniors and your 360 feedback team and strangers you come across to keep filling this table of your intellectual capital. This is your intellectual capital monitor. You can keep monitoring how you are enhancing your capital by tracking changes.

HUMAN CAPITAL: INTERNAL ASSETS OR STRENGTHS

Knowledge capital: List all the knowledge you have using all specifiable knowledge. This may run into several pages. Only go the desired level of specificity you think will help others to know you. For example, knowledge of statistics can calculate coefficients of correlation or do factor analysis knowledge of SPSS, or knowledge of methods of pricing product, knowledge of sources of working capital, knowledge of languages (knowledge workers are valued on the basis of the knowledge they possess. The more you know the more you are valued in any profession. For example, knowledgeable lawyers, doctors, insurance agents, etc.).

Skill capital: List all the skills you have or all that you can do skilfully and the level of proficiency. For example, design assessment centres, create simulation exercises, do language editing, design and upload websites, diagnose the problems in a laptop or service PCs, etc. (Doctors like Dr Trehan, the famous heart surgeon, Dr Panda of Asia Heart are known for their technical skills, managers like Krishnamurthy for their turnaround skills.

Value capital: List what you consider are the values you hold. For example, integrity. I can be relied upon to carry out or at least try my best to carry out my promises or verbal statements, or I value service and am therefore willing to put in hard work if the activity is service driven. (CEOs like Deepak Parekh, Narayana Murthy and Dr Kurien are known for their values.)

Motivational capital: Highlight significant motives you have that drive you to work. For example, achievement driven, affiliation driven, influence, extension, etc. Refer to the chapter on motivation in this book.

Emotional capital: Highlight your general emotional state and those emotions you have which help you to convert your knowledge and other skills into work and generate other forms of physical or intellectual capital. Emotional self-control gets high points. High drive gets high points. List qualitatively what you have as your emotional capital. (If I am obsessed with an idea I have sleepless nights until I complete the work. I am able to control my anger.)

Self-concept: What is the self-concept you carry. How is it an asset to you? (Leaders like Sam Pitroda, Kiran Bedi, Dr Kurien are known for their self-confidence and self-concept)

Other forms of human capital: traits, habits, practices, etc.

1. Structural capital
Education history and accomplishments
Employment history and experience gained
Other accomplishments which form structural capital include patents, papers, books published, awards, etc.

2. Social or image capital
Image in the profession

Image capital in the organizations you serve (including past organizations)

Image capital in the society or community where you live

3. Networking capital

Professional networks, membership of associations and bodies, organizational networks, membership of committees, task forces, etc.

Community networks—membership clubs of associations and societies, charities, etc.

Friendship circles and other networks of which you are a part

9

Communication

Managers who have in recent years become leaders in India have one thing in common—communication. They write, give speeches, and address meetings and conferences. Many of them have now written successful books, such as Nandan Nilekani (*Imagining India*, where he sets out a road map for India's future) and Narayana Murthy (*A Better Indian, A Better World*, a collection of his speeches and writings). After he completed his term as president of India, A.P.J. Abdul Kalam made it his mission to address students, scientists, businessmen and particularly the youth of India. He even teaches a course at IIMA along with another professor, Anil Gupta. Similarly, Kiran Mazumdar-Shaw, Anu Aga, Kiran Bedi, Deepak Parikh, Kumar Managalam Birla, Ratan Tata, and Azim Premji have become well-known fixtures at forums and convocation addresses. The new generation of Indian leaders such as Shivender Singh of Fortis, Sanjiv Bhikchandani of naukri.com, Vijay Mahajan of Basix, Vindi Banga of Unilever, Jerry Rao of Mphasis are also well-known speakers and motivators.

Communication is the only way that one's thoughts, values, dreams, experiences, actions and talent become known to others. As I explained in the chapter on efficacy, effective managers communicate to influence others. Indeed, as we've seen with some of the examples above, it can become an important component of a person's stature and influence. Nandan Nilekani became known to a wider audience after *Imagining India*. And there's a joke that Jack Welch made even more money after he retired from GE through his writing. Communication is perhaps the single largest factor responsible for many talented people to get noticed and become of use to society.

Good managers also are good networkers. Through networks they learn, articulate their goals, and disseminate their thoughts. This chapter focuses on the two unique competencies of good managers and how they communicate, network, and make a difference. There is a lot of material available on how to communicate effectively. The purpose of this chapter, however, is to look at what our managers communicate and how much they do it, what makes them effective, and what are the lessons we can learn from successful communicators.

WHAT MANAGERS COMMUNICATE

Communication is one of the qualities that really sets apart transactional managers from the transformational ones, achievers from visionaries, visionaries from missionaries. Everyone has to communicate constantly. At the low end, managers communicate about practical, work-related matters. The more effective the manager, the more they manage to tie in larger issues in their communication.

> **At the low end managers talk about:** goals and purposes, activities, methods, dos and don'ts, expected behaviour, norms, guidelines, instructions, rewards, punishments, immediate tasks to be done, consequences of not accomplishing goals, what is acceptable and what is not, etc.

At the higher end: the connection between current and long-term goals, ambitions of the company and team, impact of achievements on career goals, future opportunities, optimism, talent needs, problem-solving approaches, accomplishments of competitors, how successful people have achieved higher targets, benchmarking data, costs, efficiency parameters, need for change and how that change is possible, etc.

At the visionary level: vision, values, goals, strategies, how to influence others with their thoughts, data about opportunities, the country and its status in the world, the company and its status globally, the need to work, dreams of the CEOs and others in the organization, social needs, etc.

At the missionary level: vision, values, sustainable development, future of the world, nation, people, poverty, social responsibility of business, the glory of the work they are doing, their team's contributions to the country, appeal to conscience, need to sacrifice and share, long-term good of the country, dreams for the country and humanity at large.

While most managers have to engage in low-end communication on a day-to-day level, one of the key ways you can rise to the next level is to be aware of your communication and bring in the big picture. Connect your audience to the larger ideas and values behind what you're saying as much as possible.

Case study 1: How Dr Anil Khandelwal used communication to connect to people and transformed Bank of Baroda

Anil Khandelwal joined the Bank of Baroda in 2005 as its chairman. His remit was to revitalize the ninety-seven-year-old bank.

> The enormous changes that we were planning at the Bank of Baroda required that we engage our people at every level. For me employee engagement was a really big challenge because only this could bring about perceptible change in our image in the mind of customers. For us, engagement of employees meant communicating the vision of the bank and also developing an emotional connection with the bank's new aspirations. This was part of our value system.
>
> Just imagine an employee in one of our branches in remote Bihar or Orissa receiving instructions to implement a particular decision. He does not know the background, rationale, and compulsions for this change. He also does not know what benefits will result from this change. He may, in fact, be overwhelmed or even intimidated by these new instructions. How do we allay his fears? What is the best way to reach out and communicate to him what he yearns to know? How do we keep him informed from time to time and by what mechanism? We had to find creative answers to these questions. The success of our endeavours would depend upon this.
>
> We needed to reach out to employees at a deep psychological level through large group events that involved working together and dreaming together about the future.
>
> Based on this theme, we started a new initiative called Baroda Manthan (employee conclave). It was planned to be a large group event, over a day, of around 100 to 120 participants drawn from a cross-section of employees covering all cadres. Zonal/Regional functionaries were

expected to lend support for holding such events. The programme was woven around four key themes—building a sales and service culture, customer centricity, leveraging technology for business success, and moving towards a universal financial services organization. The entire programme was to be conducted in a highly informal and non-threatening (conducive) environment, where employees felt safe and energized to contribute. The whole objective was to get people ignited with zeal and positive images of themselves and of the bank and also to seek their commitment to the new vision.

Case study 2: How Jack Welch transformed GE through communication

In 1981, at the age of 45, Jack Welch became the eighth and youngest CEO of GE. His goal was to make GE the world's most competitive enterprise. He knew that it would take nothing less than a revolution to make this transformation. To Welch, business was 'all about capturing intellect.' More people, more ideas. But to make sure that no worthwhile idea went unsaid, organizations had to encourage people to articulate and express themselves. To spark communication and exchange of ideas, Welch turned GE into a learning organization. In a learning organization employees are given access to important information and are expected to scope out new ideas and opportunities and come up with creative solutions to problems.

Management guru Noel Tichy, who assisted Jack Welch, developed a new theory which was actively promoted in GE (discussed in the chapter on internality). According to him, good leaders should have a teachable point of view. They then should communicate their experiences and points of view to others. This is the way you create a learning organization and also develop your own leadership skills and influence. This is exactly what Jack Welch did in GE. People at all levels were encouraged to come up with ideas, solve problems, and take the organization forward. This is how communication became a foundation of GE's growth.

Peter Cappelli and his team, after studying ninety-eight Indian CEOs, identified empowering communication as one of the ways these leaders shape their organizations. 'At HCL for example, an online system allows employees to create quality control "tickets", much like those on an assembly line. These can flag product-quality problems or even personal issues related to management such as, "I have problems with my bonus". Employees can also post comments and questions on the company's "U and I" website.' (Cappelli, *et al*. 2010: 95). A similar system was used by Anil Khandelwal to connect with customers and employees at the Bank of Baroda.

KINDS OF COMMUNICATIONS

Successful managers communicate a number of things to their juniors and also encourage them to communicate upwards. The following is a sample list of things that can be communicated to influence each other and enhance utilization of employee competencies, engagement, and achieving vision. For example, when an employee is able to document and communicate his/ her talents through a personal biography, this information can be used to fully explore the individual's capacity to learn. Family-related information helps in counselling, providing organizational support and managing employee welfare. Company vision and values help individuals to connect their daily work with the customers they serve and enhances their engagement. Every employee would like to feel that they are not merely working for a pay cheque but serving someone and making a contribution to something larger.

TABLE 9.1

Content	Possible
Personal	Personal data, biographic information, experiences, feelings, intentions, concerns, fears, ideas, reactions to decisions by others, personal experiences, preferences, pain, happiness, qualifications, values
Family related	Problems, issues, happenings, wealth, relationships, health, upbringing, qualifications, work, values, status
Community related	Needs, problems, issues, conflicts, solutions, diversity, experiences, changes in other communities, events, analysis of what is good and not so good, community behaviour and its implications, conflict and sources of conflict.
Workplace related	Tasks, goals, work conditions, culture, norms, methods, values, preferences, career opportunities, rewards, policies, accomplishments, performance

Team related	Composition, Tasks, Activities, Processes, Functioning, Progress, Accomplishments, Positioning of the team, Positions, Work methods, Conflicts and their resolution, Membership, Responsibilities, Functioning, Task-related information, Resources, Roles, Responsibilities
Organization related	Vision, Mission, Opportunities, Competitor information, Performance information, Technology, Values, Systems and procedures, Culture, Success experiences, Events, Policies, Accomplishments of individuals and teams, Benchmarking data, Survey results, Customer-related information including needs, Problems, Preferences, Solutions to issues, Conflicts and their sources, Organizational processes, Financial data, People/employee-related information, Accomplishments of employees
Country, World, and Humanity related	Vision for a new world, Mission and tasks required to be done to achieve world or community vision, Values, Need for sacrifices, Collective action, Movements and plans for movements, Developments, Happenings, Predictions, Projections, Development-related issues, Needs of special groups, Happenings across the world, Philosophy, Spiritual issues, Trends, Diversity Issues, Changes in society, Organizational impact on society, Societal needs, World statistics and other related information

Good managers also use a variety of opportunities for communicating different things. For example, daily and weekly meetings are good places for communicating expectations and identifying difficulties. Table 9.2 provides a more detailed look at what to communicate to who and how.

TABLE 9.2

Target of communication	What to communicate	Medium/situation to communicate
To Juniors or subordinates and other staff down the line	Expectations, tasks, targets, goals, results, challenges, opportunities, vision and values of the company, policies and processes, changes, work procedures, culture, norms, etc.	Circulars, performance management systems, training programmes, orientation sessions, daily, weekly, monthly and other periodic meetings, internet memos, web site messages and informal sessions, vision and value workshops, newsletters
Boss, seniors and top management	Views, opinions, suggestions, difficulties, support requirements, thoughts and ideas	Performance planning and review discussions, daily and weekly meetings, concept papers, task forces and committees where opportunities are available, suggestion schemes

Colleagues and internal customers	Expectations, compliments for help and assistance provided, assistance required, support requirements	Memos, notes, inter-departmental meetings, brain storming sessions, specially requested informal meetings, newsletters
External customers, suppliers	product innovations, usages, services, expectations	Memos, notes, informal discussions, telephone calls, SMSs, greetings, special bulletins, newsletters
Public at large, investors	Company performance, accomplishments, technological and other changes, innovations	Newsletters, newspaper advertisements, websites, video films, investor meetings, special bulletins and other communications

HOW MANAGERS COMMUNICATE

Any textbook on communication will say that communication is a two-way process. It involves the sender, a receiver, a message, and the medium through which it is transmitted. All managers thus are not just communicators but receivers of information. Here is a more detailed look at how the four types of managers both give and send information.

Doers

Doer managers, in varying degrees, take but don't give information.

They take for granted the goals, tasks, and methods given to them and follow them blindly and perhaps faithfully.

Blind doer: This person does things blindly without even attempting to understand what is required of them. They communicate very little. At the bottom of the continuum they may not even seek clarifications and take everything they're given for granted. They receive distorted communication and interpret the message by their seniors, juniors, customers, and colleagues in the way that suits them.

Understanding doer: This kind of manager seeks clarification on the tasks they are expected to do. They do not take the instructions for granted and seek as much information as possible before beginning or at each step. They require continuous guidance and instructions, sometimes detailed instructions.

Questioning doer: This kind of manager not only attempts to understand everything they've been told, but also questions what is and is not acceptable. Perhaps an achiever in the making.

Quiet doer: This kind of manager seeks clarification when required, talks less but quietly accomplishes whatever asked to do. Once accomplished they keep quiet until asked. They may not even tell the boss if they have completed a task. They perhaps feel that if they announce a task has been completed, there will be more work assigned to them or they might feel a general lethargy to share information.

Talker doer: This kind of manager usually talks more than they produce. They do not do much beyond what is asked to be done but communicate all the time about their views, accomplishments, etc.

Shirker: This kind of a person shirks their work and does not do things on time. They constantly look for excuses and constraints. They have little to communicate apart from complaints, problems, and issues.

LEADERS DO NOT LISTEN

Good communication also requires good listening skills. However, Shrinivas Pandit (2001), after surveying a large number of leaders in India, came to the conclusion that 'leaders do not listen'. This was based on his finding that the leaders he interviewed were so obsessed with their vision that they often do not listen to others' point of view once they make up their mind (see chapter 5 on leadership).

Achievers

Achievers constantly communicate. They give instructions and try to understand problems. They try to ascertain from their juniors if they have understood their tasks and roles and also try to influence them to stretch their goals and apply their talent.

Non-communicating achievers: These are the managers who set high standards, have a desire to achieve something but don't wish to be in the limelight. So they are silent achievers and believe that their work speaks for themselves. They are most often the losers among achievers. They are likely to be left out except under a highly competent supervisor who can notice and reward them.

Communicating achievers: This set of managers share with others whatever they have been able to accomplish. To begin with, they share their own views and not just the goals set or the tasks and targets assigned to them, their approach, the support they require, etc. They influence their juniors to set higher goals and also communicate their personal accomplishments and goals, how they worked hard and attained various goals.

FACE TO FACE WITH ACHIEVERS OF EXCELLENCE BY AHMEDABAD MANAGEMENT ASSOCIATION, JULY 2005 SPEECH DELIVERED BY HARSHA BHOGLE (IIMA 1985)

The is it following excerpt from a speech made by renowned cricket commentator Harsha Bhogle at the Ahmedabad Management Association is a good example of the kind of communication visionaries make.

Live commentary: Initially Bhogle used to compete with his guests but soon realized that you cannot comment on a reverse swing when Wasim Akram is sitting next to you. He understood that if he made them look better, he'd look better himself.

On the secret of his success and his desire for excellence:
Being in the right place at the right time to start off with, and then by believing that every day my performance has to be the best I am capable of. It's funny but you never know who is watching what and where you can make an impact. My earliest heroes were the cameramen, engineers, and replay editors. They never went wrong and I thought I had a great responsibility as the front man to live up to their standards. My desire for excellence comes from these people.

On multi-tasking and being a team player:
The key to multi-tasking though is to focus on one thing at a time and not let them mingle with each other. I think my strength

lies in being able to switch on and off, in believing that every activity that I am involved in is very special and deserves the best I can do. If I don't do something well enough I can live with it but if I haven't given it everything I have, I will be disappointed with myself. When I first got the opportunity to be a commentator at this level, I was excited as a little kid. And I am still just as enthusiastic about presenting and doing commentary on cricket. I'd like to think I am professional and humble about what I do, often the two words go together, and I believe that everyone who works on a live telecast has to be a team player.

Arrogance is the biggest stumbling block to excellence. Shane Warne [the cricketer] lived in a 'rarefied bubble', where nobody had the courage to tell him that he was doing something wrong. It is more important to surround yourself with people who are better than you. Excellence is learning from mistakes.

Visionary managers

These managers, as we know, largely communicate their dreams and vision and may stress on the possibility to achieve them, the methods to be followed (hard work, systems and processes, discipline, etc.), and the values they and the organizations or the teams they represent. On task-related communication they will focus on big things and big scenarios. Let's go back to Anil Khandelwal.

Along with transforming the working of the bank (see Case study 1), Khandelwal decided to do a rebranding exercise when he took over the Bank of Baroda. The rebranding was of a scale that had rarely been witnessed in any government-owned financial institution in India. The makeover of the external façade of the bank was completed in fifty-three days and the new brand was launched on 6 June 2005. Within a month, the rebranding was hailed as a successful initiative by all quarters with even the sceptics becoming believers. Anil Khandelwal worked internally amongst 40,000 employees to market rebranding and the other initiatives he was implementing:

> I wrote a letter to our 40,000 employees. Our marketing chief conducted a variety of seminars in various locations. The significance of the logo of the 'Baroda sun' was explained. I think the sun is a much respected symbol and calling it the Baroda sun created a sense of pride in people. And the sun itself symbolizes energy, power and brightness. So we threw a very powerful internal communication. We also brought out a house journal, especially devoted to brand launch and conducted training programmes.

Apart from that exercise, Dr Khandelwal constantly stays in touch with his employees, addressing and listening to their suggestions and this, according to him, works wonders for an organization. He thinks it is important to travel to different branches/locations for open houses and have blunt dialogues with your employees. Dr Khandelwal says that they spoke about issues such as where they had gone wrong and how they could find solutions to address those problems. The names of employees at all branches were entered into the computer system and any circulars would be individually addressed to them, to ensure that they reached out to them and employees knew about the happenings at the bank.

Missionary managers

A missionary manager's communications is largely inspirational. They may use stories, pictures, paint the picture of those differing or those that are being exploited, and the need for helping them. They appeal to the consciousness of people and try to influence them. They try to inculcate the right kind of values in others. David McClelland, the Harvard psychologist, demonstrated beyond doubt that children who are told achievement-driven stories have grown to become better entrepreneurs.

Consider the following story related by Abdul Kalam:

In 1973 Professor Satish Dhawan (chairman of the Atomic Energy and Space Commission) assigned Abdul Kalam the job of creating a satellite launch vehicle. Kalam, with a team of thousands of engineers, 10,000 workers and staff finally completed their vehicle. On the day of the launch, 17 August 1979, and the team gathered in the control centre, filled with nervousness and excitement. At eight minutes to launch, the computer took over the rocket launch. Four minutes later, it put the launch on hold. It had diagnosed a problem in the second-stage control system: there was a leakage. Kalam turned to his experts and asked them to look into the problem. They said that the igniters, that is, oxidizers, were more than sufficient and that the launch could take place even though there was a leakage. So Kalam put the rocket in manual mode. The rocket took off. It was a beautiful launch and in the first stage the rocket seemed to be in fine shape. Then within moments of reaching the second stage, it went into a spin. Kalam knew he had lost the rocket system. Within a few seconds, instead of putting the satellite into orbit, the whole system fell in the Bay of Bengal. It was a failure.

Professor Satish Dhawan came into Kalam's room and asked him to join him for a press conference. There were hundreds of reporters gathered and they asked a lot of questions. One reporter asked, 'How can you put 20 crores in the Bay of Bengal?' Professor Dhawan admitted failure but he took the responsibility for it. Exactly a year later, Kalam did another satellite launch. This time it was successful, and Dhawan asked Kalam to conduct the press conference. He had taken the burden of failure, but handed the success to Kalam and his team.

This episode clearly indicates how good managers can empower others through their communication. In passing the credit to Abdul Kalam through his communication to the external world, Satish Dhawan also helped build a future leader. In narrating this story Dr Kalam is also communicating to the young students and the outside world the importance of empowering leadership. Effective managers should aim for empowering communication.

FACTORS THAT AFFECT COMMUNICATION

However we choose to communicate, we must be aware that there are two factors that will affect the way we do it. The first is our cultural context, the second is our personality.

Culture

Hendrik Hofstede is an influential Dutch organizational sociologist, who studied the interactions between national and organizational cultures. Hofstede's study demonstrated that there are national and regional cultural groupings that affect the behaviour of societies and organizations, and that these are persistent across time.

In his most recent book, *Outliers*, Malcolm Gladwell looks at how cultures affect communication. Referring to research by Hofstede, he outlines three cultural variables: tolerance for ambiguity or uncertainty avoidance, individualism-collectivism, and power distance. Individualism-collectivism deals with how much people in a country are expected to look after themselves. The US tops the list and the absence of nationalized health insurance in the country (until recently) is an example of this. Uncertainty avoidance deals with the extent to which a person or a culture is tolerant of ambiguity. Those who have low tolerance for ambiguity would like everything to be clearly told to them. They feel uncomfortable going to a school that is not known, or buying an item that is not new, or attending a programme that has not been fully detailed out.

Power distance deals with the extent to which hierarchy and those with power are respected. Employees not being encouraged to disagree with their managers, the extent to which older people and those in power are feared, and the level to which powerful people are given special privileges are some of the indicators of power distance. While power distance is a cultural variable, it varies in individuals of the same culture. Gladwell's analysis of air crashes in countries across the world including Korea and New York in the last three decades indicates very convincingly that the inability of the co-pilots or the first officer to communicate clearly and assertively with the commanding pilot about the targets or runways or impending problems is due to power distance.

Thus, culture and personality seem to influence communication content and style. Some people and cultures tend to communicate things in an unclear and subtle way. For example, the Japanese believe in subtle communication and Americans believe in straight-forward and fact-based exchanges. Their cultures promote these. In India there are many cultural variations. Humility as a virtue is stressed in certain families, particularly in rural areas, and as a result an individual's power of expression may not develop. In other families assertive communication is encouraged.

Edward T. Hall classifies culture into two categories. *High-context cultures* are those where long-lasting relationships and spoken agreements are valued, insiders and outsiders are clearly distinguished. There is no business without friendship and credibility is attained through relationships. Agreements are founded on trust and negotiations slow and ritualistic. India is one of these countries. In *low-context cultures*, such as Germany or the US, shorter relationships are valued and they are less dependent on friendships in business. Credibility is attained through expertise and performance, agreements are by legal contract, and negotiations are efficient.

Personality

The MBTI dimension also has an impact on the nature of communication (see chapter 4 on teamwork for a full explanation of this concept). Introverts naturally are more hesitant communicators, as opposed to extroverts. Extroverts also tend to form various forms of networks as they derive energy from other people. The intuitive person may be able to absorb more 'invisible' information than a sensing person. The feeling person may respond to the feelings of others and take decisions on the basis of people and their emotions while those who are the thinking type respond to logical communication. The perceiving person might speak freely from the heart while judgemental people may like to prepare their speech.

If you are an introvert and a sensing, thinking and judging type (ISTJ) you are less likely to communicate with your heart and need planning. You might find it better to communicate in writing than by speaking. If you are an ENFP type you may be a more relaxed, happy-go-lucky personality but as a result may communicate far too much, and sometimes unnecessarily. You may therefore need someone to help you organize your thoughts to have maximum impact. A number of senior managers and CEOs use executive coaches to enhance their communication skills and impact.

Credibility

As we know, effective managers communicate a lot. This requires them to be visible—in the media, or in their organization, at talks, etc. However, high visibility does not necessarily lead to credibility. The little they say is of value.

On a 10 point scale of credibility and visibility, effective managers should aim to be very high on credibility and moderate on visibility. Doer managers do not even attempt to be visible. Their credibility comes from hard work and by following instructions and guidelines. Achievers become both visible and credible as they are leaders in the making. Visionary managers need to be high on visibility and also on credibility. It is important for managers to establish their credibility before they can become more visible. Managers who become highly visible but have low credibility, disappear quickly. Missionaries are highly credible as they establish their credibility through personal example and a values-driven life.

PERFORMACE REVIEW DISCUSSION AS A MEANS OF COMMUNICATION

As I've said before, PRDs are excellent tools to aid communication. Studies report that managers hate appraisals and do not give adequate time to conduct a PRD. Yet management textbooks go out of their way to suggest to managers that good and effective managers spend time and conduct PRDs meticulously so that their juniors develop through the communication they pass on to them. It is said that a PRD helps develop mutuality and understanding, and empowers the junior. It also gives an opportunity to the senior to communicate his expectations to junior and encourage them to perform better than before.

Networking

Effective managers are great networkers. Networking is the ability to establish, maintain, and utilize connections with individuals and groups and communicate and benefit from them in a variety of ways. Networking is a skill that emanates from an attitude to learn and remain connected. People with networking attitudes like to establish and maintain networks. These networks may be professional or social and personal. Today a variety of methods are available to network. These include:

▶ Member ship of internet-based networks like Twitter, Yahoogroups, Linkedin, Facebook, Orkut, blogs, etc.
▶ Social clubs like the Lions Club, etc.
▶ Professional bodies and associations: Local management Associations, NIPM, National HRD Network, ISTD, AIMA, CSI, ORSI, etc.
▶ Informal networks established by the candidate himself such as his friends circles, clubs, associations
▶ Dealer networks, customer networks, supplier networks
▶ Employee unions and associations
▶ Cultural associations and networks such as associations for different states like the Bengal Cultural Association

In the initial years of naukri.com, Sanjiv Bhikchandani made use of a variety of networks for establishing and popularizing the website. He became a member of the National HRD Network, got on to the board and attended their meetings regularly and this helped him a great deal as HRD professionals are potential users of naukri.com. He also got his team to network with many other agencies and organizations that conduct workshops and seminars and co-sponsored them.

Networking is a great way to expand the world you live in. And whether you're talking about formal networking events, continuing education classes, social gatherings or other functions, they're all prime opportunities to meet new people and/or further relations with those you would like to know better. (Barry Zweibel business and personal life coach and founder of GottaGettaCoach! Incorporated)

Ways to network

Most of us would rather spend an evening with people we know and are comfortable with rather than go up to a stranger and introduce ourselves. But remember the key to networking is to meet new people. Here are some tips to make things easier:

▶ If you're shy, it is always easier to introduce yourself to a stranger who is standing alone in a gathering.

▶ Don't worry about having to be witty or entertaining. Just ask them simple questions about themselves—who they are, what they do, who they work for, who they know, what they hate about these types of parties, etc. People always open up to those who show interest in them.

▶ Ask for business cards so that (a) you can remember their names, (b) you have a record of who you talked to and how to reach them, and (c) you can use the back of the card to write down what you want to remember and what might be a relevant next step to take.

You can also turn an acquaintance into a friend:

▶ Always share information about yourself and be creative about what you want to share. The more you open up, the more they will.

▶ As mentioned above, people always open up to those taking

an interest in them. Ask them questions about themselves, think about what you might like to know about them.

▶ Go to the next step and organize another interaction—a meal, a drink, a phone call, etc.

▶ One of the simplest tricks to make friends is to give them your undivided attention.

If things get awkward, try the following:

▶ Move on if the conversation gets stuck. If you can't think of what to say, try 'Excuse me, there's someone I want to meet (that person standing alone over there)'. Another trick is to ask them if they'd like to meet anyone else in the room that you can introduce them to. Or point to someone else in the room and walk with them to the third person.

▶ If you have forgotten someone's name, don't worry. Simply say, 'Remind me of your name again' and then tell them yours.

(*Source:* http://www.questcareer.com/networking_skills.htm)

CONCLUSION

Leadership is the art and science of influencing others to do things you want done and leave them with a feeling that they have done what they wanted to do. Communication and networking are the main tools through which managers and leaders influence the world around them. Unless a manager communicates his vision, values, expectations, the people who work with him may lack direction and commitment. It is also essential for managers to advertise their abilities and achievements. The key to effective communication is not how much we communicate but how credibly we do so. Moreover, as we climb up the four rungs of managers our communications become more values- and vision led. Visionary and missionary leaders use stories to connect and inspire others and through these they communicate the missions and goals of their organizations or society at large.

APPENDIX

VISIBILITY–CREDIBILITY AND NETWORKING SKILLS INVENTORY TEST

Assess yourself on the 7 point scale given below on each of the items listed.

7 = Always (100 percent)

6 = Almost always (90 percent)

5 = Most of the time or most frequently (70 percent)

4= Sometimes or somewhat frequently (50 percent)

3 = Occasionally (30 percent)

2 = Rarely or once in a while (10 percent)

1 = Never (0 percent)

☐ V-How frequently are you noticed by most people who live in your neighbourhood or colony?

☐ V-How frequently do you make it a point to make your views known on various issues at your workplace?

☐ V-How frequently is your presence noticed? at your workplace

☐ V-To what extent do you make your views loudly in a visible way at your workplace?

☐ V-To what extent do you volunteer to give your views and opinions when problems arise at your workplace?

☐ V-To what extent do your friends and colleagues seem to miss you when you are away on tour?

☐ V-When you participate in debates and discussions how much are you noticed?

☐ V-To what extent do you volunteer to give your views and opinions to your boss?

☐ V-When you are involved in group discussions how frequently do you participate or make your points?

☐ V-When you participate in discussions with people how frequently do you speak loudly so that everyone hears you?

☐ C- In your family to what extent do your family members seek your views on various issues?

☐ C- To what extent do your boss and other seniors seem to use your knowledge and opinions?

☐ C- To what extent do your friends seem to take into consideration your views and knowledge?

☐ C- To what extent do people at your workplace seem to rely on the information you give?

☐ C- To what extent do you think the people you interact with give an impression that they rely on what you say?

☐ C- When you participate in conversations how much of what you say is listened to attentively by those whom you are addressing?

☐ C-In your conversations to what extent does people you meet outside your workplace rely on the information you give?

☐ C-To what extent do you consider yourself a credible contributor?

☐ C-To what extent do your seniors at the workplace seem to seek your opinions?

☐ C-To what extent do your juniors seem to value your views?

SCORING FOR THE VISIBILITY–CREDIBILITY QUESTIONNAIRE

Visibility

The first ten items are items dealing with visibility, that is, the extent to which you are seen by others at your workplace, in your family, society, and neighbourhood in and groups discussions and other activities. Add (sum) your scores on the first ten items, that is, item numbers 1 to 10. If your scores are above 40 you are a highly visible individual. Scores near to 70 indicate an extremely high visibility or highly seen.

Credibility

The next ten items, that is, item numbers 11 to 20, deal with the extent to which you are perceived as a credible individual. That is the extent to which what you say is believed or heard. Scores above 40 indicate a high degree of credibility. Scores nearer to 70 indicate a very high credibility.

You could be a highly visible and highly credible individual, that is, both seen and heard. Or you could be a low visibility and high credibility individual. That is a person not seen but heard. If your visibility and credibility scores are both low then you are neither seen nor heard. If your scores are high visibility and low credibility then you are seen but not heard.

NETWORKING COMPETENCE

Please answer the following in 'Yes' or 'No'

☐ I enjoy meeting new people in my profession.

☐ I make it a point to maintain contact with all my professional acquaintances.

☐ I exchange my visiting card and invite email and other communications from all those whom I meet at social gatherings.

☐ I make it a point to attend conferences and seminars for my professional growth.

☐ I am a member of some of the relevant professional associations and bodies in my profession.

☐ I maintain regular contact with all my childhood friends.

☐ I maintain contact with all my friends and acquaintances through linked or other networks.

☐ I am a member of most networking groups like Yahoo! Groups and other groups.

☐ I am a regular subscriber to professional journals.

☐ I make it a point to keep in touch with developments in my field by reading magazines, journals and other publications.

☐ I make it a point to attend most meetings and gatherings of professional bodies.

☐ I find it easy to make new friends and acquaintances.

☐ I can readily and without hesitation initiate discussion with strangers in my profession.

☐ I am considered a well-networked individual.

☐ I have a lot of social acquaintances.

☐ I have a lot of professional contacts.

☐ I maintain regular contact with my contacts.

☐ I am known to reply to my mails promptly by all my networked members.

Count the number of items you have marked 'Yes'. The higher the number of 'Yes' items, the more networked an individual you are. It is simple to enhance your networking competence. Just start doing what you have tick-marked as 'No' among the above-mentioned items.

REFERENCES

Cappelli and team in HBR, March 2010, P. 95

Pandit, Shrinivas (2001), *Thought Leaders*, New Delhi: Tata McGraw-Hill.
   http://www.ibscdc.org/executiveinterviews/Q&A_with_Dr_
   Anil_K_Khandelwal_3.htm

http://74.125.153.132/search?q=cache%3A8MHNjWozs54J%3Awww.ril.
   com%2Fdownloads%2Fpdf%2FDr%2520APJ%2520Abdul%2520Ka
   lam.PDF+APJ+abdul+kalam+outstanding+qualities&hl=en&gl=i
   n)

http://www.questcareer.com/networking_skills.htm

10

Motivation and Leadership Styles

N.M. Desai, former chairman of Larsen & Toubro, famously remarked that if one of Mumbai's red buses were to knock him down, there would be at least six others who could readily take charge of Larsen & Toubro. Good leaders help build others as leaders. In this book we have looked at the skills and qualities you need to become an effective manager. The final weapon you need in your armoury is the ability to create other leaders and managers. How do you motivate your team to become leaders? And what are the most common leadership styles Indian managers adopt? These are the questions we try to answer in this chapter.

WHAT MOTIVATES LEADERSHIP?

Henry Murray, an early nineteenth-century psychologist, tried to assess the inner beliefs and motivations of people using a test called the Thematic Apperception Test (TAT). Murray felt that people often may not recognize their own motives if they are not conscious of them or cannot articulate them clearly. He developed a series of twenty pictures and asked subjects to write stories in response to them. In writing these stories, people often revealed their own desires and motivations. Later David McClelland, a Harvard psychologist, identified three of Murray's 'motives' as significant factors behind the success or failure of managers:

▶ Achievement motivation: The need to do better than other people, set new standards, engage in doing something unique or distinguished. Some people are driven by their hunger to achieve. All successful managers are motivated by this.
▶ Affiliation motivation: The need to establish relationships, maintain them or restore them. Some managers work actively to build meaningful relationships. Public relations officers, front office assistants, marketing, sales, counsellors, teachers, etc. All are suitable jobs for individuals with high affiliation motivation.
▶ Power motivation: The need to influence, dominate, and overpower, win an argument or establish supremacy over others. 'Personal power' aims at empowering the self, but 'social power' is used for the benefit of others.

Udai Pareek added another factor to this list which he called the 'extension motivation'. By this he meant that in countries like India managers were often motivated by their need to help others and work for a larger cause. Two other work-related motivations are independence and dependence—which indicate how much working independently or being guided motivates a manager. An individual with high dependence motivation may prefer a bureaucratic set-up where there are many norms. Some of these jobs include being a civil servant, administrative officer, police officer, etc. Conversely, a manager with greater independence motivation is likely to prefer an environment that is less regulated.

The four types of managers we described earlier have different combinations of motivational profiles. Achievers are high on power and achievement motivations and low on extension motivation. Visionaries are high on achievement, and also on power. Their power needs are the desire to influence others. Missionaries are high on extension motivation.

Case study 1: Anu Aga

Anu Aga, who transformed her company Thermax after a series of personal tragedies, is a good example of a manager motivated first by achievement, then by social power, and (ultimately) by extension motivation.

Thermax was started by Anu Aga's father. Her husband, Rohinton Aga, transformed it from a small, family-run business into a professionally run engineering organization of formidable repute. When he died unexpectedly of a massive stroke in 1996, Anu Aga had to take over Thermax.

Here is the set of events according to her description given in *Forbes* magazine: (http://business.in.com/column/zen-garden/anu-aga-a-house-by-the-river/2362/1).

> The board met in two days and suggested I be the chairperson. I wasn't comfortable assuming this responsibility. Personally, I felt that I didn't deserve the position and I felt very small within myself. I kept feeling that it is the 62 percent shares which we have that has given me this position, and not my merit. We had gone public a year earlier and our share was quoted at 7 times the issue price. In those days, it was very good—my husband had done a superb job.
>
> And then came the downturn. My company didn't do well at all. My executives kept telling me that when the market is down, we are bound to be affected. Have faith in us and if you, the largest shareholder, can have patience, everything will be okay. I went along with that.

One day, I got an anonymous letter from a shareholder. It said, 'I do not know about your finances, Mrs Aga—you may have enough or may not care for money, but you have let your shareholders down'. I suddenly woke up! You can see how un-businesslike I was. Though we were a public limited company, it hadn't dawned on me that I had responsibility towards others who were not majority shareholders. I couldn't sleep that night. I felt I had let down people. That was one thing which my husband and I were very keen on—we will not knowingly let down people.

Anu Aga started a full-scale reform, aided by Arun Maira of Boston Consulting Group. Between 1996 and 2004, Thermax shed its unrelated investments in areas from software to drinking water; it dramatically reconstituted the board to bring in a new perspective, and went on an enviable growth spiral. In 2004, Anu Aga decided to hand over the legacy to the future. She had taken over a company with a Rs 605 crore turnover. Eight years later, she passed on a Thermax with a turnover of Rs 1,281 crore to daughter Meher. Since her retirement in 2004, Anu has been involved with the social sector, deeply concerned about promoting communal harmony and nurturing education. In 2010, she was awarded the Padma Shri (Social Work) by the Government of India (Ibid.)

CAN MOTIVES BE DEVELOPED?

McClelland's work has demonstrated that it is possible to develop motivation through training. The rationale for such development is as follows:

1. Your behaviour is determined by the way you think.
2. The way you think is determined by the language you use to think.

3. If language can be influenced, thinking can be influenced and thereby so can behaviour.
4. If you want people to think like achievers, give them the language of achievement.
5. If you want them to think like reformers and extension workers give them language to think in terms of superordinate goals.

EXPECTATIONS AND THEIR EFFECT ON MOTIVATION AND PERFORMANCE

Expectations also impact motivation. Borrowing Pygmalion as an analogy, Harvard Professor Robert Rosenthal and his team conducted a series of experiments on schoolchildren. They created expectations in teachers by administering some ability tests on children and classifying them as geniuses and dullards or high and low performers. They asked the teachers to teach the two groups and discovered later that the high achiever group had done far better than the low achiever group, while in reality they were of similar abilities. The teachers treated both the groups differently and unconsciously communicated their low expectations to the low achiever group and high expectations to the high ability group. It made them conclude that our expectations have a tremendous effect (positive or negative) on our subjects and influence their performance.

This is dramatically demonstrated in an exercise most organizational behaviour professors use in management schools called 'Tower Building'.

The tower-building game was first used by Rosen and D'Andrade (1959:185–218) to study the relationship of child-rearing practices with achievement motivation.

This game was used in actual family settings, and two-year-old boys were made to play the game with their parents. This game indicated some significant findings and was later adopted for achievement motivation training.

The game is played with wooden cubes or blocks. Experience shows that cubes of about 2.5 inch dimensions are useful for the game. These cubes can be bought or constructed out of ordinary wood. Usually about twenty-five cubes are required for one group. One handkerchief or cloth is also required. Usually it takes about ten to fifteen minutes to play the game—the entire process, from understanding the game to executing it takes about an hour. The instructor asks three volunteers to play: they are to act as father, mother, and child (son or daughter). Their job is to supervise their child construct a tower placing one cube on the other. The tower should be as tall as possible and the aim of the game is for the child to place as many cubes as they can, blindfolded and using the non-dominant hand. Parents are not allowed to touch the child. Before the game begins, all three are expected to make an estimate of the number of cubes the child is likely to stack to make the tower before it falls and they are also told that an average child has been found to place ten cubes or so. The child role player also estimates how many blocks he/she can use. The figures are revealed to the three of them by the instructor. If the figures are different, they are given time to discuss and make one estimate collectively. It is only after the consensus that the child is blindfolded and asked to actually make the tower.

The game is fascinating for the different behaviours it shows—what the impact of underestimating or overestimating parents is on the child's performance, the way parents argue about the capacity of the child, the way in which the three come to a consensus about the child's capacity.

Rosen and D'Andrade established that parents who had higher expectations from their children created a climate in which children had higher achievement motivation. In the case of those parents who had lower expectations from their children in this game, it was found that their children had lower achievement motivation.

The Pygmalion phenomenon seems to work well in the family, in the classroom, and also in management at the workplace. Robert Rosenthal and Jacobson (1968, 1992) cited several cases of managers showing high performance when they were assigned to high performing teams or leaders with high expectations versus those assigned to low performing leaders and teams showing low performance in tune with the expectations. These studies have concluded that expectations of superiors, seniors, and other significant people in our surroundings have a high effect on our performance.

A corollary to this finding is that motivation and particularly achievement motivations can be developed by setting the right kind of expectations for employees. The same is true with extension motivation.

HOW TO BUILD A MOTIVATIONAL CLIMATE

▶ **Create a climate of independence and interdependence**: Do not interfere unless it becomes necessary. Trust your subordinates and give them enough freedom to plan their own ways of doing their work. They are expected to solve problems and to ask for guidance only when it is needed. By encouraging initiative, and supporting experimentation and teamwork, a supervisor also helps satisfy subordinates' need for belonging, affection, and security.

Some supervisors allow their subordinates to come to them continually for advice and guidance and, in the extreme case, may not allow them to do anything on their own. If every subordinate needs to check with the supervisor and obtain approval before taking any action, the supervisor is creating a climate of dependence. Subordinates will be utterly unable to take any initiative. When problems arise, subordinates may hesitate to look for solutions, and when something goes wrong, they may not accept responsibility. Learning from experience becomes difficult because they are so used to turning to their supervisor for advice. Thus, the supervisor becomes burdened with responsibilities and problem-solving. This wastes both the supervisor and subordinates' time.

► **Create a climate of competition through recognition of good work**: Employees look forward to being rewarded for good or innovative work. Financial rewards are not always necessary; even a word of appreciation and acknowledgement has great motivational value. Although indiscriminate appreciation loses its value, a supervisor should not withhold appreciation until the formal appraisal reports. Many other ways of recognizing good work can be very rewarding—praising someone in the presence of others, giving them increased responsibility, and writing letters of recommendation when necessary. Such recognition and public acknowledgement helps employees to value their work and derive a sense of satisfaction and feeling of importance. These go a long way in motivating them to work better. They even create a sense of healthy competition among employees.

► **Create a climate of approachability and problem-solving rather than avoidance**: Some supervisors approach problems with confidence, face them squarely, work out mechanisms to solve them (often with the help of others), and constantly work to overcome problems. They derive satisfaction from this struggle—even if the outcomes are not always positive—and they inspire subordinates to imitate their initiative. Some supervisors, however, see everything as a potential headache and postpone solutions to problems or delegate them to someone else. Workers are also quick to imitate this avoidance.

▶ **Create an ideal climate through personal example**: Just as supervisors are imitated in their approaches to problem-solving, they are viewed as models for other work habits. In fact, the supervisor's styles may filter down the hierarchy and influence employees several grades below. Therefore, good supervision and good work habits make the supervisor's job easier in two ways: his/her own tasks are completed more efficiently and a climate is created for making the department or unit more efficient.

▶ **Motivate people through guidance and counselling**: The foregoing discussions point out some general strategies that supervisors can use in creating the proper motivational climate for their subordinates. However, because individual workers have individual needs, individual counselling can also motivate subordinates. Within a group of workers, a supervisor may find very efficient workers, poor workers, problem creators, cooperative employees, and so on. Therefore, the supervisor should be sensitive to their individual differences.

LEADERSHIP STYLES

A manager's efficacy depends not just on his technical competence, functional knowledge, and management skills, but also on his management style. This stems from his ideas about how people need to be managed and led. If you are not sensitive to the emotional needs of subordinates and do not use the appropriate styles of supervision and leadership, there is a great danger of crippling the growth of your subordinates. For instance, if you are an authoritarian manager, you may arouse strong negative reactions by continually dictating terms to capable subordinates, but might prove successful with subordinates who are dependent or are absolute beginners in their roles. Similarly, a democratic manager may be liked by capable subordinates, but perhaps thought incompetent by dependent subordinates. You need to realize what kind of behaviour you need to adopt with different groups of people.

What kind of leaders do Indian managers see themselves as? How do they represent their thoughts about leadership? These were the questions I sought to answer when I worked with David McClelland at Harvard. Studies of Indian managers led us to conclude that they adopted one of three management styles:

▶ The paternalistic style
▶ The authoritarian style
▶ The self-dispensing style

The paternalistic style

The paternalistic style may also be called benevolent management. Managers who adopt the paternalistic style see themselves as father figures and providers of resources. Their power to give makes them sensitive to the needs of others. They tend to be good-natured and welfare driven, are charismatic and resourceful, and go out of their way to bail out subordinates who might have gotten themselves into trouble. They are instinctively protective of teams working under them and are well loved throughout the organization. The paternalistic management style has been the bedrock of a number of Indian business empires. Jamshedji Tata's vision of social welfare shaped the formation of his company, and subsequent efforts such as actively promoting benefits for his employees and eventually building an entire town for them is one example.

In the early stages of its growth, south Indian conglomerate Murugappa group, had a tradition of posting young family members as apprentices to work under an 'Agent' (their name for branch managers) who is a paid employee of the family business. The instruction to the Agent used to be to treat the family member or Murugappa family like anyone else and have the young family members do all the work. The Agent was assessed on how well he trained the family member. As the young person matured enough to handle the branch, he would be posted to another branch as an Agent so that he was never the boss of the person who groomed him. This was the respect shown to the professional employee. It is said that G.D. Birla used to know every employee by name and would frequently enquire about the family and also provide work opportunities to family members of current employees. In the paternalistic leadership styles jobs used to be created to employ the relatives of loyal employees and take care of them. Even today the Birla group builds temples, clubs, and schools in townships to provide what they feel is the right kind of family atmosphere.

This style was practised in the nineteenth century, although today it is used by certain visionaries and missionaries who genuinely believe that the best way to manage employees or juniors is by treating them like their own children. This style continues to be practised today by a good number of managers who were socialized by their bosses with a paternalistic style. It is not uncommon to find senior managers with the philosophy that the best way to manage employees is by treating them affectionately and like their own children. Such beliefs lead the manager to be warm to his juniors, pick up and support continuously those who are loyal to them, share continuously the employee's concerns, reward those loyal to them, and also assign challenging tasks for those loyal to them. In the 360 degree feedback we counted over 8,000 such senior managers across the country. This style of treating employees is the second most frequently used after the professional or developmental style.

Take the example of manager Satyaprakash (name changed for anonymity) who was assessed by his juniors. This manager talked more at meetings, came to the rescue of his juniors whenever they made mistakes, and would get involved in policing conflicts within the office. Although he consulted only a few of those who were close to him and rewarded them by giving them selectively challenging goals, almost all his juniors rated him as a warm, affectionate manager who had generated high morale, learning and satisfaction in the department. Most of his juniors also indicated that they appreciated this style and felt personally loyal to him. Who does not enjoy a paternalistic leader who is always there to protect you when you are in trouble?

Yet research shows that those leaders who protect you and earn your loyalty, in the long run may unknowingly deprive you of learning on your own from your mistakes. The organization also may not be able to manage particularly well in the absence of such leaders. As employees get accustomed to being dependent, they are unable to take initiative without their managers to guide them.

Use the benevolent style	Sustained use leads to
▶ When the employee is new	▶ Personal loyalty to the leader
▶ When the task is new and relationships are important	▶ Enjoyment of work due to a good rapport with the boss
▶ With employees who are accustomed to paternalistic leaders, until they begin to adjust gradually to other kinds of leadership	▶ Dependence on the leader
	▶ Feeling of loss in the manager's absence
	▶ Inability to get along with other professionals or systems-driven managers
▶ With dependent employees who need more care and attention	▶ Those closest to the manager enjoy the best learning experience

The authoritarian style (also known as critical style)

Authoritarian managers reprimand, criticize, and direct. They often see themselves as disciplinarians and constantly supervise and micro-manage their subordinates, with damaging consequences for employee morale. Such managers spend a large part of their time finding faults, lose their temper easily when juniors make mistakes, do not share information freely with others, and try to dominate meetings. They believe that if they are lenient, employees will take liberties and may not work sincerely. Authoritarian leaders like to determine most policies and strategies unilaterally, and decide on the composition and tasks of teams. Such managers are commonly found in organizations that have recently turned around, or are in the process of being turned around. Manager Gupta whom we encountered in chapter 3 (Interpersonal engagement, mentoring and trust) is a good example. Often, particularly in large organizations with many different rungs of managers, lower-level managers may be authoritarian. The need to be seen as a boss is particularly high at the lower levels.

In 1964, Blake and Mouton developed the concept of task-oriented leadership, which may be regarded as a subtype of authoritarian leaders. For these kinds of managers, the concern for the task becomes so overwhelming that the human aspect is likely to be neglected in dealings with subordinates. A task-oriented supervisor may frequently question or remind subordinates about their tasks, warn them about deadlines, or show a great deal of concern about details. Employees who work with an excessively task-oriented supervisor often develop negative attitudes about their work and their supervisor. They may be motivated only by fear and may feel job dissatisfaction. They may develop short cuts that, in the long run, affect the organization's performance.

Impact of authoritarian leadership style

Use the authoritarian style	Sustained use leads to
▶ With undisciplined subordinates ▶ When norms are being violated and personal goals have taken precedence over organizational goals ▶ When indiscipline is on the rise ▶ When a turnaround and some short-term goal orientation and systems are needed	▶ Feelings of incompetence on the part of subordinates ▶ Resentment towards boss ▶ Job tension ▶ Inclination to leave the boss or job ▶ High energy levels spent on the job due to tension and fear ▶ Low self-esteem

There are instances, however, where we need a critical leadership style. For example, during the early 1980s the EID Parry group was running into losses. The Murugappa group was asked to take it over and M.V. Subbaiah was made the vice-chairman of the company. He observed that there was an easygoing atmosphere in the company, lack of accountability, and a fair number of cases of senior managers not doing their job and being dishonest. After he took over, Subbaiah introduced many cost-cutting measures, sacked a large number of employees (despite the strong presence of unions) including senior managers and brought in discipline. He describes his own style as that of a hard and tough taskmaster without any scruples. There was a complete turnaround of the company in a matter of three to four years.

The self-dispensing style

Self-dispensing managers are concerned with building their juniors as potential leaders. They are democratic, respect their juniors' decisions, and create opportunities for them to do things independently and experience a sense of ownership and empowerment. People building is the first step—and as a self-dispensing leader you genuinely need to believe that employees are capable of great things, and it is your responsibility to create conditions where they can work, thrive, and feel a powerful sense of accomplishment. Competent workers who have this kind of supervision are likely to feel increasingly confident about their work. They function better both independently and interdependently with their colleagues. All modern organizations that take competent people need to nurture self-dispensing leadership at the top levels. Unless they do, the effects on the organizations may be crippling.

It is said that Dr Vikram Sarabhai's style used to be that of a self-dispensing leader. He would find competent people and hand over leadership to them. That is the secret behind his being able to build so many institutions like the Ahmedabad Textile Research Association (ATIRA), Physical Research Laboratories (PRL), Indian Space Research Organisation (ISRO), Indian Institute of Management, Ahmedabad (IIMA) and many others. Dr V. Krishnamurthy, the chairman and CEO of Bharat Heavy Electrical Ltd, (BHEL), Maruti Udyog, SAIL, and other organizations, is an example of a CEO who was able to groom large numbers of leaders. Unilever and its Indian arm, Hindustan Unilever, also have a strong self-dispensing culture and this has contributed to its reputation as an organization that breeds leaders.

When a family-owned business decides to hand over its organization to a professional manager, it is using the self-dispensing style at an organizational level. Well-known examples of this kind of handover are of Anu Aga, chairman of Thermax and the Murugappa group. Kumar Mangalam Birla is another example of a self-dispensing leader who has been able to expand the Aditya Birla Group's business after his father's death because of this approach.

The employee-oriented supervisor is a subtype of the self-dispensing manager and presents a contrast to the task-oriented supervisors discussed above. This kind of manager makes a conscious attempt to keep subordinates in good humour, and he frequently enquires about problems that team members may be experiencing. You need to be careful though that your subordinates do not begin to perceive you as too lenient, and end up taking advantage of your concern for their well-being.

Besides developing the skills and morale of individual team members, self-dispensing managers look to become what McClelland and Burnham (1976) call 'institutional supervisors'.

They try hard, over time, to improve the department or unit as a whole. As a manager, this is certainly what you should aspire towards. The following are some of the principal characteristics of institutional supervisors:

▶ They are organization oriented and tend to join organizations and feel responsible for building them
▶ They are disciplined at work and enjoy their work
▶ They are willing to sacrifice some of their own self-interest for the welfare of the organization
▶ They have a keen sense of justice
▶ They have a low need for affiliation, a high need to influence others for social or organizational goals, and a disciplined or controlled way of expressing their power needs
▶ Impact of self-dispensing style

Use the self-dispensing style	Sustained use leads to
▶ With competent employees ▶ When it is a mature organization ▶ With technical and R&D departments ▶ With those who need to be kept independent and protected from other transactional costs	▶ Independence or interdependence ▶ Teamwork, provided it is moderated well ▶ High degree of learning ▶ Professionalism and systems orientation ▶ High satisfaction ▶ Empowerment

The adaptable manager

The need to be adaptable and to recognize the uses of each of the above styles is among the things that make you a better manager.

No single supervisory style is universally effective. The efficacy of your style depends on your employees, the nature of the task, and various other factors. If a new employee does not know much about the work to be done, a benevolent approach will help. In such a situation, a critical supervisor may be frightening and a self-dispensing supervisor would cause bewilderment. On the other hand, a capable employee may feel most comfortable with a self-dispensing style of supervision and resent a benevolent supervisor who continually gives unwanted advice. Employees with low self-discipline could probably be developed best by critical supervision, at least intermittently. Continuous critical supervision, however, is unlikely to be effective. Flexibility and perceptiveness about when to use each style are useful attributes for leaders or supervisors.

The same Mr Subbaiah who used an 'authoritarian' or directive style for the turnaround of EID Parry, changed his style a few years later. He conducted an employee satisfaction survey which indicated that he needed to rely more on internal talent rather than hire from outside. A few years later he shifted to a self-dispensing style by employing professional managers to run various companies and retiring from executive positions. As Mr Subbaiah concluded, '[Management] is a matter of managing paradoxes. You should be able to understand the paradox existing at that time and manage it. The same hand that can slap also can hug. That is the paradox' (personal comment made to the author).

CASE STUDY

Mahendra N. Patel

Mahendra Patel is a good example of a development leader with high adaptability. This 1949 born CMD of Mamata Machinery Pvt. Ltd has the credit of setting up nineteen companies and around two dozen factories. The Mamata Group was set up in 1994 as joint ventures with world leaders in different machinery fields as well as start other projects. All Mamata Group operating companies are profit making and dividend paying. Currently total Group sales are more than Rs 6,000 million a year. Patel has an all-round, hands-on, wide experience in setting up of new Greenfield and successful engineering industries in India. His expertise joint ventures with foreign companies, including government formalities, marketing, finance, organization, team building, technology transfer and absorption, etc. is evident from his wide entrepreneurial spectrum.

Patela is involved in a number of community activities which include his role as a permanent trustee of Vatva GIDC Industries Association Charitable Trust. During his term as president of AMA, established the Centre for International Trade and American Corner, revamped the remuneration system, increased the activities in many spheres of learning, and increased the financial corpus threefold. Dr Rangarajan, then Governor of Reserve Bank of India decorated him with the Outstanding Manager of the year 1993, from Ahmedabad Management Association.

Patel is known for his integrity and trustworthiness. He feels that what you want others to perform, should first be performed by yourself as an illustration of the expected behaviour. His years in the industry have made him highly skilled in dealing with people from different cultures—especially Westerners. People consider his articulation and presentation skills to be above average. He is a developer of people, managers, and entrepreneurs. He believes in multiplying. Making a hundred more entrepreneurs in a country like India would have multifaceted benefits and a step towards fighting against the industrial problems the country is facing. His toil in making Mamata a world-class pioneer in manufacturing of bag making machines with indigenously developed technology and other packaging machinery was the result of the motivation behind putting in much effort and expertise. Mamata currently exports more than 60 percent of its production, worldwide.

Empathy for people, listening and understanding ability, a calm and serene attitude (his work of anger follow a six sigma approach) are a part of his personality. Empowering people through mentoring and delegation, keeping up to date with latest developments in the concerned industry and sharing these with all customers are the management mantras which he believes in religiously.

Over the years, he has made a strong loyalty among his employees. There are many cases in the Mamata Group who started their career there and would retire from there only. He follows a very simple strategy for retaining the employees. He believes if an employee has served in one position for good two-three years, it is time for his/her relocation and promotion. This holds good for employees at all levels. You can find people who joined Mamata as peons and are now purchase officers or accountants or junior cashiers. The first peon who joined the company is now the chief accountant in the travel agency business of the group. There is freedom to study, pursue courses/classes of your interest.

He identifies himself with a 'True leader whose people would say we got the work done ourselves!'

On being asked about the leadership in the Asian context Patel emphasizes the need to break away from the feudal, hierarchical attitudes towards subordinates/employees and treating all people in organization at all levels with respect and dignity. The most important attribute to be shared by the leaders is to trust others. They should be the facilitators and should desist from intervening with impatience or ego and give a platform for performance to the subordinates. Moreover, empowerment is meant to be real and not as lip service. He says, 'There is a need to encourage continuous learning and training for better and better professionalism in all jobs.' Transparency, integrity, and honesty are the virtues which always pay in the long run. Open and understandable systems provide greater transparency in his view. A promise which cannot be met is unethical. The tendency for short cuts or short-term gains should be banished.

On being asked about how he sees his competitors, he says 'We are in the same business, so there is no question of being competitors. We are compatriots.' He does not feel the competition, in fact he advises the employees that the other person has made a niche where we could not reach, so there is a lesson that needs to be learnt for all.

Source: Interviews from '100 Managers' Forthcoming book by T.V. Rao.

Research at TVRLS has shown the principal characteristics of the three leadership styles to be as has been depicted in the tables on the following pages.

CHARACTERISTICS OF VARIOUS LEADERSHIP STYLES

Task area	Leadership Style and its Characteristics		
	Benevolent	**Critical**	**Self-dispensing**
Goal setting or task allocation	Assigns tasks on the basis of likes and dislikes for particular people	Assigns tasks in an impersonal way, without consideration for the person and his competencies. Purely rule oriented and bureaucratic	Assigns tasks according to subordinates' competencies, with a view to provide challenging experiences in a planned way. Recognizes and respects individual differences and builds people
Management of Mistakes	Comes to the rescue and salvages the situation. Protects subordinates	Has very low tolerance. Loses temper, reprimands, criticizes and even punishes subordinates for mistakes	Helps employees to learn from mistakes. Treats mistakes as learning opportunities

Articulating vision	Has a personal vision and shares it with those close to him	Oriented towards short-term goals. Not particularly vision driven	Shares vision and enthuses others with his vision. Helps them to internalize and participate in the vision. Builds on the vision of others and incorporates the latter into his vision
Managing failures	Comes to the rescue of subordinates. Tends to favour loyal subordinates by showing more affection and warmth when dealing with their failures	Cannot tolerate failure. Reprimands and punishes	Helps people to learn from failures

Managing conflicts	Decides who is right and who is wrong, and resolves conflicts amicably	Calls both parties and expresses irritation, cites the 'rule book', loses temper or rules by fear	Encourages the conflicting parties to come together and resolve their conflicts and build capabilities of conflict resolution
Rewards and recognition	Rewards those close to him but rewards selectively	Does not reward or recognize easily. Feels that it may spoil employees	Rewards and encourages all deserving cases as and when needed. Uses recognition and various forms of rewards as empowering tools

Communicating and sharing information	Shares information selectively with those close to him	Does not share information. Feels powerful by keeping information to hemself and fears the misuse of the same by others	Shares information freely with a view to build others
Empowerment	Empowers those close to him	Does not empower anyone. Keeps all power to himself	Empowers all his subordinates
Delegation	Delegates selectively to those loyal to him	Does not delegate but supervises closely, and monitors and controls all the time	Delegates and develops people to exercise discretion
Systems use	Uses systems but modifies them to suit the favoured ones	Strict disciplinarian. Follows systems meticulously for their own sake	Systems driven. Uses systems to empower and build a lasting culture

CONCLUSION

The way we lead and motivate people is the key to our effectiveness, particularly as we go higher up in management levels. Not only do we have to be good team builders and possess strong interpersonal skills, but we also need to create strong managers and leaders for the future. The three principal leadership styles—benevolent, authoritarian, and self-dispensing—all need to be used depending on the situation and the employee. However, it is worth remembering that the visionary and missionary manager will always aim to be a self-dispensing leader, for the true aim of leadership is to create future leaders.

ASSESS YOUR LEADERSHIP OR MANAGEMENT STYLE

Assess your own leadership style using the following five sets of items. Each set has three items: (a), (b) and (c). You have to distribute six points between the three items in each set. The following options exist for each set of items:

1. If a particular item is most characteristic of you and the other two are not at all characteristic of you, in that set then you can give all '6' points to that item and '0' to the other two items in that set.
2. If you feel that two of them are equally characteristic of you and the third one is not at all characteristic of the way you do things, you can give '3' each to those two items and '0' to the item that does not describe you.
3. If one of the items describes you slightly better than the other two then you may give '4' to that particular item and

'1' each to the other two, or alternatively '3' to the item, '2' to the next best and '1' to the least characteristic item.

To sum up, each question could have the following scores:

▶ 6, 0, 0 (or 0, 6, 6 or 0, 0, 6)
▶ 5, 1, 0
▶ 4, 2, 0
▶ 3, 3, 0
▶ 3, 2, 1
▶ 4, 1, 1
▶ 2, 2, 2

This distribution will help identify your predominant style.

QUESTIONS

1. How do you share information?

☐ I share information mostly with those who are close to me and are trustworthy.

☐ I prefer to keep all information to myself, and I do not share information freely unless required.

☐ I share information freely with others and try to take them along.

2. How do you manage the mistakes of your subordinates?

☐ I come to their rescue and salvage the situation whenever they make a mistake.

☐ I do not tolerate mistakes. I get emotional and reprimand people.

☐ I help employees to learn from their mistakes and encourage them to use mistakes as learning opportunities.

3. How do you manage conflicts?

☐ I prefer to make decisions by pointing out who is right and who is wrong.

☐ I tend to reprimand both parties involved and may even bring it to the notice of seniors.

☐ I tend to help people diagnose the source of conflict and encourage them to resolve their conflicts by themselves.

4. How do you reward or recognize good performance?

☐ I reward, recognize and encourage only those who are close to me.

☐ I may not acknowledge good performance and contributions made by others due to the fear that they may keep expecting more and more, and will cease to concentrate on their work.

[ ] I recognize everyone's contribution and reward those who deserve it with a sense of objectivity.

5. How do you make decisions?

[ ] I make decisions in consultation with a few who are close to me and whom I know well.

[ ] I prefer to take all decisions by myself. I don't consult as I don't trust others to make decisions.

[ ] I take decisions after consulting and involving others. I try to develop others through their participation and active involvement in decision-making.

6. How do you conduct meetings, discussions, and other team transactions?

[ ] I talk a lot and fill meetings with my own views, suggestions, and comments.

[ ] I use meetings to direct, criticize, and ensure compliance.

[ ] I use meetings to empower the team by sharing information and new ideas, eliciting participation and collective decision-making.

After completing your answers, add up all your (a) scores, then (b) and (c)—separately. So you should have three scores.

1a+2a+3a+4a+5a+6a—this is your benevolence leadership score.

1b+2b+3b+4b+5b+6b—this is your critical leadership score.

1c+2c+3c+4c+5c+ 6c—this is your self-dispensing score.

You can convert your scores into a percentage for each category using the formula: Percentage score of your style = (Your score on that style × 100)/36.

For example, if your (a) score total is 9 across all the six items, your percentage score is:

(9 x 100)/36 = 25 or 25 percent.

If the sum of your (b) scores is 6, then your critical score percentage is:

(6 x 100)/36 = 16.67 or 17 percent.

And the sum of your (c) scores will be 21. And your developmental score will be (21 x 100)/36 = 58.33 percent.

REFERENCES

http://business.in.com/column/zen-garden/anu-aga-a-house-by-the-river/2362/1

http://en.wikipedia.org/wiki/Anu_Aga

McClelland, David and D.H. Burnham (1976). 'Power is the Great Motivator', *Harvard Business Review*, 54(2), pp. 100–10.

Pandit, Srinivasan (2001). *Thought Leaders: The Source Code of Exceptional Managers and Entrepreneurs*. New Delhi: Tata McGraw-Hill.

Rosenthal, Robert and Lenore Jacobson (1968, 1992). *Pygmalion in the Classroom: Teacher Expectation and Pupil's Intellectual* Development, New York: Crown Publishing.

Rosen, B.C. and R.O. D'Andrade (1959). 'The Psychological Origins of Achievement Motivation', *Sociometry*, vol. 22, pp. 185–218.

Conclusion

This book aims at enhancing the managerial effectiveness of individuals. We have done so by looking at the factors and practices that create effectiveness in managers.

Managers start as *doers*. They try to do what they are told to do, follow instructions, organize, coordinate, plan, and manage. They do all this according to the desires of others. As they grow, they decide to do bigger things. They try to establish new goals and roles for themselves. They gain their credibility by doing more than what they are expected to do. They become *achievers*. Their achievements may take them to be entrepreneurs. They develop vision and form new organizations and thus become *visionaries*. Their sphere of influence expands as does their fame and wealth. As they mature, visionaries start thinking about large goals. It is their sustained work and single-minded devotion to social causes and self-sacrifice that makes them *missionaries*.

You can have characteristics of more than one type of manager at the same time. For example, a visionary is also a doer; a young MBA graduate who wants to work for an NGO rather than a well-paying MNC job displays missionary qualities. But there is always one in the driver's seat.

Ask yourself what kind of manager you are at present. If you are a doer, then assess what stage you are at. Are you a shirker or the one who does what you are asked to do and nothing more? If you are you have a long way to go. Analyse the reasons for such tendencies on your part. Unless you are an active doer you are not going to get ahead in life.

If you are a good doer manager that delivers results, you are ready to move to the next level of achievers. This can be done by redefining your goals. You must look at your self-perceptions and values. The chapter on efficacy has given insights into what qualities you possess, and what you lack. *Remember, the most important thing to have is purpose and a goal in life.* It is the nature and intensity of the goals you have that determines your commitment.

The following are the qualities you must inculcate. A high level of self-confidence and internality, which will affect your dealings with the world. Your interpersonal trust and teamworking abilities should help you to influence others to accomplish things for you. This in turn will help you to achieve your mission. No one individual can achieve goals. The higher the goal, the more the energy required. Good communication enables you to express your vision and also pass on your experiences and build others to help you achieve your goals. In all this your values and character are the most important ingredients. If character is lost, everything is lost.

In *The Extraordinary Manager*, a study of 80,000 managers who went through 360 degree feedback, Zenger and Folkman observe that getting results is the first step to success. If you get results and maintain good interpersonal relations and get your team to work you are already 80 percent successful. But to be a leader you need to transcend this stage and this is possible only by changing your goals. Creativity, initiative and high internality, drive you or take you to visionary and, eventually, missionary levels.

Ultimately, your role as a manager is connected to the way you are as a person. A good manager will have lived his life fully, actively and served others and left something for the rest of the world. This is what we should all aim for.

MANAGERIAL EFFECTIVENESS QUOTIENT

Assess yourself on the following checklist of items. Just tick-mark the items that characterize you.

Checklist for a doer manager

☐ I undertake activities that are largely in tune with the purpose of my job or goals

☐ I always do the work I am asked to do

☐ I spend most of my time doing what I am assigned to do

☐ I always look for directions and follow the same in my work

☐ A large part of my time goes in doing what I am expected to do in my role

☐ I spend my time working to follow the guidelines given to me in my work

☐ I get a lot of free time in my job without much to do

☐ I am not the master of activities. A large part of what I do is already set by others

☐ I am so occupied doing what I am supposed to do that there is no time to think of doing it better. Or doing it differently

☐ There is so much to do in my current job that there is no time to think of other things

Checklist for an effective manager

☐ I decide the nature of work I should undertake

☐ No one dictates me what I should do and what I should not

☐ I try to do more than what I have been assigned to do

- [ ] I constantly try to improve the quality of my work
- [ ] I enjoy taking up new challenges and new activities
- [ ] I strive to demonstrate continuous improvements in my work
- [ ] I use internal or external benchmarks and standards to improve my work
- [ ] I take challenges in my goals and targets
- [ ] I always strive to do more than what others do
- [ ] I always strive to do better than the previous period (quarter or year)
- [ ] I have generated my own vision and goals for my future
- [ ] I have larger goals to work for
- [ ] I have been able to change the goals given to me by my organization or work unit
- [ ] I have a high degree of confidence that I can achieve my goals
- [ ] I have the talent and ability to achieve my goals
- [ ] I can inspire others in my team with my goals and commitment
- [ ] I have a high degree of values which everyone could appreciate
- [ ] I am a values driven person
- [ ] I set examples to be followed by others
- [ ] I honour my commitments
- [ ] I speak whatever I feel and think and do not hide my feelings
- [ ] I always make it a point to carry out whatever I agree to do
- [ ] I respect other people's views and opinions
- [ ] I have clear goals for my life
- [ ] I have clear-cut goals for my career
- [ ] I have clear-cut goals for the next few years

- [ ] I am clear about my goals for the next few months
- [ ] My goals are of a higher order and are meant to serve a larger cause
- [ ] I am highly committed to my goals
- [ ] I have sleepless nights thinking about my goals, ambitions, and aspirations
- [ ] I breathe, dream, and constantly talk about my goals and life purpose
- [ ] I am involved in some activity or the other all the time
- [ ] My work is focused on my goals
- [ ] I trust other people's word and do not waste time following up
- [ ] I have a high degree of interpersonal competence
- [ ] I can understand and communicate to other people well
- [ ] I have faith in my ability to get things done
- [ ] I make attempts to solve problems as they arise
- [ ] I am sensitive to the feelings of others
- [ ] I get many new ideas and thoughts
- [ ] I am good at generating alternative solutions to issues
- [ ] I am a well networked individual
- [ ] I manage my time well. I don't waste time
- [ ] I use my time to develop new capabilities and learn new things
- [ ] I guide and coach others if they come to me
- [ ] I am continuously learning
- [ ] I keep sharing my experiences and ideas with others
- [ ] I actively seek the company of those from whom I can learn
- [ ] I read stories of great people or other effective managers
- [ ] I am passionate about working for a larger cause or for higher goals

If you have tick-marked all the items on the first ten questions (Checklist for a doer manager) it indicates that you are a good doer manager. You are good at doing what you are expected to do and spend a lot of time doing what others are expecting you to do. You are an asset to an organization that needs hard work. You have to see that unless you create new standards and new activities, your talent may not get developed beyond a point. It is time for you to think of graduating to higher levels. Normally your scores on the next section are likely to be on the lower side. If your scores on the next fifty items are high then you need not bother about your scores on the first ten.

Your scores on the remaining fifty items are meant to give you a broad indication of the number of behaviours you seem to be demonstrating in the direction of being an effective manager. The higher the score the more effective you are. If you scored above 40 it is a high score. If your score is below 20 you may look at items where you can work on and improve to raise your score to at least 35 or 40.

A note on the author

T.V. Rao has been a Professor at IIM Ahmedabad for over twenty years. He was earlier the L&T Professor of Human Resource Development at XLRI, the first Honorary Director of the Academy of HRD, and an HRD Advisor to the Reserve Bank of India. He has worked as a short-term consultant to several world bodies and organizations both in India and abroad.

A note on IIMA Business Books

The IIM Ahmedabad Business Books bring key issues in management and business to a general audience. With a wealth of information and illustrations from contemporary Indian businesses, these non-academic and user-friendly books from the faculty of IIM Ahmedabad are essential corporate reading. www.iimabooks.com

Would you like to participate

in the IIMA Guru Yatra?

For more details visit

www.iimabooks.com

Other books in this series

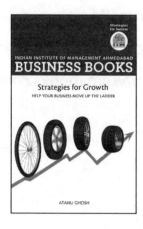